Nipping Crime in the Bud
How the Philanthropic Quest Was Put Into Law

Nipping Crime in the Bud
How the Philanthropic Quest Was Put Into Law
Muriel Whitten

Published 2011 by
Waterside Press Ltd.
Sherfield Gables
Sherfield on Loddon
Hook
Hampshire
United Kingdom RG27 0JG

Telephone +44(0)1256 882250
Low cost UK landline calls
0845 2300 733
E-mail
enquiries@watersidepress.co.uk
Online catalogue
WatersidePress.co.uk

ISBN 9781904380658 (Paperback)
ISBN 9781906534981 (E-book)

Copyright © 2010 This work is the copyright of Muriel Whitten. All intellectual property and associated rights are hereby asserted and reserved by the author in full compliance with UK, European and international law. No part of this book may be copied, reproduced, stored in any retrieval system or transmitted in any form or by any means, including in hard copy or at the internet, without the prior written permission of the publishers to whom all such rights have been assigned worldwide. The Foreword is the copyright of Rob Allen © 2010.

Cover design © 2010 Waterside Press. Design by www.gibgob.com.

Cataloguing-In-Publication Data A catalogue record for this book can be obtained on request from the British Library.

UK distributor Gardners Books, 1 Whittle Drive, Eastbourne, East Sussex, BN23 6QH. Tel: +44 (0)1323 521777; sales@gardners.com; www.gardners.com

North American distributor International Specialised Book Services (ISBS), 920 NE 58th Ave, Suite 300, Portland, Oregon, 97213-3786, USA.
Tel: 1 800 944 6190 Fax 1 503 280 8832; orders@isbs.com; www.isbs.com

e-book *Nipping Crime in the Bud* is available as an ebook (ISBN 9781906534981) and also to subscribers of Myilibrary and Dawsonera.

Printed in Great Britain by the MPG Books Group, Bodmin and King's Lynn

Nipping Crime in the Bud

How the Philanthropic Quest Was Put Into Law

Muriel Whitten

≋ WATERSIDE PRESS

Putting justice into words...

A History of Criminal Justice in England and Wales
by John Hostettler

An ideal introduction. It charts all the main developments of criminal justice, from Anglo-Saxon dooms to the Common Law, struggles for political, legislative and judicial ascendency and the formation of the modern-day Criminal Justice System.

'**Every student entering law school should have a copy and read it**': *Criminal Law and Justice Weekly*

Paperback ISBN 9781904380511 | Ebook ISBN 9781906534790
352 pages | 2009

Pit of Shame
The Real Ballad of Reading Gaol
by Anthony Stokes, Foreword by Theodore Dalrymple

A unique account of the life and times of one of the UK's most famous prisons—a fame that flows directly from an account of the execution of Trooper Charles Thomas Wooldridge (CTW) as written by Reading Gaol's best-known prisoner, C.3.3, the pseudonym of Oscar Wilde. Based on close research over ten years, and written by a serving Reading prison officer with access to official records and the Execution Log.

'**You won't put it down**' Henry Kelly, *Irish Times*

Paperback ISBN 9781904380214 | Ebook ISBN 9781906534455
192 pages | 2007

visit **WatersidePress.co.uk**

Contents

About the author .... *vii*
The author of the Foreword .... *vii*
Acknowledgements .... *viii*
Foreword .... *ix*
Dedication .... *xv*

1. **The Philanthropic Quest** *17*
   Alarming Times *17*
   The Philanthropic Plan. *24*
   The Philanthropic Network: Ideas and Interests *29*

2. **The Philanthropic Plan Put Into Practice**. *45*
   The Early Years. *45*
   The Philanthropic Children *47*
   Inside the School of Morals *61*

3. **Problems of Governance** *81*
   Domestic Economy *81*
   Ways and Means *89*
   At 'War' with Mr Robert Young. *98*

4. **Reformatory Refinements** *113*
   Network Expansion *113*
   An Act of Incorporation and the Chapel Affair. *116*
   What Might Work Better? *125*
   Education, Health and Morals *133*

5. **A Thinning Mesh of Support** *145*
   Highs and Lows *145*
   Fickle Funding. *156*
   Diminishing Returns *164*

6. Enlightenment..........................179
Change or Decay?...................... *179*
Government interest: Ups and Downs.................. *188*
An Experimental Opportunity.......................... *198*

7. The Legislative Quest.............................217
A Fresh Start.. *217*
Reformatory Returns................................. *227*
The Philanthropic Network for Reform:
A Legislative Conundrum *230*
The Philanthropic Network for Reform:
Reasons to be Cheerful.............................. *243*

8. Into the Future...................................255

Bibliography   *263*

Index   *275*

About the author

Dr. Muriel Whitten has been a youth court and family proceedings court magistrate and a member of the West Sussex Probation Committee. She lectured on criminal justice policy and criminology at Goldsmiths and Birkbeck (University of London) and more recently on sentencing theory, policy and practice at the University of Ulster. She has presented on policing issues for Centrex (now the National Policing Improvement Agency) and contributed a weekly column to the *Belfast News Letter*. She lives in County Antrim.

The author of the Foreword

Rob Allen was director of the International Centre for Prison Studies from 2005-2010. Before that he was director of Rethinking Crime and Punishment at the Esmée Fairbairn Foundation. His earlier roles include being director of research and development at the National Association for the Care and Resettlement of Offenders (Nacro) and head of the Juvenile Offender Policy Unit within the Home Office. He has also served as a member of the Youth Justice Board.

Acknowledgements

I would like to thank the trustees, director and staff of the Royal Philanthropic Society (RPS) for their unfailing courtesy when answering my queries and their generosity in taking time to guide me through the intricacies of innovating policy and practice. Many thanks are likewise due to Joyce Moseley, chief executive of Catch22, who updated me on how this national charity (formed by the merger of RPS, Rainer and Crime Concern) helps young people in tough situations make a positive contribution to their communities today.

For their forbearance, I also wish to take this opportunity to express my appreciation to staff in the British Library Rare Books Reading Room, the British Library of Political and Economic Science, Senate House Library, Guildhall Library, Southwark Local History Library, the National Archives, London Metropolitan Archives, London Borough of Hackney Archives, the Bank of England Archive, the Sussex County Record Office and, especially, to all those at the Surrey History Centre and Heritage Archives at Woking.

I owe a particular debt of gratitude to Emeritus Professor Robert Pinker for his encouragement and advice, to Dame Gillian Wagner for lending a friendly ear and to Stephanie Hayman without whose support this book would not have materialised. And lastly, my deepest thanks to Jim — for his patience.

Muriel Whitten
September 2010

Foreword

Muriel Whitten's beautifully written account of the London Philanthropic Society in the years leading up to the Reform School Movement informs and fascinates across a range of subject matter. Of course it sheds penetrating light on a period of history in which well-intentioned and largely religiously motivated individuals sought to alleviate some of the horrors of life for the poorest children brought up in the capital city—in particular those who found themselves at the mercy of the criminal courts but also those who were deemed at risk of becoming criminals; the 'orphans, needy and erring', children with inadequate or non-existent family support.

But by carefully charting the ups and downs of the society from its foundation in 1788 to the passing of the Reformatory Schools Act in 1854, *Nipping Crime in the Bud* also illustrates the changing responses to the perennial dilemmas at play in the way law, policy and practice respond to young people in trouble. How far should children be held to account for wrongdoing? Should and if so how should the implementation of sentences be modified in the case of juveniles? How should parents—where there are parents—be held responsible and under what circumstances should the state step in to replace them? Should young offenders be dealt with separately from children in need who have not been convicted or is a unified approach more appropriate? And what kinds of regimes are likely to produce humane and effective outcomes for young people who are placed in institutions?

Yet this is not a legal or philosophical text, but rather at root a story of how change was brought about over a particular period of time, and of how the intentions and actions of individual philanthropists who wanted to prevent crime and improve the life chances of young offenders both reflected and influenced the social, economic and political context. What it shows is that how we end up dealing with young delinquents—and perhaps this is as true in many other spheres of policy—depends less on the underlying philosophy than on the altogether messier matters related to implementation. Questions of funding or the availability of land, accidents of personal connections, relationships between movers and shakers and the 'ripeness' of the timing will generally do more to determine the achievement or otherwise of an initiative and the shape it eventually takes than the merits of the originating ideas or values. Many of the telling examples of life in the society's institutions suggest it provides an example of an organization — to coin a phrase — campaigning in poetry and governing in prose.

As for the measures which the Philanthropic Society promoted much has of course changed over the last 150 years. The early 19th-century was an age of institution building and there seems to have been an unwavering faith in the ability of residential institutions to improve children largely by excluding them from their former connections. This faith seems not to have been shaken by the rather mixed outcomes (at best) which have always seemed to characterise institutions for young people. Of the first 176 entrants to the society's school, 51 absconded. Yet parents were often keen for their children to be admitted exaggerating the seriousness of their delinquency in order to persuade the visitors to admit them.

Many of those leaving the society's institutions were taken to new life in the colonies or at sea or apprenticed out to employers. This was not uncontroversial at the time with some protesting that slave dealing was being promoted in the name of charity. Aftercare was, as ever, a problem with a recognition that without a home and a job young offenders would return to their old ways.

The overall approach to young people was still far from giving priority to meeting their individual needs, with institutional life strictly rule bound, and harshly enforced with work or preparation for work and religion at the absolute heart.

The society's original idea of a family-based or cottage-based institution teaching and providing agricultural skills rapidly gave way to an altogether more prison like establishment in St George's Fields, Southwark with a wall 'to prevent interruptions, counter temptations to wander and from evil communications'. *Chevaux de frise* were added after one of a series of escape attempts in the 1830s. Some of this book's most engaging passages describe how young people found ways around the rigours of institutional life through escape, intoxication or other mischievous behaviour. One boy escorting Mary Carpenter back to the station after she had visited returned drunk; and there were periodic disturbances, including a riot quelled by the Peelers. Some of the more troubling material concerns the measures to prevent or punish bad behaviour. To prevent escapes boys had logs tied to their feet. A boy who broke into the porter's box and stole the contents was publicly and severely flogged in front of the boys with the label thief on his forehead.

A 'black book of faults and merits' was kept by a regulator, no doubt to monitor the extent to which the curriculum of the time—including Bishop Wilson's instructions to the Indians and Mrs Trimmer's morally edifying tales—were having their desired effect. While the basic standard of care appears reasonable if the diets are an indicator, the institutions did not aspire that its charges should do more than find work at the lowest end of the scale. Hence it was 'important not to accustom them to conveniences and indulgences of which they might feel the want'.

The modernising superintendent of the institution Sydney Turner appears to have relaxed the discipline although it still relied on aspects of military drill. One sergeant appeared not to be able to get the boys to obey him and was replaced. As with institutions today, achieving compliance was no easy matter. The society found it hard to devise effective incentives for young people for whom 'the future is comparatively nothing and the present everything'.

The move from St George's Fields to the Redhill Farm School may have allowed for some further replacement of physical discipline with cords of love but by now the society was on the verge of forming a closer relationship with government, of becoming a prototype approved school. The demands of taking more boys who had been convicted of serious crimes, the duties arising from taking government funding and the inspectorial regime that went with it—Turner became the first Inspector of Reformatory Schools—will have created new dynamics.

It is the journey to this brave new world that the book's subtitle, *How the Philanthropic Quest was put into Law*, refers to. The Philanthropic quest was very much a child of the Enlightenment. This was an era of a growing and sometimes breathtakingly wide-ranging belief in the power of knowledge, analysis and evidence to provide the best approach to addressing and solving social problems. The Philanthropists were linked to another group who undertook research on the causes of delinquency, identifying the key issues as 'Improper conduct of parents, want of education, want of employment violation of the Sabbath and gambling in the streets'. As for tackling these causes, it was an era of surprisingly widespread exchange of international practices. The society sent a delegation to the French institution at Mettray, founded in 1840 by the reformer Demetz. Foucault wrote that were he 'to fix the date of completion of the carceral system … the date I would choose would be 22 January 1840, the date of the official opening of Mettray. Or better still, perhaps, that glorious day, unremarked and unrecorded, when a child in Mettray remarked as he lay dying: "What a pity I left the colony so soon".'

No doubt the elaborate power structures embedded in the precisely ordered and controlled community at Mettray could be seen to epitomise the carceral approach, but the institution, limited to boys and young men from age six to 21 years old, did at least mean the youngest were kept out of adult prisons. Demetz's ideas had been developed on a visit to the United States of America in 1836, but American visitors had already been to the Philanthropic Society's institution in London nearly 20 years before. The Quaker John Griscom was cheered to find that so many wretched children were snatched as firebrands from criminality and ruin and restored to the prospects of respectable and honourable life.

The interest in international developments reflected the wide-ranging concerns of the Philanthropists who were however not only interested in the evidence but prepared to put their time into the enterprise and their reputations on the line. There were limits to this. When members of the society were invited to act as guardians for those leaving only four volunteered in the five months up to August 1797. But *Nipping Crime in the Bud* is littered with examples of the rich and powerful intervening on behalf of individual children whose paths they crossed in various ways.

Indeed it is the interplay between the Philanthropic Society and the authorities which has particular contemporary resonance as the British Government formed in 2010 looks to respond to a range of contemporary problems—including delinquency—through the creation of the so-called 'big society'.

The story of the Philanthropic Society illustrates some of the familiar pitfalls facing the voluntary sector. For much of the period covered here the society was well-connected but short of money. It was periodically tempted by government to take on particular types of young person—for example boys from Parkhurst or Millbank—or to merge with other organizations such as

The Refuge for the Destitute. There were discussions about the most appropriate funding mechanisms — local or central, core grants or per capita fees.

The society saw a major falling out with its founder, Robert Young, a serial social entrepreneur and somewhat larger than life figure who had difficulty taking colleagues with him in respect of some of his more ambitious schemes and whose accounting seems to have left something to be desired. He spent time in the Fleet debtors prison, and worked as a government spy in France as well as finding time to set up an establishment in Sussex to help resettle ex-prisoners.

Like modern voluntary organizations, Young and his successors and the powerful network they created sought not only to provide a service but to shape the legislative framework governing the treatment of young offenders. The book illustrates the important part the Philanthropic Society played in the period running up to the Acts of Parliament which brought reformatory and industrial schools into a national system. There are countless examples of the savagery of the penal response to children as young as eight years of age. Mary Crawley aged eleven was sentenced to death for shoplifting in 1797 but pardoned and received into the society's Female School. A large number of the children were admitted following their parents' imprisonment, transportation or execution.

There are many examples of discretion in the execution of sentences with courts and the executive seemingly able to apply the law as they saw fit — but with an inevitable sense of the law as something of a lottery. Is this perpetuated still through the retention of an unusually low age of criminal responsibility?

The society's chairman is quoted as saying in 1852 that:

> It was a great characteristic of England that in this land many problems were solved by private enterprise by private benevolence and by the spirit of Christian religion. Difficult questions were first approached and were often finally solved by the efforts of individuals with which the public law and the institutions of the country would never have ventured to grapple.

Contemporary youth justice offers several opportunities for this sort of big society approach although a 21st century version of the Philanthropic's 'preventive policing' is likely to be predominantly community-based rather than custodial. National Citizen Service for 16 year olds will soon add to a range of preventive initiatives which involve local people as mentors to young people at risk and grassroots organizations offering educational, sporting and cultural opportunities. Local volunteers could play a greater role in the justice process itself—by expanding referral order panels—or by increasing options for restorative justice.

Devolution of power could see local authorities take greater responsibility for meeting the high costs of custodial placements where these are needed or re-investing resources to develop more effective alternatives, especially in neighbourhoods with the highest concentrations of children in trouble. More diverse providers—including charities and social enterprises could also run community-based or even custodial services. A voluntary sector proposal for a Young Offenders Academy in East London is perhaps a contemporary analogue of the Philanthropic's work.

The big society, whatever it may mean, may of course prefer not to get involved in this field. *Nipping Crime in the Bud* notes elements of charity fatigue blighting the Philanthropic Society's prospects, with the Lord Mayor wishing some temporary retirement from charitable activity and a sheriff desirous of some little relaxation. It may be of course that the government look to the private sector to do more—it was after all to that sector that the last Tory Government looked to establish the latest form of closed institution for young offenders the secure training centre. It would do well to consider the danger—highlighted by the Parliamentary committee which, during the period covered by this volume, rejected Jeremy Bentham's ideas of contract management—'that a pecuniary advantage would be made the most prominent object of attention rather than the reformation of the prisoners'.

More fundamentally, the government would do well to consider Turner's defence of his boys—that though nominally convicts:

> ... they are not criminals in the real sense of the word and deserve and want the moral discipline of a school much more than the penal correction of a prison.

Rob Allen
September 2010

Dedication

For Melissa, Camilla and Davina

CHAPTER 1

THE PHILANTHROPIC QUEST

Alarming Times

It was in 1788 that a little group of men met in the St. Paul's Coffee-House in London, to discuss a problem which had been exercising their minds for some time. They were worried by the increasing number of homeless children infesting the Metropolis, who only managed to keep alive by begging and dishonesty. Some of these were no older than three or four years; many were homeless, others were trained by their relatives to win what they could by theft. There seemed little ahead of them except execution on the public gallows or a lifetime of imprisonment.[1]

Saving these forlorn children from the perils of the streets and the terrors of the laws was a laudable mission for the Philanthropic Society's gentlemen to undertake. This was an era when boys and girls could be exploited, abused and neglected by parents or employers yet had few rights and protections afforded them in law. They might even be sentenced to death for committing a felony. Even though a presumption of *doli incapax*[2] extended over children between seven to 14 years, this easily could be rebutted. These still were the 'very modern times' in which, as Blackstone observed in his *Commentaries on the Laws of England* (1769), cases similar to that relating to this boy of ten years old could be found. Convicted on his own confession of murdering a bed-fellow, yet being perceived to display 'in his whole behaviour plain tokens of mischievous discretion', the judges unanimously agreed he was a proper object for capital punishment. Their justification was, that:

> sparing this boy merely on account of his tender years might be of dangerous consequence to the public, by propagating a notion that children might commit such atrocious crimes with impunity.

---

1. Alabaster, (n.d.).
2. Incapable of criminal intent; that is, without sufficient understanding of right and wrong.

Still, while compassion is not to be discounted, we can gain a deeper understanding of what propelled the philanthropic gentlemen into action by considering the broader climate of concerns in which the society's enterprise embarked. These certainly were unsettling times of ferment. The ignominy caused by the loss of American colonies in the revolutionary War of Independence had traumatised the nation and was firmly fixed in recent memory. What was more, the terms on which peace had been achieved bred turmoil, rather than tranquillity, in the political sphere as factions fought over who to blame for the debacle.

Fears about what was happening in the realm of France were also mounting. *The Times* could well remark that the exertions French citizens were making to attain rights and liberties 'must naturally be viewed by every enlightened Briton in two opposing lights'.[3] Even so, to Britons of pessimistic bent, news that a rebellion against paying taxes to the government of that country was not a 'mockery and fabrication',[4] rekindled worries about seditious plots at home. Indeed, the destruction of private property and prisons during the Gordon Riots of 1780 had already sent shock-waves through the land and heightened anxieties about the erosion of what had been thought relatively stable social relationships of authority and deference. These disorders had also brought the inadequacy of existing civil powers for quelling the 'the mob' into anxious focus.

Entwined with these alarms were those fuelled by escalating levels of Poor Law expenditure. With roots in the thirteenth century, this means of administering relief to the poor had, from time to time, been tweaked and adjusted to suit local conditions under the requirements established by Tudor statutes. But by the end of the eighteenth-century, a rapidly expanding and mobile population of the poor was putting the system — and rate-payers — under increasing stress. The mounting financial burden was noticed particularly in the Metropolis. By then the largest city in Europe, London had long been a magnet for those who sought work or fortune by legal — or illegal — means. But, as the agrarian and then industrial 'revolutions' gathered pace and dis-

---

3. *The Times*-10/7/1788.
4. *The Times*-5/8/1788.

placed people from the countryside, the problem of supporting the urban poor became a matter of ever-rising concern.

Anxieties were intensified by perceptions of crime being on the upswing. The extent to which this was actually so is hard to confirm as no official national statistics on committals for indictable offences in England and Wales were collected before 1805. And, even where crimes were recorded at a local level, the information gathered is extremely patchy, especially in regard to summarily tried offences. Nonetheless, with the peace of 1783 leaving hordes of demobilised soldiers and sailors free to contribute to an upsurge in cases of assault brought before the courts, these certainly seemed alarming times. They also saw a 40 per cent increase in committals to the Old Bailey for felony over the three years to 1786. This awesome achievement was accompanied by an extraordinary escalation of executions carried out in London between 1783 and 1787; at a rate 82 per cent higher than in the previous five years.[5]

In this context of worry and alarm, it is understandable why the burgeoning numbers of poor children at loose on the streets—and kept alive only through begging or dishonesty—could both inspire compassion and conjure-up the spectre of 'the mob' on the rampage. Even the disorderly behaviour of boys on *exeat* from Westminster School could 'outrage' and 'terrify' nearby residents[6] and lead *The Times* to trumpet:

> The *Westminster* Boy that offends the Peace should be taken up by a Constable, and instead of complaints against him to the Master, he should be had before a Magistrate and committed to Bridewell, though the offender were heir to a Dukedom. This would soon quell these riotous lads.[7]

That remedy might well have been counterproductive. The insalubrious state of bridewells, gaols and other places of confinement did not elicit overwhelming admiration. 'Gaol fever' was rampant and might carry-off as many prisoners awaiting trial as would suffer a State sanctioned sentence of death by hanging.[8] Spreading with equal ease through captive populations

---

5. Ignatieff (1978:87).
6. *The Times*-10/8/1788.
7. *The Times*-16/8/1788–original emphasis.
8. 'Gaol fever' was epidemic typhus, transmitted by lice. The outbreak during an Old Bailey session in 1750 not only dispatched more than 60 prisoners but also added the Lord Mayor, two

were vices of all varieties. This moral contamination was just as dispiriting to some observers. As prison reformer, John Howard, commented in his *State of the Prisons* (1777), not only were half the robberies committed in and about London planned in prisons 'by that dreadful assemblage of criminals, and the number of idle people who visit them', but:

> Multitudes of young creatures committed for some trifling offence are totally ruined there. I make no scruple to affirm, that if it were the wish and aim of magistrates to effect the destruction, present and future, of young delinquents, they could not devise a more effectual method than to confine them so long in our prisons: those seats and seminaries (as they have been very properly called) of idleness and every vice.

Yet, what could be done to prevent crimes and depredations? The existing panoply of punishments did not appear to have a deterrent effect. As was reported by *The Times* in an Old Bailey 'Intelligence':

> The numbers convicted last session ... are a melancholy proof of the inefficacy of our laws, and ought to stimulate our Parliament to an alteration of the system for punishing crimes ... [as] ... hanging, most certainly, has not sufficient terrors to prevent those crimes for which it is the punishment.

This sad defect in the Bloody Code of penal law inspired *The Times* to then thunder:

> Instead of death, the sale of our capital convicts to the Barbary States—or a present of them to the Dey of Algiers, would be more terrific than death, and consequently have a greater effect on the conduct of those inclined to depart from the letter of the law.[9]

The exercise of discretion throughout all stages of the criminal justice process also stirred currents of concern. While some crimes of felony were not prosecuted out of sympathy for the likely fate of the perpetrators on the gallows, mercy might also be extended in the form of a Royal pardon after a capital sentence had been imposed. Juries likewise played their part: sometimes with the nudge of judicial guidance displayed in this account of the case of

---

judges, an alderman and an under-sheriff to the death toll.
9. *The Times* – 22/9/1788.

Hannah Rowley. On her appearance in court on indictment, charged with stealing a prayer-book from St. Giles's Church and pawning it the same day for 2s/6d, 'Mr Recorder observed that this was Sacrilege and a Capital Felony, by a statute of Edward IV, unless the jury could find the value of the book below 12d'. The verdict? Hannah was found 'Guilty of stealing to the value of 10d'.[10]

In this climate of uncertainty over the rule of law, the 'State of Crimes and Punishments in London' became a subject of particular scrutiny. This readers of the *Whitehall Evening Post*[11] were appraised of by way of an abridged report on Newgate Prison. Therein they saw that over the year from 28th September 1785 to 28th September 1786, one thousand seven hundred and ninety-six prisoners had been received under the 'Sheriffalties' of James Sanderson and Brook Watson esquires. As was customary, these gentlemen had been elected by the Lord Mayor and Court of Common Council to hold the office of sheriff for one year, during which they were responsible for ensuring that prisoners delivered to Newgate did not escape. Facing substantial fines (and a blight on their prospects for advancement in public office) should this occur, they made sure that a close eye was kept on the fate of these 1,796 prisoners. It was recorded as follows:

```
Executed . . . . . . . . . . . . . . . . . . . . . . . . . .  68
Sent to hulks  . . . . . . . . . . . . . . . . . . . . . . 350
Dead  . . . . . . . . . . . . . . . . . . . . . . . . . . . . .  16
Discharged . . . . . . . . . . . . . . . . . . . . . . . . 891
```

The remaining 471 were then placed into the hands of sheriffs Paul le Mesurier and Charles Higgins 'in the usual form' and a further 1,536 prisoners were added by 28th September 1787. They were disposed of thus:

```
Executed . . . . . . . . . . . . . . . . . . . . . . . . . .  87
Transported to Botany Bay[12]  . . . . . . . . . . . 117
```

---

10. *The Times*–16/9/1788.
11. *Whitehall Evening Post*–24/6/1788.
12. There was also uncertainty about this new penal venture. *The Times* of 17th September 1788 comments: 'It is possible that we may never hear more of our Botany Bay convicts. Accounts

> Sent to the hulks 225
> Dead 56
> Discharged 969
>   1454

And, with those 'remained under the sentence of death and transportation etc.'

> 553
> Making in all   2007

These statistical 'accounts' were claimed to be 'the first of the kind which have ever been made out'. Likely complied by the sheriffs themselves, they were brought into play to argue that:

> when people complain of the sanguinary nature of our laws, and the frequency of our executions, they have not sufficiently balanced one circumstance against the other.

Not only did these figures illustrate 'how small the proportion of executions is to that of commitments, and what proportion the number convicted bears to the number acquitted', but also, while people might 'think it a shocking circumstance that eighty-seven persons are executed in one year, they should consider that this is eighty-seven out of two thousand and seven'. If they did so:

> [the] number then will not appear so great, and it will appear less if we consider that of those sentenced to die, two thirds are in general pardoned, or their sentence changed to transportation.

Whether or not these observations were intended to deflect criticism from existing sentencing practice, they were connected to an additional concern. This was, that 'of the vast number discharged in any one of these years, even Charity herself will not permit us to think that many return to industry

---

from them should have reached England by this time, as they certainly, if safe, must have been met by many vessels, after leaving The Cape'.

and honesty'. With this in mind, the 'accounts' had been presented to the public in the hope they:

> may be useful to the curious enquirer into the state of crimes and punishments, and who wish[es] to devise some plan to operate as a general preventive.

This offer was extended at a time when the establishment of a professional and centrally co-ordinated body of police officers in the Metropolis was being vigorously resisted. The foundations of such a crime preventive measure—in the form of foot patrols that helped preserve the security of citizens and their property—already had been laid and supervised by the Fielding brother magistrates at Bow Street Court.[13] Yet when proposals to extend this scheme, in co-operation with the Government, were mooted after the Gordon Riots fiasco and incorporated into Pitt the Younger's Police Bill of 1785, opposition had been successfully mobilised. This rested largely on the grounds that the scheme smacked too much of a State despotism perceived to reside in the French system of government of funded and organised police 'spies'. Introducing any such police of this kind would, undoubtedly, coercively interfere with the precious liberties of free-born Englishmen.

'Police', nonetheless, carried wider connotations in this period. Besides embracing activities directed at preventing future ills, in eighteenth-century usage it included those which maintained order in a civilised society. Closely bound-up with the goal of benefiting the 'common weal' it was considered not solely the remit of politicians or a professional corps of police but an important duty of all responsible citizens. In these interconnected senses, the call for a 'general preventive' would have been seen by contemporaries to be in continuity with ideas expressed by Jonas Hanway. In a series of letters outlining *The Defects of Police* (1775), he had proffered various propositions for 'the establishment of general plans of Police on a permanent basis'. These, he believed, by dealing more effectively with immorality, the regulation of paupers and the reform of prisoners, would benefit the 'national security and happiness'. With some irony, he further commented that:

---

13. These patrols complemented the work of the Bow Street 'Runners' who were more concerned with detecting crimes and apprehending the criminals.

> The word Police is not universally intelligible, so little have we attended to it; and consequently we must expect that many proposals for it will be treated as utopian or romantic, tho' they may be salutary and necessary regulations. If the people are not kept in good order, and just apprehension of what they owe to themselves, their God and their country, no event ought to surprise us. For my own part when I consider how lame and deficient our Police is, I wonder things are not in a worse state than they really are.

Not that Hanway was content to float mere proposals in the air. Besides being involved with the Magdalen Asylum's efforts to reform 'common' but 'penitent' prostitutes and the Foundling Hospital's child-saving activities, Hanway sought to ease the plight of chimney-sweepers' apprentices. He also helped found the Marine Society in 1756. Established with the patriotic aim of supplying disciplined men and boy sailors who could help defend the nation in times of war and assist mercantile trade in times of peace, by the time of his death, in 1786, that enterprise was mainly training poor boys for service in the Merchant Marine or the King's Navy. Sweeping from the streets 'vast shoals' of 'the children of thieves or the deserted offspring of idle or dissolute parents',[14] it exemplified how policing for the social good could be achieved by active citizens.

The Philanthropic Plan

Did the Philanthropic Society set out to do likewise? Frustratingly, we cannot be entirely sure. Despite the extensive archival sources that remain, the *Minutes* of its very first meetings have disappeared. Nevertheless, from scant details provided in an *Abstract of Proceedings*, it seems that the inaugural meeting was held at the home of Robert Young Esq. on the 5th of September 1788. During this, the assembled gentlemen decided to form a society aimed at 'the Prevention of Vice and Misery among the Poor'. By the sixth meeting, Young had been appointed Intendent, the Marquis of Carmarthen designated President and the society had determined that its enterprise was 'not to have surrounding walls'. It was thus to be an 'Asylum not a Prison'.

Helpfully, surviving publicity literature relating to the society's earliest years gives some indication of the concerns that gripped its founders' imaginations

---

14. Radzinowicz and Hood (1986:134).

and which they believed would capture interest—and purses—elsewhere. While the latter consideration reminds us to be cautious of rhetorical gloss and flourishes, these texts reveal a complexity of imperatives at play. Foregrounded to hook public attention was not so much the plight of vagrant and destitute children who were at risk from the perils of society. Rather, privileged in the rhetoric was the intention to maintain order and prevent future ills through rescuing and reforming children who presented a risk to society. Hence, the enterprise was explicitly portrayed as a *Philanthropic Society Instituted for the Prevention of Crimes* which would begin the task by seeking children:

> in the nurseries of vice and iniquity in order to train up these embryo robbers and nuisances, to useful purposes in life; and thus to draw riches and strength to the state even from sources of impoverishment and decay.[15]

This strategy, it was argued, would be welcomed by 'every friend to order and public good who sees with concern the daily outrages and indecencies of those who are abandoned to profligacy and vice'. After all:

> Notwithstanding that great sums are annually expended in the country for the service of the Poor, it is a melancholy fact that much want and misery still exist. And although the necessary severity of the laws and the frequency of punishment are subjects of general regret, vices and crimes continue to prevail and even increase to an alarming degree.

These evils unquestionably confirmed the 'inefficacy' of the means that had 'hitherto been attempted' to banish them from the land. Their persistence also pointed to the 'necessity of trying measures altogether of a different kind'. Although the 'calamities' that beset the poor could 'call forth the warmest emotions of pity', it appeared to the founders that much of the charitable 'bounty' of the nation had been bestowed 'without proper discrimination' and was 'annually employed in the support and consequently the reward

---

15. The texts drawn upon are the Philanthropic Society's *First Report* and *Second Report* (1789), *Address* (1789), *Appeal* (1790) and *Address* (1792). In this section, references have been consolidated so as to trace thematic strands. Original emphases and spelling in these and other primary sources have been retained here and throughout.

of idleness'. Since the 'class of labouring poor' was the 'first in the scale of civil society and the basis on which all higher gradations rest', charity thus threatened to 'operate in an alarming degree'. If not directed towards a productive end, 'the springs of the wealth of the nation will no longer flow'.

Charity's drain on national prosperity was compounded by the operation of the Poor Laws. Their 'great defect' also was the 'want of discrimination between merit and demerit, amounting virtually to the discountenancing of honest industry and rewarding indolence and vice'. In making provision for everyone that could make a claim to settlement in a parish, they removed 'the necessity of providing against the love of ease inherent in all men' and fostered 'the evil dispositions prevalent in too many'. In short, parochial benefits created dependency and:

> although the workhouse is sufficiently irksome to the poor when they come to reside in one, it nevertheless affords, while in prospect, a support to their minds, and a pretext for indulging in present vicious inclinations.

Nor did the code of criminal laws offer solace. It was 'by no means a power adapted to correct the depravity that pervades the vast body of the poor'. Not only were 'the thefts committed under the gallows at times of public execution … striking proofs of this truth', but, 'Justice, by waging war upon men's passions' seemed 'to have rendered their vices more formidable' and made 'dangerous enemies of neighbours whom a wise and gentle policy' might have attached as 'valuable friends'. 'Governments, the province of whom it is to watch over the collective welfare of communities', had ignored 'society's essential interests'. Instead of planting the 'seeds of virtue':

> with the retainers and retinues of justice, with the iron hand of the law, the plough and harrow of litigation, they over-run the ground and tear up the soil, carrying with them only desolation and misery, and still leave the roots of evil to shoot up anew, and the seeds to germinate with fresh vigour in the loosened earth.

In contrast, the philanthropic remedy would not be found wanting. It would strike at the roots of evil and:

lead to the reduction of every species of public burthen, which vice and misery induce; poor rates, hospitals and prisons; and to the restoration of peace, good order and personal security.

These benefits would, surely, flow from attending to a 'sound principle' of trade in which 'giving ever has a return with interest' in mind. It was this important 'principle of policy' that had been too little regarded in establishments supported by voluntary contributions and by the legal provisions for the poor. It was also sadly lacking 'in the alms given to beggars and the private donations of individuals' which altogether made 'a sum surpassing belief'.

Admittedly, incorporating 'prospects of gain' might be alleged to be a 'pollution of the spirit of pure benevolence'. Yet charity, when 'divested of any views of return', was a perpetual 'current from the purses of the rich to the miseries of the poor'. There it 'stagnated' and, in merely keeping people alive, threatened to be 'destructive of the main pillars of civil society'. This made a sorrowful comparison to the approach taken by 'great trading companies and capital manufacturers' which did not neglect to calculate the return on their investments and understood how 'the order of society has linked other interests to their own'. Thus, the Philanthropic Society intended:

> to unite the spirit of charity with the principles of trade by erecting a Temple to Philanthropy on the foundations of Virtuous Industry.

It would, moreover, see the 'sum of happiness augmented beyond what has been hitherto known in any former period of mankind' by:

> [commencing its] operation on lives which in their present state are below the zero point in the scale of estimation; which not only have, already, no positive value, but which on the contrary have a positive *disvalue*; if it may be so expressed, in the balance of which the evil prevails over the good.

To this useful end, the Philanthropists would seek out in the 'Augean stable of filth, disease and iniquity which disgraces the Metropolis' and train-up to 'virtue and usefulness in life, the children of vagrants and such who are in the paths of vice and infamy'. Then, since 'corruption must inevitably be propagated from race to race, so long as children were brought up in the society and example of their parents', the first step would be to separate the young from the old 'who would corrupt them'. The next was to 'impress a contrary impression on their minds, virtuous dispositions, and industrious habits and lastly to find them the means of an honest employment and livelihood'.

Objections would, no doubt, be raised at the prospect of the society relieving the 'burthens of bad members of the community, in preference to those of honest and industrious persons'. The danger of any 'ill consequences' was 'obviated', however, by the choice of 'objects': being children, they '*cannot form a deliberate purpose to become wicked* and cannot look to charity with hope'. These children certainly were not undeserving. Neglecting to provide for their moral education and employment posed even greater dangers, for:

> They are a class which belongs to no rank of the civil community; they are ex-communicates in police; extra social; extra civil; extra legal; they are links which have fallen off from the chain of society and which going to decay, injure and obstruct the movements of the whole machine. A just policy requires that these links be replaced, by re-uniting the vagrants of the country, to the classes of labourers and mechanics.

There were, besides, other imperative reasons for targeting such zero-sum children. They were the 'only subjects that could be employed for a grand experiment' directed 'to the improvement of knowledge' and 'designed to ascertain and fix the principles of a general reform'. These children, indeed, offered to 'an experimentalist in mind … an opportunity that was beyond price'. If they were rescued and the first lessons taught them was 'forgetfulness, and disuse of all they had hitherto learned and practised', each would be 'as a blank, ready to receive any impressions or forms, which were designed for it'. Then:

> when the influence of moral education was experienced on the very lowest and worst description of people; when there should be change, by this means, so as to produce the best characteristics; when from the children of vagrants there should be formed a superior class of mechanics and servants; honest, industrious, affectionate, faithful, examples to others, and preferred before them, it would be impossible but that every order in society would be eager to wipe away the disgrace of being left behind in the race of virtue by those whom they had been accustomed to hold in contempt.

By reforming the offspring of 'the most degenerate class of poor' and raising them 'to a degree of superior utility', the philanthropic enterprise would thus provide a 'magnificent, striking and commanding' model to 'attract the eye of the nation'. The society's 'new mode for a plan of education' was, furthermore, not an 'obtrusion of a new Utopian vision on the world'. Rather, it was 'the result of much study', was based on 'facts' and designed for execution by men who were 'prepared to commit their time and reputation on its event'. From this it derived a credibility lacking in the merely 'speculative projects thrown on the mass of opinions which issue continually from the press'. It was, in fact, a practical Plan of Police that would 'prevent the growth of evil and snatch the innocent from destruction ... deprive the jails from their inhabitants ... [and] ... add citizens to society'. In doing so, it would appeal to diverse interests, for:

> If we regard humanity and religion, this institution opens an asylum to the most forlorn of the human race. It befriends the most friendless, it saves their souls from perdition.
>
> If we regard national prosperity, and the public welfare, it is calculated to increase industry in the most helpful and necessary channels.
>
> If we regard self-interest; its immediate object is to protect our persons from assault and murder; and our property from depredation; that our wealth should not endanger our lives, our repose be interrupted by thieves, nor our dwellings be exposed to the desperate design of midnight incendiaries: and this is a point in which the most selfish among mankind are most concerned, and which makes it in the interest even of avarice itself to be the most liberal.

The Philanthropic Network: Ideas and Interests

It is impossible to trace here the roots and gestation of all the ideas articulated in these philanthropic refrains. Bringing children of an apparently dangerous class into high profile was not an innovation. This progeny had even fuelled fears about the ravages which the Elizabethan 'sturdy beggar' might wreck on society. As well, the adage that 'the devil makes work for idle hands to do' had not only been a recurrent theme in child-rearing but also had circulated around the establishment of many charity schools of industry. The

Philanthropic Society's response to children, deemed 'the most important object of police' was, nevertheless, particularly redolent of Enlightenment modes of thought. Strongly coloured by Lockean convictions about the malleability of human nature in its earliest stages of development and melded to an environmentalist theory about the roots of crime, it followed the empirical tradition by aiming to study human nature 'not as it was found in books, but as it is in fact'. It was, indeed, the society's 'peculiar distinction and boast' that its members sought an 'acquaintance with wretchedness in the last and lowest sources' which only was to be had by 'painful researches in which few will engage'. Already they had visited places where its objects resided and discovered:

> indescribable misery, which no friendly hand had reached, nor pitying eye had seen. The most abominable filth renders their habitations to the last degree offensive; swathed with rags, begrimed with dirt, the traces of the human figure, in them are almost lost; a person cannot go upstairs without apprehending danger to his limbs; an empty apartment, or at best, furnished with a broken chair, and a bundle of rags for a bed, is their wretched existence ... Sometimes there are two or three in a room. Begging and stealing are their ordinary means of subsistence; drunkenness, lying, quarrelling, profaneness and prostitution, are their manners and way of life. The springs of honest industry, in their minds are wholly unbent.

So, who were the Philanthropists who believed it important to embark on this experimental crime prevention quest? Why might they have been concerned to restore outcast children to the 'civil community' and 'to the right knowledge of their God'?

Robert Young

Although we cannot scrutinise all the personalities associated with the society in its earliest years, it seems more than apt to begin with Robert Young. As glimpsed from the publicity pamphlets, this founder renders the Philanthropic Plan with the assured tone of a gentleman of the Enlightenment, imbued with an optimistic spirit of scientific enquiry and a confidence in the possibility of solving social problems through the application of reason. In this he exhibits 'the engaging self-assertiveness'[16] of the age and displays

---
16. Gay (1969:8).

competence in distilling from a currency of contemporary opinion, assumptions and theories, a solution for social evils that gripped the imaginations of a considerable network of Philanthropists. Young appears, indeed, particularly conversant with many of the concerns and remedies discussed in the coffee-houses, taverns and drawing rooms of London in the shadow of Adam Smith's *Wealth of the Nations* (1776) and Thomas Gilbert's *Plan of Police* (1781) which advocated reform of Poor Law administration.[17] He also displays a familiarity with sentiments expressed by the Reverend Townsend, whose arguments against indiscriminate charity and condemnation of how the Poor Laws promoted evils they were meant to prevent, made a substantial impact when published in 1786. That same year also saw Hewling Luson, a clerk in the Navy Office, publish *Inferior Politics: or, Considerations of the wretchedness and profligacy of the Poor*. In this, Luson deftly propounded on the defects of the existing system of penal and parochial laws and proposed the establishment of asylums where children of convicts—and other neglected and pauper children—would be provided with 'maintenance, employment and instruction'.

Paying reverence to the Beccarian notion that it is better to prevent crimes than to punish them was likewise not ignored.[18] As Young took pains to stress, the Philanthropic rationale rested on the conviction that:

> long experience has shewn that punishments cannot subdue vicious propensities deeply rooted in the mind; and that the characters of men commonly depend on the impressions they receive in early life. The combined forces of habit, example and necessity, drag to their ruin those who are at once entangled in the snares of the wicked; and were justice armed with additional terrors, it would still be unable to stop the torrent of corruption, impelled by so many powerful causes. Increased severity would but make men more artful and more desperate, would occasion new devices and new crimes to assist or conceal the old.

Although credited with establishing an Institution so often mentioned in the annals of juvenile justice and welfare, little is known about Robert Young's

---

17. Many of Gilbert's recommendations were embedded in the *Act for the better Relief and Employment of the Poor* (1782).
18. Young may also have been paying an intellectual debt to Montesquieu on this matter.

background. What is remarked upon, however, is the irony of this moral entrepreneur's subsequent disgrace and banishment from the society. Within a few years, money collected by him for Philanthropic purposes had not, allegedly, found its way to that end. This led to a Special Meeting being called on the 19th of August 1790. A Constitution of Regulations and Rules was then drawn-up in the hope of ensuring the society's welfare — rather than an individual member's fortune — was secured. It was also decided to circulate 'cautionary notices' to warn that:

> The Philanthropic Society find it absolutely necessary to inform the public that Mr Young is no longer Treasurer to, or hath any connections with this Institution–a deficiency of 1,200£ and upwards having been found in his accounts, by Auditors appointed by a general meeting of Subscribers to inspect the same. Of which deficiency he himself admitted to the amount of 1,075£ on an examination before a very full committee.[19]

We might speculate on the possibility of the funds being used as venture capital for other schemes Young had in hand. By March 1792, he was confidently promoting his *Undertaking for the Reform of the Poor, of which a principal branch is the Asylum of Industry, consisting of eleven houses in East Street, Walworth, in the Parish of Newington Butts*. With an Office at No. 22 Downing Street, Westminster, this enterprise had been in operation for a year and — like the Philanthropic Society — it aimed to instil virtue. It was, however, more ambitious in scope being intended to embrace:

> Youth discharged from gaols, female prostitutes, seamen and soldiers in want, vagrants, and in general, all who are willing to labour but who cannot procure employment.

Even grander designs were in contemplation. In 1790 Young had published 'Proposals for Raising a Capital, for erecting and stocking a settlement for the employment and reform of discharged convicts, criminals, and others'. This *British Settlement, for the Reformation of the Criminal Poor, Adults and Children* was projected in greater magnitude. Estimated to require £15,000

---

19. For some time after 1790, Philanthropic publicity material continued to draw upon passages from earlier texts which can be attributed to Robert Young.

to establish 'in a centrical Situation of the Kingdom on some waste or cheap land', it had secured Earl Grosvenor as president and his son, Viscount Belgrave, as one of the vice-presidents. This venture had a further twist, however, in that its buildings 'consisting of cottages, workshops, and ware-houses' were to be erected on their discharge by:

> persons who have suffered imprisonment ... whether they have been acquitted of a crime laid to them or have undergone a term of confinement by the sentence of the law.

These schemes were not the limit of Young's fertility of invention or ambition. In 1790 he was also promoting a *Social Union Formed for the Improvement of Civil Society*. This, he confided, was to be 'an association composed of various parts, organized into a grand machinery of active powers, having virtue for its spring, reason for its guide, and happiness for its end'. Its range was broad. The Social Union was to be comprised of committees for:

> the redress of injuries, the Constitution, the Laws, the Police, Public Justice, Medicine, Charities, Political honour, Education, Parochial Affairs, Literature, Culture and science, Elocution, New discoveries and Foreign correspondence.

It was, furthermore, 'Founded upon a science which may be called the Science of Society, because its object is to reduce the knowledge of domestic policy to principles and methodological arrangements'. Labouring for the benefit of all mankind, 'theoretically as well as practically', the Social Union also aimed to:

> [disseminate] through all orders a knowledge of the social science, so that the concerns of life may be reduced to a system and method; and that light and certainty may accompany man's pursuits of future interest and happiness, instead of the darkness and doubt in which at present they are involved.

Cross-fertilisation of ideas

This Enlightenment Manifesto draws more explicitly on Humean ideas about the possibility that a science of man could be developed than is evident in the

Philanthropic Plan. In the latter, however, there is such a heightened emphasis on the principle of utility, which would become popularised through the writings of Jeremy Bentham, that we may wonder whether Young's works would have been quite so overlooked had he not been discredited.

Still, while Young's scribblings sank into relative obscurity, Bentham's plans for establishing a panopticon penitentiary attained notoriety. With details of its design published in 1790, this ambitious scheme had the following beneficial ends in view:

> Morals reformed, health preserved, industry invigorated, instruction diffused, public burthens lightened, Economy seated, as it were upon a rock, the Gordian knot of the Poor-Laws not cut but untied.

And, if its calculated utility bears a close similarity to that claimed for the Philanthropic enterprise, Bentham's plan for a subsidiary to the parent panopticon — the paedotrophium — carries eerie echoes of the society's deliberations on adding value to zero-sum children. As he would later reminisce:

> According to the calculations which had then been ... made, the pecuniary value of a child at its birth,–that value which at present is not merely equal o, but equal to an oppressively large negative quantity, would, under that system of maintenance and education which I had prepared for it ... have been a positive quantity to no inconsiderable amount.[20]

Bentham's National Charity Company proposal of 1797, likewise aimed to pass the Philanthropic's utilitarian test for an effective police; namely, adding to the sum of happiness. Insofar as this plan to improve pauper management envisaged setting poor children to labour in the countryside, rather than being allowed to congregate amidst the contamination of towns, Bentham's ideas already had been rehearsed by Jonas Hanway in the 1760s. They were also reworked by Robert Young when proposing that his British Settlement should be located in the 'waste-lands of Derbyshire'. They are evident too in the philanthropic paean on 'agriculture' being the 'grand source to which

---

20. Cited in Semple (1993:294).

the Society looks for employment for their Wards'. This was held to have particular utility. As the Philanthropic Society's *First Report* declares:

> Our populous cities and towns are already too much crowded with manufacturers, mechanics and menial servants who flock from all parts of the country ... [To] ... preserve the just balance, let us then, send to wholesome air and exercise, the miserable wretches who are now perishing upon dunghills in London, and from them a hardy race of husbandmen, from the waste of society, to populate and cultivate the waste and barren parts of the country.

This cross-fertilisation of ideas is characteristic of the Enlightenment movement which flourished across Europe — and the New World — with the support of members from the aristocracy as well as from the professional strata of society that encompassed the clergy, lawyers, medical men, educationalists, manufacturers and administrators. Busily disseminating knowledge through writing letters to each other, publishing tracts and gathering together in learned academies, they also met in coffee houses and drawing rooms. One such British exemplar was the Lunar Society of Birmingham. Providing a forum for the exchange of knowledge on discoveries that would help foster the growth of industrial production, this society complemented other groups established by members who were united in an amateur love of science and a desire to be involved with practical improvements in diverse spheres.

The Philanthropic Society can shed some illumination on a London scene in which gentlemen were instilled with a belief that their crime prevention experiment would contribute to the improvement of society. If we look at the membership in its earliest years, we can find a Jeremiah Bentham, of Queen's Square Place, Westminster, on the Committee list of 1790. If — allowing for the vagaries of spelling that prevailed at the time — this is Jeremy, it is understandable why the society's declared utilitarian ethos could have attracted his interest. Likewise, the promise it afforded for an 'experimentalist' with Baconian/Newtonian pretensions to study and mould the minds of the young accorded with his dictum that 'observation and experience compose the basis of all knowledge'. As well, the rendering of the Philanthropic Society's preventive rationale would have been admired for its reflection of Beccaria's reasonings on the severity of punishment which emboldens men to commit the very crimes it was meant to prevent.

This reference to 'Bentham' needs to be handled with caution, nonetheless. It more likely refers to Jeremy's father—Jeremiah Bentham—who was a prosperous attorney and a magistrate on the Middlesex Bench. It was due to his prompting that Jeremy published the *Introduction to the Principles of Morals and Legislation* (1789) which encapsulated the utilitarian argument that all laws should work for the greatest happiness of the greatest number. Jeremiah did not, however, promote his son's panopticon project to the same extent. Underpinned by the principle of the 'all-seeing eye', its plan had been inspired on Jeremy's visit to the Russian manufactory designed by his brother Samuel. Once constructed, the panopticon was to be run for profit under privately contracted management. As stated in an *Outline* (1790), Jeremy believed the panopticon principle could be applied to:

> any other establishment, in which persons of any description are to be kept under inspection: such as Prisons in general, Poor Houses, manufactories, mad-Houses, Hospitals, and Schools.

Whether Jeremiah Bentham's magisterial observations on the prevalence of vice in London suggested that investing in the Philanthropic enterprise would accrue more immediately beneficial returns,[21] he amassed a considerable fortune through dealing in property. This Jeremy inherited on his father's death in 1792.[22] It was thereupon used to further his panopticon ambitions and promote the many other ideas embraced in his wider agenda for remedying the ills of society. His vision of how this could be achieved may have been of a less evangelical cast than that displayed by his friend, William Wilberforce, who established a Proclamation Society, in 1787, with the aim of reforming the morals and manners of the nation and repressing the vices that propelled so many perpetrators to the gallows.[23] Nor did

---

21. A preponderance of Philanthropic gentlemen would be party to a similar courtroom perspective.
22. After 1792, the name of Jeremiah Bentham disappears from the Philanthropic Committee lists. Jeremy only took up residence at Queen's Square after his father's death.
23. This society was founded in response to the Royal Proclamation, of June that year, which had called for the encouragement of piety and virtue and the prevention and punishment of vice, profaneness and immorality.

it prevent Jeremy declaring that the equally pious prison reformer, John Howard, was one of the most extraordinary men of the age, with his *State of the Prisons* providing:

> a model for method and for the sort of stile that is competent to his subject ... He is accurate to the extreme: takes nothing from report: and asserts nothing but what has come under the cognizance of his senses.[24]

Bentham was not alone in this reverence for Howard whose exposure of defects in custodial arrangements had fuelled the passage of a Penitentiary Act through Parliament in 1779. The two model penitentiaries envisaged in that legislation did not, however, materialise. The failure to do so stemmed, in part, from the government's reluctance to make a commitment to the financing and direct management of such a project. It was also partly due to Howard—and the two other gentlemen appointed to oversee the construction—not being able to agree on suitable sites. Ironically, one of these gentlemen was Howard's close friend John Fothergill. A Quaker physician who established a very successful medical practice and treated many prominent Nonconformist families involved in banking, commerce and industry, Fothergill was part of a coterie of medical men whose spirit of scientific enquiry helped transform the practice of hygiene and management in hospitals, poor houses and prisons. Renowned for being the first person in England to clinically describe diphtheria in his *Account of the Sore Throat* (1783), he was also deeply involved in the development of the dispensary movement. At a time when illness could cost the poor what modest means they had, dispensaries offered free advice and medicine to those who could attend on an out-patient basis or who required to be visited in their homes. They thus afforded physicians an opportunity to increase their knowledge of disease, poverty and distress and, in turn, publish their observations.

John Cloakley Lettsom was another wealthy Quaker physician and Fothergill's protégé. He too was involved in the dispensary movement and his *Hints,* designed to promote '*Beneficence, Temperance and Medical Science*' (1797), played an important part in scientific philanthropy's attempt

---

24. Cited in Semple (1993:75).

to diffuse useful knowledge.[25] Many of his *Hints* would be published under the auspices of the Society for Bettering the Condition and Increasing the Comforts of the Poor (SBCP). With some of its goals prefigured, to an extent, by Robert Young in his Social Union proposal, the SBCP can be considered another Enlightenment project in that it aimed to enquire into 'all that concerns the poor' and make 'all that concerns their happiness a science'. Acting as a sort of trading-exchange for collating and disseminating information on the latest scientific enquiries conducted by its members and like-minded parties at home and abroad, it was founded by the Bishop of Durham, Thomas Bernard and William Wilberforce in 1795. These last two gentlemen's names appear in the Philanthropic Society's early subscription lists along with that of the Evangelical Henry Thornton MP, a banker, economist and cousin of Wilberforce, with whom he founded a Committee for the Abolition of the Slave Trade in the summer of 1787. That endeavour was in keeping with the Quaker community's efforts to promote the stand against slavery and, by that time, Lettsom already had emancipated the slaves on his West Indies plantation at Tortola. By 1788, however, he was being exhorted to join with Howard so as to give of 'their talents as well as their purses' in order to relieve the miseries of:

> Those unfortunate little boys, doomed to ignorance, filthiness, and the consequent diseases of the body and mind, the Chimney-Sweepers.[26]

After Howard's death, Lettsom helped sustain public interest in prison reform through publishing a series of letters in which he promoted James Neild's further enquiries into the state of prisons. In the sixth of these, he expresses sympathy with the 'reasonings of the benevolent Neild' who believed that

---

25. Lettsom's *Hints respecting the Immediate Effects of Poverty* (1780) provide a graphic account of the abject social conditions (very similar to those depicted in Philanthropic texts) which he encountered on a visit to a family residing in a little court off Aldersgate Street. These, he observed, made a stark contrast to the 'plenty and elegance which reigned within the extent of a few yards only' and showed 'how greatly the sight of real misery exceeds the description of it'.
26. Letter signed 'Eusebia', *Gentleman's Magazine* (1788, vol.58). That year, a small measure of relief was provided by an Act For the Better Regulation of Chimney Sweepers and their Apprentices.

the steps taken by many to the gallows could have been prevented by the promotion of virtue and industry by parish officers. Lettsom further comments that, as 'the seeds of future vices, which are often sown very early in life, ripen by example, and mature by age', it was of the:

> greatest importance to the community that the roots of these noxious plants be early removed; that the bad propensities of unguarded youth be corrected before they are exemplified by practice, and become familiar by repetition ... [and] ... as the most usual sources of early depravity may be ascribed to the want of a decent education ... which enables its possessor to apply his powers to the emoluments of industry ... prevents idleness, and fortifies resolution to withstand vice ...[the] ... man of feeling and piety contemplates, with high gratification, the increasing establishment of Sunday and other Schools, for the benefit of the rising generation ... and a pleasing source of future happiness.[27]

Some other key members of the Philanthropic Society

In view of the close affinity of sentiments, we may not be too surprised to find that Lettsom had been attracted sufficiently by the Philanthropic Plan to become associated with the society's enterprise. Indeed, in 1790 he was a committee member in the company of Jeremiah Bentham, Samuel Whitbread, John Julius Angerstein and Thomas Boddington. At that date, James Sims, George Hardinge, and James Sanderson were Philanthropic Society vice-presidents.

These individuals may not all be historically illustrious figures on the national stage. Even so, a brief examination of their interlacing circles of acquaintance provides a snap-shot of the diversity of interests and expertise brought together in the Philanthropic community of Preventive Police. Vice-president Hardinge served as Solicitor General (1782) and then Attorney General (1794) to Queen Adelaide. He was a senior judge on the Welsh circuit (1787-1816), an MP for the 'pocket' borough of Old Sarum (1787-1807) and acted as counsel—in the House of Lords—for the East India Company. Besides these legal and parliamentary involvements, he was interested in the

---

27. *Gentleman's Magazine* (1804, vol.74).

arts and sciences and—like Lettsom—acquired the status of Fellow of the Royal Society and Fellow of the Society of Arts.[28]

Vice-president James Sims, MD and LLD, would be one of the most active Philanthropic players. The son of a dissenting minister and born in County Down, he had been helped further in his medical career by Lettsom. Rising to become the president of the Medical Society of London, Sims's published works included a *Discourse on the best methods of prosecuting Medical Enquiries* (1774) and *Observations on the Scarlatina Anginosa, commonly called the Ulcerated Sore Throat* (1803). Thus adding to the sum of medical knowledge, Sims accumulated charitable credentials and extended his own education in poverty and disease by serving as a physician at the Surrey Dispensary as well as the General Dispensary, Aldersgate Street. Along with Lettsom, he also helped advance the work of the Royal Humane Society which promoted techniques for the art of resuscitation of 'persons apparently in a state of suspended animation'.[29]

It is not clear which Samuel Whitbread belonged to the Philanthropic Committee in 1790. If Samuel senior, besides accumulating a vast fortune in the brewing business, he was John Howard's neighbour and friend and helped secure both the Discharged Prisoners and the Health of Prisoners Acts of 1774. Although hardly implemented, that legislation enabled Magistrates to pay acquitted prisoners' fees so they could be released from custody. With the prevention of gaol fever as a goal, it also empowered magistrates to direct that prisoners be periodically washed and provided with proper ventilation and separate sick rooms. They could also select surgeons or apothecaries to attend the prisoners and report their condition to the Quarter Sessions. If this is Samuel Whitbread junior, however, in 1790 he became MP for Bedfordshire on his father vacating that seat and would be a leading political light in campaigns to advance the cause of Poor Law reform and for the provision of free education.

Philanthropic vice-president James Sanderson we have already met as one of the sheriffs who calculated the 'accounts' on Newgate Prison. As a wealthy

---

28. *Dictionary of National Biography*. The *DNB* is drawn upon heavily, but not exclusively, for the profiles of Philanthropic personalities.
29. That is, persons who had suffered 'from drowning, asphyxiation, lightening stroke or other mode of unconsciousness' (Brown, 1961:342).

banker and hop merchant, his commercial interests probably brought him into association with the Whitbread brewing family and their reforming concerns. Sanderson's interest in a Philanthropic Society that offered to nip crime in the bud might also have been encouraged by what he observed while doing his public duty in Newgate and as an alderman presiding over the Guildhall Sessions. In the latter office, the experience of flexing his civil powers to quell riotous assemblies that frequently erupted in the Metropolis might likewise have provided an impetus. When Lord Mayor of London, he would be thanked by the City Corporation for accomplishing that public duty in 1792, the year he was first returned as an MP. Also a member of Wilberforce's Proclamation Society (as was Jeremiah Bentham), Sanderson became a baronet in 1794 and, besides being involved in Philanthropic affairs, found time to serve on the committees of the Emanuel Bridewell, the Foundling Hospital and Magdalen Asylum.

The Magdalen also features in Philanthropic committee member John Julius Angerstein's charitable profile. Russian born—but a naturalised Briton under a private Act of Parliament—he was at various times head of the largest trading firms in the city. He too was a MP and, with Enlightenment enquiry and exactitude, devised a system of State lotteries that was taken-up by government. His business interests, however, enabled him to acquire a sufficient fortune to amass valuable paintings which later formed the nucleus of the National Gallery collection. Besides being an underwriter at Lloyds and reforming the arrangements under which its business was conducted, Angerstein was one of the Evangelic brotherhood involved in the Society for Bettering the Condition and Increasing the Comforts of the Poor (SBCP) and supported the Marine Society's enterprise. He also sought to end the misery endured by chimney sweepers' climbing boys and would be noted as having particularly thanked Patrick Colquhoun for the efforts made by that gentleman on behalf of the Society for Improving the Condition of the Infant Chimney Sweepers.[30]

Colquhoun was one of the first magistrates appointed to the Police Offices set up under the Middlesex Justices Act of 1792. We will later meet him expressing interest in the Philanthropic Society's endeavours but, for now,

---

30. *Iatros*, (1818:42).

we can note that he was a close friend of Lettsom and took part in the SBCP enterprise of providing cheap food to the poor. Amongst Colquhoun's publications, however, his *Treatise on the Police of the Metropolis* (1796) attempted to quantify the incidence of (and stressed the connection between) poverty, indigence, vice and criminality. This formed part of his campaign for a systematic reform on a national basis of the existing fragmented and localised policing system of night-watchmen, constables and justices of the peace.

Although Colquhoun's efforts in this regard were thwarted, he was more successful in seeing his ideas for a Marine Police bear fruition in 1798.[31] This privately established preventive police unit was designed to tackle the property losses of businessmen, such as the West India merchants who provided most of its finances. Its apparent effectiveness in reducing thefts from the quays helped smooth the passage of the Thames River Police Bill through Parliament in 1800.[32] This Bill was not, however, the one enthusiastically drafted by Colquhoun and Jeremy Bentham, both of whom had been called as witnesses before a Parliamentary Select Committee enquiring into the state of Police and Convict Establishments in 1797. By that time, Colquhoun had supplied statistical information used in framing Bentham's National Charity Company scheme and had been invited to dinner by its author to discuss the subject of building penitentiary houses at the end of the previous year.[33] They may, perhaps, have even mulled over these matters with Thomas Boddington who had served on the Philanthropic Committee alongside Jeremiah Bentham and Lettsom in 1790. This would have been possible in this small world of interlaced interests. Boddington was most likely familiar with the impact of crime and interested in its prevention being a West India merchant, a director of the London Dock Company, the Royal Exchange Assurance Company and the Bank of England. A common councillor of the City of

---

31. Colquhoun's scheme was anticipated by John Harriott who became resident magistrate on its implementation.
32. The 'mob', however, was not deterred by the River Police innovation which had robbed many of work 'perks' previously enjoyed. In the summer of 1799, Colquhoun was standing close-by to an 'officer of justice' who was killed by a shot fired from amidst 2,000 rioters who were attempting to pull down the Marine Police Office, in Wapping.
33. Milne (1981:325).

London, he also was on the committee of the Marine Society and supported the Society for Promoting Christian Knowledge Among the Poor (SPCK).

Quite how individual strands in this complex web of personal relationships and humanitarian concerns came to meet and interlock may remain a mystery. Even so, the configuration of ideas embraced within the Philanthropic Policing Plan had undoubtedly captured the imagination of influential men with diverse but often overlapping interests in the arts, politics, religion, commerce and the law. Having scrutinised the sources of disorder in society, they had identified a particular constituency of poor children as a problem connected to prevailing concerns about the health, wealth and security of the nation. Whether inspired by compassion, the public welfare or even self-interest, theirs was a practical response at a local level and was fuelled by a conviction that social improvement was possible. With Enlightenment belief in the power of education to shape young minds, these Philanthropists confidently set out to explore how their crime prevention experiment could be charitably applied to meet the utilitarian end of adding to the sum of national happiness. Their preoccupations, as we shall see, would continue to shape the Philanthropic Society's endeavours.

CHAPTER 2

THE PHILANTHROPIC PLAN PUT INTO PRACTICE

The Early Years

Having painted the social and intellectual back-cloth and introduced a few of the Philanthropic actors, it is time to see how the preventive Policing Plan was enacted. As confidently envisaged by the founders, this was no speculative 'bubble' that might 'rise and break and to the sea of fancy return'. Within a few months of commencing operations, the society could announce to the public that:

> There are now above THIRTY CHILDREN under the Society's care. As soon as these wards have, by persons appointed in town, been freed from their rags, filth and loathsome diseases, they are sent to houses hired at *Cambridge Place, Hackney*, for their more convenient instruction in virtuous principles and useful labours.

These numbers had grown from the placement of a single child 'out to nurse'. Then, when the Philanthropic 'objects' amounted to 12, a small house had been rented in which a matron was installed to superintend household concerns and the government of the society's wards. Little difficulty was experienced in finding young 'ex-communicates in police' and two more houses were swiftly hired nearby. In these, the children under its protection learnt 'knitting, spinning or some such employ as may be useful to them in old age and infirmity'. The girls and boys were then separated. With the former being educated as 'menial servants', a shoemaker instructed the elder boys in one house and, in another, a tailor tutored his younger wards. Soon six carpenters, six tailors and six shoemakers were engaged and an additional small plot of land was rented on which 'the boys assisted the gardener in their leisure hours'.

Publicising the rapid progress of this collective 'reform' was not neglected by the society. With the 'mode of living in distinct houses, as separate families' designed to approach 'common life' and with each manufacturer and his wife regarding the wards as their own children, the Philanthropists could soon proclaim that their establishment was beginning to:

> give the semblance of a little village, which, in order and industry, and good morals, is a pattern to the poor.

Yet, pursuit of the Arcadian idyll was abandoned. Rather than being preliminary to setting-up an 'establishment in the country for purposes of agriculture', by 1792 that 'grand and fundamental part' of the original design had faded from view. Instead, the society was embarking on a larger-scale operation in St. George's Fields, Southwark, on a plot of ground leased from the City of London 'on very liberal conditions'.

As to the rationale underpinning this shift in direction? In part, it was justified in terms of economy for it would enable more children to be instructed in 'such trades as may qualify them by their labour, to diminish the expenses of the Institution'. Even more crucially, it was a means of ensuring that the children's reformation would be more efficiently secured. As the public was informed:

> The Committee of this Society are fully convinced by observation and experience, that it will be impossible to effect the great purposes of this Institution, to RENDER INDUSTRIOUS AND VIRTUOUS THE IDLE AND CRIMINAL POOR CHILDREN ADMITTED INTO THIS REFORM, unless they are enabled absolutely to exclude them from their former connections.[1]

To this important end, the Philanthropic gentlemen now proposed:

> to enclose the whole in a high Wall, in order to preserve the children from interruptions in their business, from temptations to wander, and from evil communications.

Quite what was encompassed by this retreat from the society's initial ideal of establishing an asylum without prison-like walls can be seen in a 'memorial'

---

1. Although the village of Hackney was renowned for its market gardens at this time, the St. George's Fields area was hardly built upon. According to Weinreb and Hibbert (1983/1993) it was used as a training ground for soldiers and as a Sunday resort for Londoners. It was where the Protestant Association assembled before provoking the Gordon Riots of 1780.

of May 1793. This related to the 'Sum wanting to complete the buildings already begun' and was penned by Mr. Peacock, the Surveyor. By then, he was able to inform the committee that:

> The ground has been enclosed by a Wall twelve feet high and about eighteen hundred feet in circumference, on the north side of which and adjoining the said wall is erected a range of workshops five hundred and forty five feet in length, with a rope walk underneath, which I compute to be sufficiently capacious for the employment of four to five hundred boys.

Pursuing this new—and expansionist—Philanthropic vision also involved a radical revision of the original family system of care. Three dwelling houses already had been built 'each of which is calculated to contain a master and mistress and forty five boys', with the basement storey of each house converted into a temporary general kitchen, pantry, and wash-house. Plans were also in hand for constructing 'cells of confinement for refractory objects' at the St. George's Fields site and a 'prison' had been 'fitted up' in temporary premises rented in Bermondsey.

So, what knowledge of the potentially 'obnoxious' members of society had led to these expedients? Indeed, what children had actually been deemed deserving of rescue and reform? In order to explore the Philanthropic world and how it worked we need to turn the pages of the society's *Admissions Registers* and *Description Books*. Along with *Committee Minutes* and *Superintendent's Journals*, these ledgers present the 'facts' in an embryo case-history format. They note the social background of the children and contain observations on their character. They often outline the trades children were put to, whether they were apprenticed, when they were rewarded or punished and who recommended them to the society. Importantly, the ledgers provide a glimpse of how the penal and pauper laws of the day played around them.

The Philanthropic Children

The categories of poor children to be taken under the society's protection were rather loosely defined at the outset. This vagueness appears to have placed the reprobate founder, Robert Young, in additional difficulty. Oddly enough, although intent on demonstrating how carefully targeted philanthropy could reap socially beneficial rewards and despite stressing that poverty *per se* was not a sufficient qualification for admission, his lack of discrimination in the selection process drew Philanthropic ire upon his head. This can be detected in the case of Stephen Stemp who had no father but his mother was:

> a very decent woman who maintains herself & another child by millinery work–the boy is in every respect an improper object–one of those admitted by Mr Young.[2]

If the society's disapproval stemmed from Young selecting children not distinguished under the criteria of being vagrant or without friends, family or parish to support them, the following entries give some indication of the range of those who were deemed deserving:

> John Cole (age 7) admitted 1789–An orphan found in the streets almost starved and knows not to which parish he belongs.

> William Cotton (age 8) admitted 1789–father and mother are beggars and being Americans can claim no relief from any parish.

> Thomas Hurst (age 13) admitted 1789–Has no father, knows not where his mother is. In summer worked in the brick-fields–in winter, maintained himself by begging. Had not slept on a bed for near two years.

> John Major (age 13) admitted 1790–A vagrant in the streets; lived in St. Giles'—recommended by the Revd. Mr Southgate.

> Mary Crawley (age 15) admitted 1790–cruelly treated almost starved, and turned into the Streets by a Brutal Father in law [stepfather] who consumed his earnings in drunkenness. This girl was exposed to every danger of seduction and ruin–but for the timely succour of this Society.

> George (age 13) and James (age 12) Bucknell admitted 1792–father and mother are both dead; were taken from wandering about St. George's Market, sleeping in carts and in a complete state of vagrancy.

---

2. Other clouds seem to have been cast over Young's reputation. Concerning a child aged seven when admitted in 1792, the entry reads: 'This boy and his sister, a girl of nine years of age, was under the care of Mr. Young and by him left to starve, having nothing to subsist on'.

> Richard Starkey (no age given) admitted 1792–has no father nor mother–wandered up to town out of Somersetshire–was found in the streets sick and almost starved.
>
> Margaret Hagan (age 11) admitted 1794–this girl has neither father or mother–from her infancy was put out to nurse by Aldgate Parish and afterwards apprenticed to a woman of infamous character by whom she was so ill treated that she could not continue with her ... has been in a state of vagrancy and almost starving on the streets.

The boundaries between poverty, vagrancy and criminality could, however, slip and blur. This can be seen in the case-history of Henry Humble, aged 13 when admitted in 1792. Henry's experience may, indeed, have reinforced the society's unfavourable view of the operation of the Poor Law. When illness had hindered his father from earning a living as a coal porter, indoor relief had been claimed from the parish. The application succeeded but afterwards 'the boy was turned out of the workhouse on account of his father's being incapable of paying a debt he had contracted there'. Henry had then taken to thieving.

The fate of many other children of the streets was to endure a spell in custody under the vagrancy laws. Flowing from the Poor Law statutes, these could be employed to apprehend, confine and punish persons suspected of less than good intentions when found loitering abroad or lodging in barns and outhouses. They may have helped capture Richard Shepperd in the first instance. Aged 14 when admitted in 1793, Richard was found to be:

> A wanderer without any regular employment subsisting by begging & sleeping in the streets–when unable to provide two pence to pay for a night's lodgings was committed to Bridewell for stealing a Horsecloth.

William James Perry was likewise confined. His custodial experience may not have been so unusual at a time when it was at the discretion of the keepers of bridewells and gaols whether bedding—and even food—would be provided without payment. William, also aged 14, was rescued by the society in 1792 after being:

> Taken up as a vagrant and committed to Clerkenwell Bridewell and when received into this Reform was in the utmost state of wretchedness having been four and twenty days in confinement and sleeping only on boards without any covering.

Besides the want and woe that could draw upon compassion, concern over the consequences of parental neglect also took many children through the Philanthropic portals. One such was Edmund Moon who was admitted in 1793:

> Born at Witley in the County of Surry–very much neglected by his father who is a bricklayer. This boy has been guilty of diverse acts of pilfering and threatening the lives of children younger than himself to obtain their victuals and was, on the 10th April, confined in a solitary cell for one month.

Also brought under the Philanthropic's care and control — but on account of other reasons for the neglect of his welfare — was William Sanders. He was aged 12 when admitted in 1795:

> The father of this boy was drowned about ten years ago–and his mother was out of her mind for a considerable time–is now tolerably rational, except at intervals–during the insanity of the mother, this boy has been left to himself. Has been absent for a fortnight or three weeks together, in which time he was connected with thieves and existed on what he could steal–his mother being totally incapable of taking charge of him he was recommended as a proper object for this Institution.

The following scene of London life reveals how James Fordree's pathway to the Philanthropic was paved by a vigilant victim. Brought before a magistrate at Bow Street court, he was admitted in 1796, aged 13, after being:

> charged on the oath of Michael Mintor with having picked his pocket of a pocket handkerchief. Michael Mintor stated that on Monday last, as he was coming out of Drury Lane Theatre, the prisoner Fordree followed him and picked the handkerchief out of his pocket–that the witness had tried to take him, but he was prevented by the prisoner getting among the carriages that stood about the Play House door–that yesterday evening he was again at the Theatre and seeing Fordree had him secured.

James's danger to society was, moreover, compounded by the aggravating circumstance of his mother's reputation. A washerwoman who also sold play bills and lodged at Mr. Dickson's, Cock Court, Tottenham Court Road, she appeared on James's behalf, but:

> was found to be a woman of very bad character—and destitute of the means of supporting him in any way which might tend to rescue him from his present depraved state.

Children 'at risk' from their being the offspring of convicted felons were also amply represented. Included in this category was George Hicks, aged 7 when admitted in 1797:

> Son of William Hicks, formerly of Cheshunt, Herts., who was committed to Newgate for feloniously stealing from the Powder Mills at Waltham Abbey in Essex, a large quantity of Salt Petre, the property of His Majesty; was removed to Chelmsford, tried at the Assizes, March 1796, held there for the County of Essex, was Capitally convicted, but pardoned on condition of being transported, and is now on board the Hulks.

These hulks were the old sailing ships—moored on the Thames and other river estuaries and harbours—which had offered an expedient custodial alternative to transportation when the revolutionary War of Independence cut-off the supply of British convicts to American colonies. That event provided an impetus to the quest for a new penal colony and, after some tentative experiments in African venues, Botany Bay had become operational. As the Newgate 'accounts' revealed, its potential had been swiftly embraced. This destination does not appear to have proved so attractive to the father of William Lilley—a boy who was aged 8 when admitted in 1790. Confined in Newgate before being sent abroad, William's father was noted to be:

> one of the miserable beings who made their escape from Botany Bay in an open boat, was ten days without food, and brought to England in a Dutch frigate.

Henry Sheers was aged 9 on his admission to the Reform in 1798. His father was even less fortunate. The Philanthropic ledgers disclose that he had been 'executed for forgery'. They also note that he left:

a widow and four children as appears by a certificate from Mr Kirby, Keeper of Newgate. The mother is very poor and earns a scanty livelihood by her needle and hawking fruits in the streets.

Mention of Mr. Kirby draws attention to an important source of referrals at this time. This Keeper of Newgate Prison had also recommended William Lilley to the society and he appears again in the following account:

> Francis Ross (age 6) admitted 1794–This boy and his sister, received in at the same time, are children of Francis Ross, at this time under sentence of death in Newgate, having been Capitally convicted during the last sessions of a forgery–sent by Mr Kirby to the Committee of the Philanthropic Society as proper objects for their humane attention, who confirms the truth of the above account by a letter addressed to the Superintendent. The mother is living and gets her bread by going out a-washing &c. and lives at No. 14 in the Gallery, at the Bull and Gate in Holborn.

The Philanthropic ledgers do not reveal whether Mr. Kirby was motivated to increase the supply of objects to the society from altruistic sentiments or in consideration of some form of pecuniary reward. The following case, however, suggests that at a time when there was no guarantee that children of prisoners would find a place of safety in the world outside, an anxious parent could initiate the referral process:

> Patrick Ryan (age 9) admitted 1795–Son of Dennis Ryan who was executed at Kennington Common 27th April last and who earnestly requested before his execution that this boy, his only child, might be recommended to this Society in order to be taken into the Reform. The father was a native of Ireland, but [had] no parochial settlement, nor any person to take charge of this unfortunate child, excepting the Revd. Mr Winkworth, Chaplain to the County Jail of Surry who benevolently undertook to recommend the case to the Committee of this Institution.

These ledgers also remind us that many children could experience the terror of hearing a death sentence pronounced upon them. Indeed, although there is a paucity of evidence relating to the numbers of children actually executed in this period,[3] the process of having a capital sentence imposed,

---

3. While Bayne-Powell (1939) cites a contemporary account of the hanging of boys of 14 who had been involved in the Gordon Riots, Knell (1965) notes that no child under 14 years was

respited and replaced by a sentence of transportation, then conditionally pardoned and placed into the Society's protection was the lot of quite a few Philanthropic children. As an alternative to the gallows — or even to long-term incarceration in the hulks or other contaminating custodial institutions — it certainly was a benign disposal. This route, nonetheless, still entailed a substantial period of prior imprisonment. For George Cornelius Sharpless it appears to have lasted around two years. George was admitted, aged 13, in 1798 after:

> [having] the sentence of death passed upon him July 13th 1796 at the Assizes at Nottingham for felony; was afterwards ordered to be transported for life and put aboard the *Hillsborough* for New South Wales; and at length pardoned by His Majesty on condition of his being received into the Philanthropic Reform.

No further details of George Cornelius's background are mentioned in the Philanthropic records. But, remarkably, fragments of petitions — sent on his behalf — still survive amidst Judges Reports, held in the National Archives.[4] Those referred to are dated from the 5th to 20th May 1797. They are mostly addressed to Daniel Parker Coke, Esq. of Inner Temple in the hope he would pass them on to the Home Secretary of the time, the Duke of Portland. Included is one signed by some good citizens of Nottingham. While knowing that mercy already had been extended and the boy would not face the gallows, they observe that he was still under sentence of transportation:

> to which [they] had hoped that the extreme Youth of the prisoner would have given irresistible weight in the merciful disposition of the King had not unfavourable reports regarding his Parents unfortunately reached the royal Ear.

With this unhappy circumstance in mind, these worthies then vouched for the good character of his father, George Sharpless, who had worked for them 'in his business of Jobber of Beasts' and had always 'behaved with exemplary fidelity and honesty'. His mother, Matilda, also deserved 'the same

---

executed after receiving a capital sentence at the Old Bailey between 1801 and 1836. However, John Any Bird Bell, aged 14, would be convicted of murder and executed at Maidstone, in 1831.
4. HO–47/21.

character'. In further letters (possibly written by herself), Matilda states that she was presently 'indigent haveing no work at my Needle, being for some years employed in making Gloves for the Army but has had no Orders for several months'. Her 'poor Child', however, had been in the local gaol for a year 'upon Straw & Double iron'd as tho' he had been of adult age'. As she now had heard that George Cornelius was about to be 'banished from his native land and doomed to all the horrors of a life of bondage', his loss would shortly bring her 'Grey Hairs with sorrow to the Grave'. The correspondence was passed on to William Baldwin, Esq., at the Treasury, thus:

> Mr Coke presents his compl^{ts} to Mr Baldwin – is very sorry that his Duty compels him to send the enclosed papers but he does not follow them with any request.

These documents do not reveal how George Cornelius harpless afterwards came to the attention of the Philanthropic Society. Likewise, the precise route taken by Mary Mander into its reform is not identified. Admitted, aged 11 in 1797, Mary was described as follows:

> This girl was tried and convicted at the Old Bailey by the name of Ann Crawley for shoplifting and received a sentence of death but afterwards obtained His Majesty's Pardon on condition of her being received into this Institution–her father is a bricklayer's labourer and her mother is employed in making hammocks.

The Philanthropists could, however, be pro-active in setting the admission process under way. Stephen Lee was ten years old when admitted to the Reform in 1796 and appears to have received merely a sentence of secondary rather than capital punishment. But, with 'the case having appeared in the publick papers' and Stephen seeming a 'proper Object' to be 'rendered a useful member of society', the society dispatched a letter to Lord Chief Baron Macdonald. As is noted:

> This boy was tried with his mother at Reading Assizes, before the Lord Chief Baron, for a robbery and found guilty, but appearing to have acted under the influence of his mother, was sentenced to only six months imprisonment–at the Committee's request, His Lordship applied to the Secretary of State, by whose means His Majesty's pardon was obtained on condition that he should be delivered over to the Society.

The society's records also illuminate how magisterial discretion could be exercised in favour of diversion from the criminal justice system. As we see from the case-history of James Cooper, who was nine years old when admitted in 1793, his 'tender age' played a crucial role in the decision making process:

> This boy [with Edward Poole, age 8, son of Poole the Highwayman] were convicted on February 7th Sessions last for stealing a child's frock–but on account of their youth were not punished but sent to the Institution by the recommendation of the Magistrates at Hatton Garden Police Office. The boy's father is in St. Martin's Workhouse, his mother is a washerwoman.

Likewise, some Shadwell magistrates would take this mitigating factor into consideration in the case of Daniel Arrogant. As Daniel was 12 years old and appears to have committed a felony for which other children might receive a capital sentence, his case-history helps shed further light on how the full stretch of the criminal justice system could be circumvented. Daniel had:

> neither father or mother–apprenticed about eight months to Mr Peale, Taylor, Ship Alley, Willclose Square (from the Workhouse) by the officers of the Parish of Aldgate. Charged by the said master on oath before the magistrates at the Public Office, Shadwell, with having on the [.?.] day of [.?.] in the absence of his master in the country, forced open a door with a pair of tongs, and with a large spike, the lock of a till in the room, into which he had broken and with having stolen thereout two gold seals, a gold breast pin &c.–and upon the discovery of this offence, he also confessed the having robbed his said master at several times of halfpence–which his master had missed without being able to account for it.
> The above magistrates committed him to the House of Correction in Cold Bath Fields for a further hearing, instead of fully committing him for tryal on account of his tender age, and a view to an application to the Philanthropic Society in his behalf, for which purpose the said magistrates, very humanely, sent him in the care of an Officer with a letter, dated October 27th, expressing a wish that this Society would take him under their care, as it was not the desire of his master to prosecute him — but which must take place if he be not received by the Philanthropic Society.

We are not informed whether pressure had been applied to Daniel's master in order to sway his intention to prosecute. But at this time, more than 80 per cent of prosecutions were conducted by the victims of crimes themselves. They could, nonetheless, be persuaded to let the matter drop and sometimes were satisfied to have the culprit verbally admonished when the case appeared before the court. This was less likely to happen in cases of felony. Magistrates were legally required to refer these to Quarter Sessions or Assize Courts on indictment rather than deal with them summarily. A degree of flexibility could still, nonetheless, be exercised in deciding which acts should be treated as felonies. Misdemeanours, however, offered the bench rather more scope for discretion and the opportunity to dispose of cases by way of informal mediation between interested parties. Such negotiations may have occurred in the case of Jeremiah Willett, aged 12 when admitted in 1795. Jeremiah was the:

> Son of Jane Willett (Naked Boy Court, No.5 Ludgate Hill) who was left a widow with eight children and who since her husband's death has had another now at the breast, making in all, nine. The mother bears the character of a very honest hardworking sober woman and as such respected and assisted by her neighbours.
> The above son, on the contrary, a very bad one. Has frequently robbed his mother and once of nine shillings which he spent on a boat on the Thames at sixpence an hour–has robbed several of the neighbours of different articles and escaped prosecution, particularly in one instance by Mr Purden out of tenderness and respect for his mother.

If the mitigating circumstance of his mother's good reputation underpinned Jeremiah's fortunes, other children were directed to the Philanthropic Reform after prosecutors failed to turn up in court. This occurred in the case of Michael van Coulster, who was admitted in 1794 aged 12 years old. Michael had been:

> Born in Scotland Yard–his father was a Doctor of Physic–died 6 years ago–his mother died about 4 years ago–he lived with his mother until about half a year before her death–she got her livelihood by washing and sent him to sea as a servant to Lieut. Peacock of the *Satan* where he staid two years and a half–left the ship at Portsmouth about a year ago when the ship was paid off–he had lived with his godmother Lady Price in the King's Bench Prison as an errand boy ever since–he went every evening to his sister who lives in Drury Lane–a p———-t-. He was asked by some boys to steal a rope from the ship which he did and sold it [for] 5/s.–he stole a till from a Chandler's Shop in Bishopsgate Street about three months ago and was committed by Mr Addington–but not convicted for want of prosecutors applying.[5]

---

5. Although Michael's godmother's abode was usually reserved for debtors, the conditions they could enjoy therein depended on what could be paid for from their remaining finances

The victims of Charles Smith's repeat offending were not reluctant to prosecute. Charles can be placed in the 'one last chance' category of offender welcomed into the Reform. Adding to the Philanthropic's stock of knowledge on human nature, he was 13 years old when admitted in 1796, after being found:

> totally ungovernable—at various times absented himself from home without the least provocation ... he was on Tuesday the fourteenth of February detected in robbing a Church in Cornhill, on the fifteenth committed to Bridewell to Hard Labour and to receive the correction of the House.

This did nothing to deter Charles. After his time inside expired he went home and:

> [on] April the fourth, found means in the night to get out of bed and leave the house, taking with him a canvas bag, tinder box, flint and steel, matches, candles and key of the door.

Armed with these accoutrements, Charles entered a nearby house and hid before the family went to bed. On being discovered he 'confessed his design was to have let in a gang of thieves [to] strip the house'. Upon this information he was 'taken and committed next day to take his trial'. However, owing to some 'error' in the indictment, the Bill for the same was thrown out 'to the surprize and mortification' of his parents. They then had him confined by the Lord Mayor 'having now no recourse left but the expectation of getting him admitted into the Reform'.

The prospect of placing their son in the Philanthropic's corrective custody may also have afforded comfort to the parents of James Dalziell. James was ten years old when admitted in 1793 and had 'at sundry times been guilty of pilfering and stealing alone, and in company with other boys'. Most other options available to his responsible parents had failed to produce a good citizen, for:

---

and those of their friends. Weinreb and Hibbert (1983/1993) note that in 1828 it would be described as one of the most desirable places of incarceration in London. In its courtyard tailors, hatters, piano-makers, chandlers and oyster sellers plied their trades and 120 gallons of gin were sold weekly.

His father, who bears a good character, has hitherto tried every means to reclaim him from his wicked ways in vain, both by encouraging him to do well and also by severe punishment for his thefts. He has two other children younger and as he is absent from home on his business except at meal times or in the evening, cannot attend so much as the urgent necessity of this boy's care demands to his conduct; the mother also is in a great measure, by her younger children, prevented from checking his wicked courses. They had placed him in a School of Industry, but his lying and stealing practices were injurious to the other boys, from which cause he has been removed.

Even more meagre evidence of being beyond parental care and control proved acceptable to the society. In 1796 James Brady, aged nine, gained a place in the Reform on the basis of barely emergent 'vicious' propensities:

His father in law and his mother bear a good character, they are poor and cannot afford to put the boy to school, having two other children–this boy is of ungovernable temper and behaves very ill to his mother who can maintain no influence over him; he once robbed her of three pence half-penny, the only instance which appears of dishonesty, though he is in utmost danger from the bad company he keeps.

Although the Philanthropic net might appear randomly cast, some guidance on the selection procedure had been provided in the regulations drawn-up after Robert Young's downfall. These stipulated that four visitors should be 'selected from the subscribers at large' to find and report 'Objects for the reception of the Society'. They were also to act as intermediaries through whom subscribers and friends might recommend candidates. The visitors were then expected to undertake the 'business of investigating their true circumstances'. As this entry indicates, their investigations could garner quite detailed facts:

Christiana Carter (age 12) admitted 1797–Apprenticed from Cripplegate without St. Giles Workhouse the 15th November 1796, to Richard Allison of Newington Street, Holborn, St. Giles in the Fields, umbrella maker, until of age. Her master says the girl was recommended by Mr Bond of Bow Street to be brought to this Committee, charged with diverse thefts at different times, instigated by her Mother who is in the same Workhouse, and an Aunt called Mrs Orsall, Mary le Bone, a woman shoemaker. The girl confesses several thefts. The master works for Adams Umbrella Manufactory, 207 High Holborn, opposite Bloomsbury Square. The girl's Father's a Taylor, but gone to Sea in the Shark Sloop now at Halifax. The above case, on enquiry of Mr Adams, umbrella maker, by Mr Coxe, Visitor, being fully identified, the girl was ordered admission.

The visitors also investigated whether changed family circumstances might allow children to leave the Institution. These enquiries could arise when parents who previously had been in a state of financial distress then claimed they could support their offspring. Occasionally, children were returned once the visitors confirmed that formerly dissolute parents had themselves been reformed. As Edward Sutton's case-history illustrates, even transportation could produce this beneficial effect. Edward was nine years old when admitted in 1790 and his father had been sent to Botany Bay. But when Edward ran away from St. George's Fields in 1797, his father brought him back. At a time when returning to England without government permission was itself a grave crime, suspicions about this circumstance led the society to check on the situation. The father had prospered, however, for:

> Colonel Harnage having reported to the Committee that the father of this boy, who was transported and released, had by his good conduct obtained from Governor Phillip his discharge and had since not only been appointed storekeeper by the Governor, but had also returned to England with an excellent character, had applied to have his son, who has been in the Reform ... delivered to him in order to take him and the rest of the family back to Port Jackson, to which he is now returning with the consent of the Government. Ordered that Edward Sutton be delivered to his father—and necessary clothing given to him.[6]

These Philanthropic visitors can be regarded as social explorers who became intimately acquainted 'with wretchedness in its last and lowest sources'. Accumulating such knowledge already had been a by-product of the medical endeavours of the Philanthropic Dr. Lettsom and Dr. Sims in the Rookeries of London. Another medical gentlemen, William Houlston, Surgeon, gained similar expertise. In the company of J. H. Hooper, Apothecary, he had been a committee member alongside Jeremiah Bentham in 1790 and

---

6. Governor Phillip was the Navy captain under whose command the first fleet of eleven ships had carried 750 convicts and 250 marines to Botany Bay in 1787. When the marines wouldn't take part in the preparation or government of this new penal settlement, Governor Phillip had resorted to finding all his overseers – and the first police force – from the ranks of the convicts. They were encouraged by perks and privileges: at first by 'freedom from toil' and then by being allotted convicts for their own use and, further, by the 'granting or promise of pardons' (Hirst, 1995:237-9).

took his turn in attending to visitorial duties. Mr. Coxe (who investigated Christiana Carter's case) does not appear to have had any medical interests but is probably the Daniel Coxe who was also on the committee of the nearby Lambeth Asylum and was a common councillor. However, the Reverend Mr. Richard Southgate (who rescued John Major from the streets) had an interest in the arts and sciences and held the position of assistant librarian at the British Museum. As curate of St. Giles in the Fields he was to be found:

> through the last years of his life ... every day (with but few intervals of exception) consoling the afflicted, and pointing out the true grounds of consolation to the wretched inhabitants of St. Giles's.[7]

James Bosanquet (who recorded George Hicks's case history) was a member of a prominent Philanthropic family which included Samuel Bosanquet, a city merchant and banker, a justice of the peace and high sheriff for Essex. Elected a vice-president of the society by 1792, he served as Governor of the Bank of England from 1791-93 and was father to Philanthropic committee members Charles and Samuel (junior). While Charles would gain renown for his treatises on a variety of economic topics, Samuel (junior) supported the SPCK, was a member of the SBCP and subscribed to the Marine Society. He may also have been impressed to see the transforming results of the Philanthropic enterprise at the Anniversary Dinner of 1793, when:

> the children under the Society's protection walked in procession round the room–First, upwards of thirty girls, preceded by their mistress: after these, near one hundred boys; each department led by their respective masters, the carpenter, printer, shoemaker, & taylor; the Superintendant & Steward also attending.

> The decent appearance and orderly demeanour of the children filled the minds of the spectators with the most pleasing sensations, the natural result of contemplating the happy change which had been wrought in the situation of this numerous little group, lately in the high road of vice, now leading through the paths of Industry and Virtue to character and happiness. Thus a fair prospect opened of their becoming useful

---

7. *The Gentleman's Magazine* (1795, vol.65).

members of that community of which, but for a timely and benevolent interposition of the Philanthropic Society, they must soon have been the dread and annoyance.[8]

This gratifying spectacle, as we shall see, could be dispelled by disorders reigning within the world of the reform.

Inside the School of Morals

The Philanthropic venture had commenced with the intention of receiving children no more than six years old. But, when children of nine or ten came under notice, the society's members 'felt it a duty not to consign such to ruin, without affording them a chance of salvation'. That humane impulse, blended with a pragmatic concern to select children 'capable of immediately engaging in useful labours', soon led them to accept children of up to 14 years of age. This 'important alteration in the Plan' also stemmed from the gentlemen's Enlightenment pre-occupations. Gripped by faith in the 'plastic power of education' through which 'virtue and industry ... are articles that can be manufactured and the stock increased at pleasure', initial studies of their wards revealed that:

> the mischiefs many had feared from the evil habits of the children of so ripe an age must have contracted in bad company, and a vagrant life, were found within the power of seasonable correction and good government to prevent.

So, how had this Philanthropic feat been achieved? Indeed, what methods were employed to exercise the children's minds in the 'social character' so that the qualities wanted in man would be 'called forth in youth, put to tryal, brought under government ... and confirmed by habit'? At the foundation of the Philanthropic design was a 'School of Morals'. Therein, a catalogue

---

8. Mary Smith most likely joined this procession. She had been admitted in 1792, aged nine, and was declared to be 'one of the most artful and depraved characters of her age that in all probability ever was heard of'. We might ponder over this assessment. To 'exemplify the truth of this assertion' her history was related as follows: 'The person under whose protection she had been having often found it necessary to correct her died and during the time he was in the coffin she stole an opportunity unseen of getting into the room – and uncovered the sheet and spoke to the corpse in these terms: "I don't mind you, you can't hurt me now".'.

of vices and virtues was displayed to remind the children which they were to practise and which to shun:

Virtues	Vices
industry	idleness
honesty	dishonesty
piety	impiety
obedience	disobedience
good temper	ill temper
kindness	cruelty
decent language	immoral language
gratitude	ingratitude
contentment	discontent

To ensure that moral improvement proceeded as intended, each week a 'Regulator' tallied what had been recorded by the children's masters and mistresses in the 'black book' of faults and merits. That personage then dispensed tokens of honour or disgrace on a system explicitly 'adopted from the practice of Mr Raikes of Gloucester, Institutor of Sunday Schools'. By 1792, this embryo mark-system of punishment and reward was being administered by a chaplain-superintendant appointed to be 'resident near the spot'. Besides providing instruction in the principles of morals and religion, he was expected to report every instance of ill conduct on the part of the children to the committee at their weekly meetings. When the society moved to St.

George's Fields, most of these duties came under the remit of a non-clerical Superintendant Durand.

With industry given a privileged place in the virtues to be inculcated, yet believing that 'no good is done to humanity or the state' if 'honest men' were thus 'turned out of bread', the society set out to employ their wards 'primarily, in the produce of such things as they would consume'. To some extent, self-sufficiency had been achieved through selecting trades which provided shoes and clothing. But, to keep the boys employed and provide opportunities for instructing them properly, outside orders were soon sought. Additional industry and income were generated by placing printing on the Philanthropic programme. This was joined by the rope-making trade on the transition to Southwark. Choosing such trades had the particular 'utility' of protecting the children from the contaminations of the Metropolis. Early experience had, indeed, led to the trade of bricklayer being discontinued:

> because as the buildings in the late situation of the Reform near Hackney were completed, the boys could not be employed, unless they went out to work, by which means they would have been removed from inspection, and greatly endangered in their morals by mixing with various characters, and frequently resorting to public houses.

By the beginning of 1793, the numbers of children in the Institution had increased to 127 and were simply classified as follows:

```
At the Reform . . . . . . . . . . . . . . . . . . . 91 boys
At the Female Reform . . . . . . . . . . . . . 30 girls
At Retford . . . . . . . . . . . . . . . . . . . . . .  6 boys
```

Mention of Retford here, alerts us to the decision to accept the Revolution Mill Company's offer to take some children into a worsted manufactory, located near Nottingham, in 1792. Apprenticing pauper children out to such mills was a common practice of Poor Law guardians and was also followed by the Foundling Hospital trustees. The Philanthropic initiative in this field was, nonetheless, presented to the public as an expedient measure for over-coming the problem of maintaining 'some of the younger children of both sexes whose labour would be productive of little benefit to the Institution'. Being aware that the chosen children might suffer adverse treatment when they arrived at Retford, the society attempted to deflect dangers by ensuring they were 'placed under the immediate care of a gentleman of known humanity'—a Mr. Teschmaker—who soon was able to give a satisfactory account of the boys under his care.

This experiment was short-lived. By 1794 only one boy remained at Retford and a later request from Pendleton Mills for children—particularly females—was refused by the committee. Once settled into St. George's Fields, the society's usual practice was to set boys to work under the guidance of master-tradesmen within the walls of the Reform. If they were old enough and proved to have some aptitude and liking for their master, they were then apprenticed to his particular trade. These arrangements also followed Poor Law practice in being formalised before magistrates. In some cases the apprenticeship premium was paid by the committee, in others the parents paid what they could or, where the ward's place of settlement was known, the parish was invited to do its duty.

Sometimes, downturns in one or another Philanthropic trade led the society to 'place out' boys with masters whom the visitors vetted for their moral probity. Vetting of potential employers would also be undertaken when choosing where to place girls out as servants. Placement was, nonetheless, a fraught task. As committee members lamented when reporting on the state of the Female Reform in 1796:

> the difficulty of disposing of these girls is considerable–a menial domestic servitude is almost the only situation to be looked for, it has been found for several of them; very minute enquiries into the character of the parties with whom the girls have been placed having in every instance been made–the Committee has not always been successful–the girls have disliked their places, or their conduct has not been approved of by their masters or mistresses.

We will leave the girls in the background for the moment to note that when suitable masters—outside the Philanthropic walls—were found for boys already apprenticed within the reform, the children were taken before a magistrate to have their indentures cancelled. This could be facilitated by members of the wider network of Philanthropic support. In January 1793, for instance, the superintendent was asked to investigate how to deal with

Thomas Denbigh, a boy 'of the most atrocious character' who had 'eloped' and was afterwards 'taken up as a vagrant by a Constable'. Mr. Durand then:

> waited on Mr Colquhoun, one of the magistrates of the Police Office, Shoreditch on account of Thomas Denbigh–who is to be taken proper care of until Friday when he is to be brought up to the Committee for further examination ... Mr Colquhoun expressed his satisfaction with the laudable intention of the Society and informs your Superintendent that he should be at all times ready to give every assistance in his power.

In February this promise was kept. After waiting on the secretary of the Marine Society to ask whether that enterprise would accept young James Davis, the superintendent was requested to return with the boy who would then be examined for 'size and state of health'. With the examination proving satisfactory, Mr. Durand was given a 'note addressed to the magistrates signifying that the boy J. Davis should be received when his indentures were cancelled'. At this, he went to the police office and found Mr. Colquhoun who happily obliged. Thereupon, James was sent to the Marine Society at four o'clock and 'with many others set off that evening for Portsmouth'. For William Lowe, however, the destination was the King's navy. Having had:

> his indentures cancelled at Union Hall, [he was] sent under the care of the Porter, J. Dunn, and placed on board His Majesty's Ship *Southampton* commanded by the Honourable Captain Robert Forbes, under whose care he was placed.

Although William volunteered for a career on the ocean waves, sending boys to sea frequently featured in the panoply of Philanthropic punishments. Indeed, while many boys would be keen to earn gratuities for their productivity in the workplace and have their general good conduct rewarded by small gifts of 'Articles of Play, [such] as Batts, Balls, Tops, &c. or in good wholesome Fruit of the Season', some failed to calculate that these pleasures outweighed the pains of the world outside. Amongst those who proved resistant to the society's reforming strategies was Thomas Burn, aged 13 on admission:

> Bred a thief from his cradle–his mother was transported for uttering counterfeit coin and his father was hanged for housebreaking–the boy was imprisoned for a burglary, in the Compter.

Thomas was placed with the shoemaker in January 1790. In October he deserted. The ledgers reveal that he had been found 'perfectly incorrigible'. Likewise hardened was James Still, who was admitted in 1789 aged 15. On his desertion it was observed:

> This boy never shewed the smallest marks of reformation but on the contrary was continually relating his old tricks with pleasure–had a very sullen temper–a most vindictive disposition–possessed of great cunning and had he not been particularly watched must have corrupted many of the other boys.

Such failures did not prevent the society giving recalcitrant wards more than one probationary 'tryal'. One beneficiary of this policy was William Causer. William was twelve years old when admitted, on 7th July 1792, from Newgate where he had been confined for having stolen a pair of plated buckles. He escaped from Philanthropic custody quite quickly but, on 10th July, was brought back by his mother and father. Their display of assiduous parental responsibility possibly had some impact on the society's deliberations over whether he should be readmitted. William's history continues thus:

> 12th July . . . . deserted
> 24th July . . . . re-admitted
> 28th July . . . . deserted
> 14th August. . . . . re-admitted
> (brought back by a Constable employed for that purpose)
> 18th August . . . . made his escape
> (from the place of confinement)
> 30th August. . . . . re-admitted again

Philanthropic patience was exhausted. Although no subsequent misdemeanours are recorded, on 4th September William was 'Expelled the Reform'.

Whilst William may have been cast out to prevent a harmful counter-culture pervading the Institution, expulsion from the society's protection had been brandished as an exemplary punishment from the commencement of its operations. This branch of the Philanthropic system of discipline also included badges of disgrace, early bedtimes or floggings as well as confinement in the cells on diets of bread and water.[9] More formal means might be employed in regard to children who had been indentured by the society. They could be taken before a magistrate and, as refractory apprentices under the Poor Laws, receive corrective whippings or a short spell in a bridewell. Yet, as this incarceration tended to cancel-out any virtues a Philanthropic sojourn had instilled — and with many boys not competent or old enough to be apprenticed — the society searched for other solutions.

By the beginning of 1793, the Philanthropic gentlemen were looking to the sea with hope. That year did not start well. On the first day, the master carpenter informed the superintendent that several of his boys would not obey his orders — 'viz. Lynch, Lewis, Vinney, Stewart, Mitchell, Seddon and Tucker'. At this 'intelligence', the superintendent went with him to the field where he saw the boys making their escape over the wall. They were pursued, some were captured and when Lewis, Vinney and Mitchell returned in the evening they were separated from the other boys 'until the committee's pleasure [was] known what to do with them'. On the 4th of January, an expedition of Philanthropists set out for the city to meet with the Lord Mayor. As is recorded in the *Minutes*:

> The Superintendent attended Mr Harman, Mr Boldero, and Mr Jackson to the Mansion House–these gentlemen being deputed to consult with the Lord Mayor on some mode to punish the before-mentioned refractory boys. From his Lordship they went to the Marine Society office and then back to the Mansion House.

If this to-ing and fro-ing makes the Philanthropic gentlemen appear all at-sea, their explorations brought an interim reward. The superintendent afterwards received:

> a note from his Lordship addressed to the magistrates at Union Hall and also his Lordship's orders to wait on Mr Pasdon to enquire if there were separate places of confinement for disorderly apprentices in their prisons.

---

9. No Philanthropic girls appear to have been flogged although they were 'chastised' and also confined in cells.

Hopes were dashed, however. Joining the superintendent on his onward journey we find that:

> Mr Pasdon being from home, [I] enquired of one of the Officers of Police—was told there were. I then presented the note to the magistrates and was informed by them that there were only two places of confinement and they were occupied.
>
> They desired I would return to his Lordship and acquaint him how they were at present circumstanced—and were sorry it was not within their power to assist his Lordship's good intentions, as they were at all times willing to lend every aid for the good of the Society.

At this less than heartening news, Superintendent Durand returned to the Mansion House and was 'desired to attend his Lordship the next day at 12 of the clock'. Having done so, it would seem that whatever his Lordship's good intentions precisely were he couldn't carry them into practical effect. Indeed, the matter of being *ultra vires* appears to have loomed, for:

> after his Lordship had consulted a person whom he then called in, desired that his compliments might be presented to the gentlemen and acquaint them he was extremely sorry that he could not do them the service he intended, it being a stretch of his power which he found it was not advisable for him to pursue.[10]

If the superintendent's subsequent search for captains willing to take refractory boys on their ships was underpinned by the belief that 'he might then, with the committee's concurrence, save a few more from destruction by sending them to sea', a few determined lads would afterwards escape the rigours of maritime life and return to the perils of mainland society. One such was Thomas Pearce, aged 13 when admitted in June 1790. His catalogue of vices over the next three years led vice-president Dr Sims to desire that the superintendent should submit 'to the Committee for their consideration the propriety of consulting an impress captain' in order that Pearce—and two other boys—might be:

> sent to sea as from their general conduct and considering their age and the time they have been in the Reform, there seems little reason to expect they will answer the Intent designed.[11]

---

10. This Lord Mayor was Philanthropic vice-president and soon to be Sir James Sanderson
11. In 1796 Dr Sims's advocacy of this exclusionary disposal practice was expressed thus: 'There

Having been banished into the care of 'a Captain William Lucas of the ship *Mentor*, bound to the South Seas for three years', Thomas was discovered at the back gate of the reform in April 1794. He was not re-admitted. Enquiries established he had run away from the ship and then wandered about the country while subsisting by begging. The superintendent ordered him to be taken back to his master. But, as Captain Lucas had sailed, Thomas was consigned into the care of Mrs. Lucas 'in order to be immediately sent on board a Man-of-War'.

To go aboard a man-of-war with the prospect of the King's bounty or prize money in view, was a compelling attraction for many boys. Indeed, the lure of the sea began, disconcertingly, to pose a problem. The day after James Davis had marched off to the Marine Society, James Kidd was sent in the same direction. Word of this opportunity for adventure appears to have spread and the superintendent felt obliged to report that:

> Some of the boys having expressed a desire to go to sea last night–and your Superintendent considering this and intending it as a punishment when he mentioned it to the Committee for this purpose–he found it necessary to address them on the subject lest instead of ... [preventing] ... their absconding–the novelty and youthful desire of change might induce them to it–by which means his intentions would be frustrated.

Superintendent Durand's search for additional modes of punishment can be appreciated. The recital of escapades contended with included 'elopements' out of skylights, down chimneys, through drains and over the walls to go birds-nesting, black-berrying or searching gardens for peaches and nectarines. John Amory had different matters in mind. In October 1798:

> It being a rejoicing evening on account of the naval victory obtained by the intrepid Admiral Nelson ... [he] ... got over the wall and absconded–it is imagined to see the illuminations.

---

are now in the reform ten or 12 boys whom there are little hopes of reclaiming; whose association with the others may be highly pernicious to the rest; and who ought therefore to be got rid of, as soon as any tolerable situation can be found for them – perhaps it may be well to place them with some masters of vessels in the South Whale Fishery Trade or any other long voyages'.

Nathaniel Sturch and James Bailey prepared for even greater adventures. This pair of 'audacious offenders' absconded early in the morning of 9th September 1793:

> [and] took with them a box containing one shilling and eight pence, two New Testaments which your Superintendent had given them last week, three hats, two pair of breeches & their best shoes. They were sent after and directions given the route they were likely to take and were found by Mr Williamson and the Porter in a Hole between Blackheath and Shooters Hill—they had disposed of their breeches and shoes and had bought white metal buttons which, after cutting off the Buttons of the Reform, they had sewed on their jackets—the Buttons of the Reform being strewn about where they sat—they were immediately brought back.[12]

Failing to return after being sent on errands was another item in the boys' repertoire of misdeeds. Such *exeats* may seem surprising in view of the intention to keep them segregated within the walls of the Reform. Allowing some to venture out was, nevertheless, in keeping with the Philanthropic philosophy of treating the boys like ordinary apprentices. It also provided an opportunity to assess whether they would conform to the society's rules for such excursions. Most displayed a willing obedience. However, one boy failed to return after expressing interest in being a spectator to the dramatic aftermath of houses falling down (and burying 16 people in the ruins) at Clare Market in 1796. The desire to be a spectator at an execution drew another boy away from the path of virtue.

Minor mischiefs could, alas, escalate into riotous assemblies. When such circumstances arose, handling the boys was no easy matter. As the superintendent relates—somewhat breathlessly—on 16th May 1794:

> this evening I found the boys in a state of disorder, on my inquiry into the cause was informed that some of the boys had been making a very vigorous noise in the shoemaker's shop and that they had before squirted water at the Porter who had reprimanded them for this conduct—and was gone to the bottom of the Field to some of the little boys who were throwing stones.
> But hearing so great a noise, and Mr Russell [the Steward] coming out of his office to enquire the cause, he returned and Mr Russell followed him, when, on entering

---

12. The Philanthropic buttons were embossed with a symbolic beehive of industry.

the shoemakers shop several of the boys made their escape out of the windows upon the grounds and those he found in the shop he corrected as they would not tell who was concerned, one of which (Watts) struck him and got a hoe in hand and said he would split the Porter's skull, and the others advanced as if to fall on him, which the Porter prevented, after which he came to his lodge and several of the boys threw stones at him–he came out and prevented any further mischief.

On the 17th of January the previous year, the superintendent had not been so fortunate. When punishing some boys for being insolent to hired workmen, another group took advantage of his attention being diverted and kindled a fire with wood shavings. Upon the watchman relating he was afraid to touch the boy bringing the shavings 'for fear of his life', the superintendent sent one of the carpenters in pursuit. The boys surrounded the carpenter 'and threw anything they could lay hold of at him'. Catching-up at this point, the superintendent received 'a stroke on [his] face with a large Battledore — and a blow from a brick or stone on the thigh'.

This alarming episode led the society to set up a 'Committee of Enquiry into the Cause and Effects of the ill conduct of several of the boys in the Reform on Thursday last'. Having evaluated existing disciplinary practices and after examining the boys' ration of leisure hours, the Committee decided to establish an 'evening school'. On the 21st of January a further improvement was set in hand when:

> The Carpenter went this afternoon to Deptford and received every information necessary for making the machines ordered by the Committee for refractory boys, six of which will be made as soon as possible.

It is conceivable that these 'machines' were some benign contraptions designed to provide safe and sanitary conditions of confinement. They might even have been designed to deliver a rationally calculated portion of pain. But, as there is no record of such being employed, we might assume that the carpenter contrived to fashion some constraints in the shape of a collar. These were certainly ready when James Ferry and George Wills made an escape the next month 'the former with a Collar about his neck and the latter with a Fetter'. Yet, while both types of device were used to restrain convicts, slaves and maritime mutineers in this era, the innovative Philanthropic collar appears to have provoked a complaint about cruel — if not unusual — punishment.

This found its way to outside authorities. The superintendent records that Ferry was brought back to the Reform the next day by his mother:

> after having been before the justices in Worship Street, and his mother there complaining of the cruelty he had sustained by having the Collar put upon his neck–and which had been taken off by some person on the street after much difficulty.

The opening months of 1793 had, however, been particularly fraught for Mr. Durand. Not only had the boys proved troublesome but he had to contend with the society's new neighbours at St. George's Fields. On the 11th of January, he visited the person who kept the grocer's shop opposite the Reform and was told that 'a boy had acquainted him that he saw three of our boys who had stole a box from him which I understood contained plumbs, and likewise a piece of bacon from his neighbour'. The superintendent then contrived to be:

> in the Reform as soon as it was light in order to see if I could find the bacon, box, or any of the plumbs hid. I searched every one of the Shoemakers boxes, Taylor's room & desired the Carpenter to look behind the doors but could make no discovery
>
> I then went to the person who had lost the articles and desired they would stop in future any boy of ours that should come to their shop and send for me and I should attend immediately.

Later the same day:

> The Carpenter informed me that [Richard] Starkey, one of his boys, had got very much affected by Liquor–and in a few minutes–as he had seen him but a little while before and he was perfectly sober. On enquiring, I learnt he had been at the Alehouse [at] the corner of the Reform where he had got some Liquor.
>
> I went to the House and reprimanded both the master and mistress for selling spirits to any of the boys–and desired they never would hereafter permit any of the boys to have Liquor, or enter within their doors. They promised a strict compliance with this request.

We might suppose the superintendent was commended for attempting to put such temptations on the doorstep out of bounds. Although 'small beer' was an acceptable refreshment—being one of the safest liquids to drink in these less than sanitary times—the Philanthropists frowned upon the consumption of spirituous liquors. As the Philanthropic Dr. Lettsom graphically illustrated by means of a 'Moral and Physical Thermometer', beverages such as water, milk and small beer could induce health, wealth, serenity of mind and happiness. In contrast, the progressive consequences of consuming even a little drop of spirits were punishments associated with vices and disease; namely debt, rags, hunger, the poor house, jails, whipping, the hulks, Botany Bay and the gallows.[13]

The next day didn't augur any better for the superintendent. Even without the aid of intoxicating substances, some boys forgot the catalogue of virtues they were supposed to digest. As he had to report:

> James Hicks and Henry Humble went away this morning–the latter returned at three o'clock and I immediately ordered him to be tied up and chastised him ...
>
> Thomas Barrer, one of the Taylors [boys], being caught gambling, confined him in the Solitary Cell.

In the evening, the superintendent visited the boys in the field. On returning to his house he found another neighbour:

> a Gingerbread Baker, who lives in the road and near the Reform [who] complained to me that one of the boys had broke his window–and said the same boy had brought him a bad shilling to be changed – but on refusing to take it [the boy] bid him take care of his windows.

The superintendent's day of trial had not ended. Following this report of threatening behaviour, the person who served the reform with vegetables came and:

> said he had lost two bunches of turnips and he thought some of my boys had stole them.
>
> I told him I believed he was mistaken–as I had ordered the Carpenter's boys to be locked in and the others were under the care of their masters.

Then, a little later:

---

13. Lettsom, (n.d.) *Hints Respecting the Effects of a Little Drop.*

the Blacksmith, who likewise does business for us, came to inform me that his son had picked up a bunch of Turnips, with a long string, part of which appears to have been artfully slung around them—and by which means they had been drawn off.

With exasperations accumulating we can appreciate why Superintendent Durand then curtly 'desired the Smith to return them to their proper owner'. We can also note he begged leave to observe:

> that tho' it is not his intention to take the part of the boys improperly—and indeed he has very little reason—still, among such a bunch of Wretches with which the Market abounds, he trusts that the Committee will consider that every Robbery laid to the Charges is not always committed by them—culpable as they are—and this he has been perfectly convinced of.

The superintendent probably was correct in his assessment. Having just moved into St. George's Fields, Philanthropic boys provided a new target for the displacement of blame. The boys, nonetheless, still had much mischief to do. They 'tossed up for halfpence' and continued their picaresque 'evening and morning excursions'. The superintendent was concerned and:

> fearing the ill consequences that might ensue from [..?..] boys being loose on the Town, he thought it proper to go to the Union Hall and desire some of the Runners endeavour to take them.

He then 'went to Tower Hill, the place of their usual resort' but on being informed that 'the afternoon was the most probable time to catch them' returned to the reform to put other boys to work. He set off again, taking two men with him and 'traversed the Quays, Tower Hill … Whitechapel, Moorfields and the most noted places', but without success. Next day, however, one of the runaways was brought back and 'confined until one of the machines is ready'. The superintendent also informed the committee that:

> a letter has been sent to his Grace the Duke of Leeds [the Society's President], reflecting on your Superintendent's Character as having been cruel to the boys under his care.

As the collars were not yet available, the cruelty most likely referred to another mode of punishment. This, possibly, was one which the Reverend

Mr. Southgate considered 'improper' when visiting to address the boys in May 1794. As was reported:

> Mr Southgate on his leaving the Reform mentioned to your Superintendent that the boys had complained to him about the Porter's chastisement and afterwards asked to see the Porter and what he usually chastised the boys with –
> On being shewn the Cane, and having been informed, for the other offences, a cat-of-nine-tails was generally used–both of which he said was improper, and that a rod was sufficient–Mr Southgate desired that this remark might be reported to the Committee and he should mention it to the Revd. Mr Agutter who would speak to the Committee on the subject.

The superintendent certainly seems to have experienced difficulty in fitting punishments to offences with a Beccarian exactness. Indeed, as we will later meet the Reverend Sydney Turner similarly exercised in dispensing a just measure of pain to Philanthropic children in the 1840s, it is of interest to find Mr. Durand now reminding the committee, that:

> ever desirous as far as his power to act conformable to the Committee's commands & to whom he looks up to for sanction and support in his situation, [he] hopes they will take the above into their consideration and having as hitherto endeavoured to proportion his corrections according to the offence committed and being eye-witness of the same when carried into effect, to prevent any accident or improper correction, respectfully requests the Committee's orders for the mode of punishment in future as he is anxious not to incur their displeasure–at the same time to preserve that discipline which he from experience finds extremely necessary for the good government of the peculiar Objects which the Committee have entrusted to his care–he begs leave to add that it is his constant practice never to inflict punishments until proper warning has been given & other means tried for their amendment.

The case of Thomas Trimbath provides an illustration of how the Philanthropic amendment process could proceed. Although a-typical in regard to his route of referral, the efforts made to reclaim Thomas are reflected in the case-histories of many other boys:

> Thomas Trimbath, alias Murphy, age 14, admitted on the orders of the Committee, August 1797. Found under a hedge in Germany, draped in an old Drummer's uniform,

by His Royal Highness the Duke of York & supposed to be the son of some soldier who had abandoned him to the wide world.

The Duke and Dutchess were remarkably kind to him & he was placed in the capacity of Groom's Boy in the Duke's Stables, but having testified a strong disposition to thieve, His Royal Highness applied in his behalf to His Grace the Duke of Leeds who recommended him by letter to the Committee.

28th August–Placed with Mr Thompson, Framework Knitter, on trial, having expressed a desire of being employed at the stocking manufactory.

16th October–Absconded this evening over the wall by the hemp Dresser's shed. He made an attempt to abscond some time ago but was prevented & has in general appeared dissatisfied.

25th October–Thomas Trimbath, the boy who had absconded was this day brought back by one of the servants of His Royal Highness and being interrogated before the person who brought him back–the reason for his going away he replied [was] a desire to see his friends–learnt that he had been at His Royal Highness the Duke of York's seat at Oatlands–and had there reported that the cause of his running away arose from his not having sufficient food.

Thomas was 'afterwards log'd'. Heavy or light logs were used to prevent boys from absconding and would be chained to ankles and then to work-benches. They did not always have the desired effect. Richard Starkey (who we met in a state of intoxication) had one applied after he 'struck another boy with a hammer on the face and … [had] given him a black eye'. That rascal then not only contrived to saw-off part of the log 'but also got the fetter off his leg & went away'. The log, nonetheless, kept Thomas on the premises and on 3rd November he was 'Liberated'.

On Christmas Eve:

Colonel Huugull visited at the request of the Duke of York to enquire after Trimbath whether he had again absconded and was informed he had not since attempted it and appeared to be in a state of reformation.

Unfortunately, appearances could be deceptive. On 2nd January 1798 and with 'the boys being this day allowed their usual holiday', Thomas spotted an opportunity to abscond. On 16th January he was recaptured and:

> Was this day brought to the Reform by His Royal Highness's servant who reported that His Highness had informed the boy that if he ever again absconded he should, when taken, be treated as a vagrant and punished accordingly–placed him on his return in solitary confinement.
>
> 18th January–Expressing marks of contrition and promising not to offend again–he was liberated and set to work.
>
> 22nd January. He soon again attempted to abscond, but was prevented–[for] this and other improper behaviour, gave him a smart chastisement–and is log'd.

Yet, if Thomas proved resistant to what might appear harsh lessons, the society had provided an asylum from a world in which many children were left to ruin and despair. Having looked at the background of those who had been brought under its protection we might sense, indeed, that the compassion underpinning this Philanthropic appeal for funds was no mere rhetorical sham:

> If, ten years to come, a malefactor at the Gallows should be heard to say, 'when I was young, necessitous, unprotected, and compelled by my parents, by friends, by blows and by hunger to steal for my daily bread, I abhorred my condition and dreaded the fate which now has arrested me; at that time I begged of you the bread of industry–I entreated the means of employment–I sought your protection from my miserable parents and friends–I had the mortification to be left, while my companion was received into the Reform.

The companion could well have been a boy like George Lefoy or even William Pearce. George had assumed the No. 1 position in the Philanthropic ledgers. He was admitted, in October 1788, having been at peril from living 'in a notorious resort of thieves in Goldsmiths Alley, St. Giles' with his 'father & mother very abandoned characters'. William had been admitted in 1792 having been 'guilty of many petty thefts and bad conduct'. He was the brother of Thomas who had been directed towards a man-of-war in 1793. By April 1798 both George and William were about 18 years old. With spring in the air they brought another reminder of the difficulties involved in taming 'strong and restless impulses':

The Superintendent, having stopped a letter from a girl which was directed to G. Bradbury, one of the boys of the Reform & having perused the same–desired the assistance of two of the Masters to attend out of the Reform in the evening after eight, when some little time after, Mr Morgan, observing Pearce, who had got over the Wall (without being noticed by the Watchman–tho' charged to keep a careful outlook) give a letter to a girl in company with two others, whom I had not long before seen & heard use a Bird Call.

Mr Morgan caught the letter & brought Pearce to the Reform, who slipped away again and absconded, it being very dark.

Mr Morgan has since reported that G. Lefoy has before his companions boasted of the means that may be used to prevent a future discovery of this kind, and whose conduct had latterly been very reprehensible, altho' advice, restraint, and punishment have been used to produce reformation without effect.

The Committee, he hopes, will excuse the length of the foregoing report, but conceives it his duty to point out the youthful temptations which appear to him the cause of these young men so frequently absconding–and which require strict attention in those persons who are to endeavour to prevent the pernicious effects of such natural but dangerous conduct.

These observations did not produce overwhelming gloom. On examining the ledgers, a Special Committee was able to determine that of the 176 boys admitted from the society's formation up to 1796:

51	have absconded
17	gone to sea, some of their own desire others sent by the Committee being considered incapable of reform
5	sent to the Marine Society two of these at their own request
3	have been expelled
10	delivered to their relations who were found to have been of good character and now able to maintain them
7	have been placed out; six of them to trades and other servitude
3	have died — two of these drowned, bathing.

The high number of 'elopements' over the period was certainly troubling. But, the Philanthropic gentlemen could, nevertheless, remark that it was 'with peculiar satisfaction that your Committee report that during the three last years only eight have absconded'. Their research had produced equally satisfactory results regarding the girls, of whom:

7	have been delivered to their friends
7	placed out to servitude
5	have absconded
1	has died.

Although the absence of children's narratives does not allow us to understand how they viewed their situation, these Philanthropic records highlight the diverse range of poor boys and girls brought into the society's care by various routes of referral. Thus providing the Reform with its human stock-in-trade and enabling the Philanthropists to increase their knowledge of youthful behaviour, they also presented ample evidence to suggest that the task of educating young minds to follow the path of virtue would not be easy.

In these early years, the Philanthropic gentlemen were sailing in the uncharted waters of experimental enterprise. But, with a blend of Enlightenment curiosity and compassion they sought to implement their preventive Policing Plan within the bounds of economy. In doing so, elements of the original design were amended and a pattern of response to institutional problems began to emerge. As this was not set in a rigid template, we now turn to considering how Philanthropic talents were harnessed to other key aspects of governance that would require adjusting in the light of experience.

CHAPTER 3

PROBLEMS OF GOVERNANCE

Domestic Economy

If the year 1793 had opened by testing the Philanthropic system of discipline, it ended with the nation engaging in war with France. This heralded a decade of economic crisis in which food shortages and inflationary prices had an acute impact on the poor. It also found swelling sales of Paine's *Rights of Man* fuelling fears over the spread of Jacobin plots and fusing with suspicions provoked by the Corresponding Societies' agenda for Parliamentary reform:

> Taxes diminished, the necessities of life more within the reach of the poor, youth better educated, prisons less crowded.

These were troubling times which saw the appearance of the Treason and Seditious Practices Act as well as the suspension of Habeas Corpus in 1794. They also, we may recall, found members of the Philanthropic network both involved in controlling disaffection when it precipitated into riot and engaged in the SBCP enterprise of establishing principles on which various forms of poor relief could be dispensed. This era likewise saw Bentham formulating his National Charity Company solution for dispersing the burdensome poor and Colquhoun offering the Home Department his plan for a Village of Industry. Somewhat prefigured by Robert Young's British Settlement scheme, this advocated the utility of providing shelter and the honest means of employment to minor convicts and discharged prisoners.

Amongst the growing number of local schemes for coping with the effects of economic downturn was that devised by Speenhamland magistrates in that same year. Whether or not compassion underpinned this initiative for linking poor relief to the price of bread and size of family, ameliorative efforts at national level included Samuel Whitbread junior's Minimum Wages Bill of 1795. Designed to endow magistrates with powers for adjusting wages in line with the cost of living, it failed to make progress. Likewise unsuccessful was William Pitt's Bill for the Better Support and Maintenance of the Poor (1797). As the preamble indicates, this was framed in an attempt to ensure:

> that provision should be made for amending and enforcing the laws for the relief, instruction and employment of the poor; in order as far as may be, to improve their condition, and to insure a more comfortable maintenance and support to them and their families, to encourage the general habits of industry and good order; and thereby gradually to reduce the excessive amount of the poor rates.

The demise of these legislative proposals owed much to inept drafting. Resilient opposition to State regulation and other forms of intervention also played a part. Indeed, the strong currency of resistance which had motivated the Philanthropic founders to defend the establishment of their voluntary enterprise, re-circulated in Sir Frederick Eden's *State of the Poor* (1797). In this, Eden criticised both Whitbread and Pitt on the grounds that their advocated statutory measures would undermine individual exertion, foster idleness and altogether undermine a family's moral responsibility for its economic well-being. Yet, while Malthus's *Essay on the Principles of Population* 1798) stoked further ideological conflict by setting out a case for abolishing poor relief (on the grounds that it worsened the condition of the poor by encouraging them to have children they could not support), the Philanthropic Society did not beat a loud drum in this debate. Instead, it was preoccupied in fashioning its affairs upon sound principles of trade. A variety of arising exigencies, however, would put the Philanthropists on their mettle.

Concern about the running-costs of the enterprise loomed large on the Philanthropic agenda. At the outset, the society had believed it important to convince subscribers that their benevolent bounty would be applied with 'utility only' consulted in every arrangement for the children's maintenance. From this, and mindful that:

> [as] the wards are forming for their humble station of labourers, it is thought an important care not to accustom them to conveniences and indulgences, of which afterwards they might severely feel the want.

the society's *First Report* noted, with some satisfaction, that the dietary regulation of 'two Banyan days every week, or days when meat is not allowed' had been imposed.

There is nothing to indicate that the society's trustees subsequently indulged in undue extravagance or that subscriptions sharply contracted. Nevertheless, by the time the society was preparing to shift into Southwark, the high cost of maintaining an increased number of children had come under the scrutiny of a Special Committee of Enquiry into affairs of Trade and Finance. By May 1793, its members were ready to lay out solutions. Unsurprisingly, the 'first object' of attention was reducing expenditure. To this end, a range of retrenchments was advocated. These included the purchase of a washing machine to lessen the consumption of coals and the use of lamps instead of candles in the workshops during the winter months. The gentlemen of this sub-committee also begged leave to observe that 'if an oven could be erected, a further saving of £70 *per annum* in the present consumption might be made by baking bread, meat and puddings at home'. What was more, although no additional savings could be made on the 'article of woollen and linen cloathing', they had:

> ordered the hats to be purchased ... at one shilling and four pence each, by which a saving is made of two pence per hat [and] also ordered stockings at one shilling and six pence per pair, by way of experiment, instead of those formerly used at two shillings and have adopted sundry regulations for the due care of the cloathing.

Being seen to exercise frugality also led to an item of girls' apparel being amended, just after they had processed around the room at the Anniversary Dinner of 1793. Although their 'decent appearance and orderly demeanour' helped raise over £600 on the occasion, shortly afterwards the society felt obliged to record that:

> It having been represented to the Committee that the trimming of the girls hats is more than is necessary or seemly for children of this Institution, it was ordered that the Superintendent shall have the same taken off all, except the binding and tie strings.

While the further detail of furnishing the girls with 'bonnets instead of hats' would not be overlooked on account of being 'cheaper and more lasting', considerations of the children's health, as well as economy, also entered Philanthropic calculations. This blend of imperatives inspired vice-president Dr. Sims and committee member Mr. Coxe to conduct the 'experiment' of allowing boys to go without shoes and stockings in the summer of 1794. The initiative was short-lived. With the extreme heat abating — and with the superintendent reporting that a rascally boy had laid the cause of his 'elopement' down to being 'obliged to go without stockings' — the order relating to the matter was quickly rescinded.

Items of food and drink, however, provided ample scope for Philanthropic economy. The 'considerable saving' expected from restricting the boys' access to small beer by keeping it 'locked up in the cellar under the care of the Steward' is not quantified. But, that to be gained by making a 'reduction in the quality of cheese allowed for supper' was estimated at £20 *per annum*. In addition, with the committee having found the 'article of milk very heavy', a new contract was soon entered upon 'by which, together with a reduction in the quality, in the proportion of two quarts of water to one of milk', an annual saving of £55 was anticipated. As for the children's diet? The even more substantial saving of £116 *per annum* was expected to accrue from adopting the following 'regulations' for dinners:

Sunday............Beef roast or baked potatoes or greens and bread as usual
Monday...........Broth & bread, instead of mutton, broth, potatoes & bread
Tuesday...........Boiled mutton, potatoes or greens & bread; instead of boiled beef &c.
Wednesday......Baked suet pudding: instead of pease soup
Thursday..........Leg of beef & bread as usual
Friday..............Broth & bread, instead of broth, mutton, potatoes & bread
Saturday..........Boiled mutton & beef, potatoes, greens & bread instead of suet puddings

Although this suggests the children were entertained to a still reasonable bill of fare, by the end of 1795 a very bad harvest had led to rations being subject to further retrenchment:

in consideration of the present alarming scarcity of wheat and wheaten flour for the use of bread which has so much excited public attention and calls for the strictest economy in all public charities and the use of every substitute in lieu thereof.

With this patriotic imperative in mind, the society then:

Ordered: that until such scarcity be happily removed, potatoes only, in lieu of bread, be constantly served at dinner to all the children within the Reform–allowing nevertheless such a specific and due quantity of bread to be distributed to each of the children at breakfast and supper as the sub-committee of trade and finance may think proper to direct.

Whereupon — and having in view the sub-committee's deliberations on the matter — it was resolved:

that in conformity to their recommendation a bread of such a mixture as shall comprise two thirds wheat and one third barley be immediately adopted at the rate not exceeding two quartern loaves per week for each boy of the first class, two quartern for those of the second class and one quartern and an half for the third class and as soon after as in point of health may be judged convenient for such a change, the mixture of bread may be equal parts of wheat and barley.

As for the girls' allocation of provisions? This was to 'be divided into two classes and ... the first class of the girls be served equal to the second class of the boys and the second class of the girls be equal to the third of the boys'.

The canny Philanthropic gentlemen did not omit consideration of being prey to fraud in this time of scarcity. Precautions were taken to ensure that the mixture of bread was as 'pure and unadulterated as possible' by having the steward personally 'purchase the wheaten and barley flour necessary to the composition of such bread'. He was then to employ a baker who would 'work up the same in the Reform according to the proper weight and quantity, under his inspection'. Afterwards, the loaves were to be dispatched for baking elsewhere 'with an Impression on each loaf so as to prevent Imposition'. It was also ruled that this mode of baking was to be continued after an oven was erected in the Reform. As might be expected, once the oven was installed, these strictures did not prevent some crafty boys smuggling loaves of bread out of the kitchen and hiding them ready for later consumption.

In the spring of 1796, the society noted that 'by the regulations lately adopted in the domestic economy there will result a considerable diminution of the expenses — the bill of fare for the boys lately established will be considered frugal'. It was as follows:

For Breakfast
bread, with milk & water

For Dinner
Monday............Broth & potatoes — no bread
Tuesday............The meat of which Monday's broth was made & potatoes
Wednesday ....Puddings of potatoes and flour
Thursday...........Legs of beef stewed and potatoes
Friday...............Beef & mutton & potatoes stewed
Saturday...........Rice puddings
Sunday.............Baked beef and potatoes

For Supper
Alternatively, bread with milk & water and bread & cheese

The diet for the girls was the same 'with the exception of rice milk for dinner Tuesday instead of meat'. This item, having 'in many instances been found prejudicial to the health of the girls', was later ordered to be changed to 'rice pudding' on the orders of the society's medical gentlemen.

If this frugal diet helps explain why Thomas Trimbath would run away to sample the servant's fare provided at the Duke of York's residence in 1797, the one offered in 1794 had appeared just as meagre to several of the master shoemaker's boys. Their grievances on the matter were transmitted to the superintendent who duly reported them to the committee. Cynically noting that 'their having broth twice a week is what they allude to and that without any meat ... these boys are very new to their eating and draw a comparison ... to ... how they used to live before', Mr. Durand added that:

> as a proof of their niceness, on a leg of beef day, which is a dinner no ways unpleasing to the palate or unsatisfactory as to nourishment, these boys are not pleased with

it and though I have had frequent occasion to remonstrate on this highly culpable conduct still as I endeavour to use such means as to me appeared necessary to remedy this defect, I conceive it unnecessary to trouble the Committee with a report on this part of their conduct.

In view of the prevailing frugality, it is not surprising to find that work incentives came to include the prospect of having baked mutton for dinner—at least, for boys who earned nine shillings a week or upwards. The girls had to wait for a similar indulgence until June 1801, when those who were 'industrious in housework and washing' were given 'baked mutton with potatoes or greens, on Mondays, instead of soup'. No doubt this was welcome. With the scarcity of flour continuing to keep prices high, the allowance of bread for breakfast had been ordered to be 'reduced one half and that such reduction be supplied with oatmeal and milk, sweetened with molasses'.

In regard to work incentives, the 'experiment' of dangling pecuniary rewards before the boys had been introduced 'as a stimulus to their exertion' as early as 1793. This was based on a plan submitted by Mr Peacock, the surveyor, who had pointed out the 'particular advantages' that would thus 'arise both to the Institution and the boys'. It is difficult to determine the extent to which this scheme actually added to the profits but it would appear that the rewards accrued in some Philanthropic trades could be substantial. The society sometimes also exercised supplemental generosity. By the time Thomas Carter's apprenticeship with the Printer had expired, the balance of his earnings amounted to £29.1s.0d and this was made up to £35 on account of his 'uniform good conduct'. Benefiting likewise was Charles Plant, whose rewards of £33.17s.0d were rounded up to £40. John Bailey, 'guilty of many petty thefts' and aged 9 when admitted to the society in 1792, did not accumulate quite so much by the time his apprenticeship expired in May 1804. Nevertheless, when he attended the committee:

and the Superintendent having reported his general good conduct, he received from the Chairman a Certificate stating the same and the balance of his rewards – amounting from his earnings the sum of twenty pounds, fourteen shillings and 3d.

These sums are of contrast to those achieved by the girls when employed in 'menial' service. Martha Brown, born in America and with both parents dead, had been aged 13 when received into the society in 1789. First apprenticed to the matron in March 1794 she was afterwards placed-out with Mrs. Gardiner, No. 193 Bermondsey Street, at the 'stipulated sum of £3.10s.0d to be paid quarterly'. In 1796 Martha attended the committee in order to receive her gratuity and, having been of 'good conduct as a Servant during the term of nearly three years', she received the sum of three guineas.

Ann Franklin was similarly recompensed. She was ten years old when admitted in 1789 with her father dead and her mother about to be transported to Botany Bay for fourteen years. She also was apprenticed to the matron and then, in 1796, placed-out as a servant to Mrs. Rhodes, of Castle Court, Aldersgate Street, at four guineas per annum. After 12 months, Ann was reported to be of good conduct and received a gratuity of one guinea from the committee 'as an encouragement'. The next year, she was rewarded a further two guineas in view of her continued good conduct and 'having remained two years in the same place'.

Mary Anne Hill initially fared a little better when placed-out as a servant to Mrs. Fenner, of No. 9 Prospect Place, at £5.5s.0d per. annum in 1808. But with Mrs. Fenner 'not approving her', she was returned to the Reform. Still, Mary Anne did have something of substance to look forward to. She had been admitted, aged 7 in March 1793, when her mother was in Newgate Prison awaiting transportation. Her father, who lived at No. 7 Sweeting's Passage, Grub Street and carried out coals at a coal shed, died in October that year. He had, however, left her:

> £9.10s 0d monies arising from goods sold ... and likewise the following articles which by his earnest request were to be kept for the use of the said Mary Anne, viz. a looking glass – sewing glass – tea board – and one gold ring.

The Society then placed the 'monies' in the hands of its Treasurer and requested it to be invested in 3% Consuls and put in trust for Mary Anne.

Another cost-cutting item on the agenda would, however, further erode the society's original family-based system. Finding the 'experience of some years has proved that the maintenance and accommodation of the wives and children [of the masters] within the Reform are attended with great inconvenience and expense', the gentlemen of the Trade and Finance Committee were moved to:

> recommend to the General Committee the expedience of allowing in future to the printer, the shoemaker and rope-maker the sum of seventy pounds annually in lieu of their present wages and board, house rent, coals and candles–for which annual sum, to be paid quarterly, they are to attend daily at the Reform as usual to instruct a certain number of boys in their respective trades, attend them at their meals and on Sundays to Church, instruct them in reading and writing three evenings in the week and be present with them during prayers and play hours untill bed time, when the masters shall be at liberty to return to their respective families, who are not to reside within the Reform.

The knock-on effects of this rationalisation of resources had also been considered. It resulted in the domestic care of the boys being placed in the hands of a matron:

> a widow free from encumbrance, between forty and fifty years of age ... who would have her constant residence in the Reform to superintend and direct the conduct of the cook, to take care of the boys linen, to mend their stockings, to act as a nurse whenever any of the children are ill and to take the youngest boys under her particular care at all times to see that the persons of all the children as well as their dormitories are kept perfectly neat and clean.

And, to ensure no disadvantages would arise from the depletion of residential staff, the gentlemen further suggested:

> the appointment of a nightly watchman ... to go round within the Reform every half-hour; that he have a key to the dormitories of the boys, that in case of fire, illness or any other emergency he may give immediate notice to the Superintendent, Steward or Matron, if the presence of either of them should be necessary.

While the future matter of furnishing the watchman 'with Fire Arms, to be delivered to him loaded, as soon as the boys are returned to bed', conveys a hint of dangers to life and property lurking around St. George's Fields, other vexing problems of governance loomed large at this time.

Ways and Means

A melancholy refrain on the 'low state of finances' hovered tenaciously over admissions policy from the outset. By 1794, this worrying constraint had led the society to announce to the public, with some reluctance:

that in the present state of their funds and buildings they can admit only such objects as have been brought before a magistrate, liable to be discharged for defect of evidence, or some such other cause altho' a strong suspicion of their guilt still remains; or such as have been tried and convicted but from favourable circumstances are objects of mercy; and those only on the recommendation of the magistrate or judge before whom the culprit was examined or convicted.

That directive would happily soon be relaxed and in the Philanthropic Account of 1797 the society was able to relate that, of the girls and boys received the previous year, 21 were the children of convicts, 20 were criminal children admitted by magistrates or from prisons and three were deserted or vagrant.[1]

Persistent cash-flow difficulties also impeded the planned expansion of the Institution. In 1791, the Building Committee had taken a cautious approach to the matter by pledging to erect buildings 'only as are absolutely necessary for the accommodation of the children and those upon the most moderate and economical plan'. This committee also had decided that subscriptions should be solicited for that particular purpose, rather than taken out of general funds. Yet, whilst the terms under which the ground lease obtained from the City Corporation allowed the society to release surplus land in order to raise capital, with few takers for the plots on offer and with the flow of subscriptions rather slower than expected, the Philanthropists were soon immersed in the task of borrowing funds at acceptable rates.

The Philanthropic gentlemen were also faced with the difficulty of having penalty-clauses about to be invoked. Indeed, with the low state of the finances placing restrictions on food provisions as well as the admissions policy in 1794, we can suppose they were more than a little perturbed to receive 'repeated directions from the Committee of City Lands to begin building on the Lots of land adjoining the Reform'. At this prompting, however, it was discovered 'expedient' to erect a house to contain 150 girls at St. George's Fields. This move was considered particularly 'prudent'. Firstly, it would 'comply with the Injunctures of the City—which are become very peremptory'. Secondly, it had economic benefits, for:

---

1. Around this time, the society appears to have ceased the practice of accepting children rescued from the streets by its members or supporters. While no explanation for this shift is given, children more formally captured under the vagrancy laws were still admitted.

to hire other premises for the girls, which must cost at least £60 annually, would be giving away more than the interest of the money that would accomplish the above purposes.

By May 1795, the girls were settling into a new Female Reform[2] at St. George's Fields, under the care of their own matron. With a laundry maid superintending the washing and a house-maid assisting in the cleaning, the wages bill for these employees amounted to £47 per annum. And, as for the girls? They did not lead an idle life. After investigating 'whether it might answer to take in some needlework for them', the society found they could hardly do any more work as:

> it appears that all, except the young ones (and there are many very young) are fully employed in making and mending their own gowns, and all their own linen; and that of the boys; washing the same; the stockings; sheets and house linen and keeping the house clean.

Despite this work-load, Philanthropic industry may not have been quite so onerous as that demanded of the older girls when placed-out as servants. Like Ann Franklin and Martha Brown, many girls did find satisfaction with their lot. But, as a high proportion quickly left their placements and returned to the society's fold, the Philanthropic gentlemen enquiring into this matter wryly commented that:

> it does not seem probable that the life which the girls lead in their gloomy apartments in the Reform, will induce any to quit a comfortable servitude.

Likewise alarmed by reports on the misbehaviour of both boys and girls in their placements outside the Philanthropic walls, the society was soon led to consider 'the propriety of appointing guardians to superintend their conduct in their several situations'. By March 1797, it was agreed:

> That the Secretary send the names of any of the children in the list now laid on the Table to such members of the Society as reside in the neighbourhood of the children apprenticed, or in service, and that the said members be requested to accept the office of guardians to said children & that they from time to time call upon them when

---

2. This department was often referred to as the 'Female School'.

necessary & also to report on their conduct at every Quarterly Meeting in order that the accounts in the Description Book of Characters &c. may be continued up to the termination of their several terms of apprenticeship.

This experiment in community after-care and surveillance does not appear to have elicited an altogether resounding response. Only four members had volunteered to be guardians by the following August. Although such 'patronage' would be an admired component of the French reformatory system established at Mettray in the next century, the Philanthropic Society now had to be content with tracking the children's progress when they came to the committee and claimed a portion of their rewards after two years satisfactory service, or, when they attended anniversary dinners. Unsuccessful careers, such as that of William Bradbury, were sometimes detected in press reports on criminal proceedings. When his apprenticeship ended in 1798, he had received his rewards in full along with a Certificate of Good Conduct. Despite this fine start in life, Superintendent Durand noted, in 1811, that:

> In the publick papers, a person of the same name, probably the same person, was pronounced as having been tried (with an accomplice) & found guilty of felony at the Assizes at Warwick.

The prevailing climate of financial stringency also led the society to embark on novel funding explorations. In May 1794, a potentially fruitful source of money supply was spotted and pursued. This was, a government grant. The quest for State aid was not, however, based on the premise that the Philanthropic enterprise fell within the remit of Poor Law provision. Rather, it was connected to ideas abroad in the penal realm, for:

> It appearing to the Committee that an application is now before Parliament for the grant of a sum of money for the purposes of constructing Penitentiary Houses for the reception and employment of such adult criminals whose crimes are not of sufficient malignity to subject them to transportation, the Committee are of opinion that it is a favourable opportunity for representing to [the] Administration the utility of this Charity in providing for the reformation and instruction of Criminal Infants.[3]

---

3. The society often applied the term 'infants' to children over seven years old at this time. Those below this age were described as 'mere nurse children' and therefore not 'proper' objects.

The society is, most likely, referring here to the provisions of the Penitentiary Act which passed by Parliament that year. This was largely stimulated by two Bills drafted by Jeremy Bentham and based on his panopticon ideas. These had caught the attention of Prime Minister Pitt who, the previous year, accompanied Home Secretary, Henry Dundas, on a visit to Bentham's abode with the purpose of examining some model designs. By June of 1794, Bentham had heard that a development grant of £2,000, from the Treasury, was coming his way.[4]

Quite how rumours of this bounty were transmitted through the Philanthropic Parliamentary network must remain a matter of conjecture. Nevertheless, the minutes reveal that the society lost little time in requesting committee member, Mr. William Knox, to:

> wait upon the Right Honourable Mr Dundas and the other Ministers with the plan and description of the ground and buildings and to solicit such a donation as might enable them to effect their purpose.

By the 6th of June, Mr. Knox could relate:

> that Mr Dundas was pleased to express his approbation of the Institution and desired to have another copy of the Plan to shew to Mr Pitt, and said that when he had time to consider of it he would send to desire to see him again upon the subject.

Access to corridors of power may explain why Mr. Knox had been chosen to represent Philanthropic interests. He almost certainly is the William Knox, MP who had been Provost-Marshal of Georgia and Under-Secretary of State for the American Colonies from 1770 until 1782. Disappointingly, he was not re-called to the Home Department.[5]

The matter of securing government aid was not forgotten. Next year, a Special Meeting, convened to consider the state of the finances, resolved:

---

4. The Bill for this Act, drawn-up by government lawyers, was very much briefer and less embracing of panopticon ideas than the two previously attempted by Bentham.
5. The 'Home Office' is usually referred to as the 'Home Department' by Philanthropic members. Created in 1782, it absorbed many of the America Department's military responsibilities until those were transferred to the War Office in 1794.

[that] the following Memorial be immediately transcribed fair and when done to be signed by the President and presented to the Right Honourable William Pitt, Chancellor of the Exchequer &c.[6]

This memorial clarifies how the society's debt had arisen. It also sets out the socially useful grounds on which the Philanthropists believed their bold application for £5,000 was justified. Commencing with an exposition of the society's aims and objectives, they attempted to cultivate Ministerial interests by stressing their 'policing' achievements:

> In the pursuit of purposes so strongly inculcated by Christianity and so conformable to the mild spirit of the British Government, which wishes to prevent rather than punish crimes, your Memorialists have the great satisfaction to find their labours have not been unattended with success and they can with confidence appeal to the general observation to justify their assertion that the streets of this metropolis are less infested with young thieves, prostitutes, and vagrants since the commencement of their Society than they formerly were.
>
> A happy change! which will be readily accounted for when it is known that in the short space of the seven years which their Society has existed they have received into their Reform no less than two hundred and eighty eight Infants of both sexes … all of whom were in the road to infamy and most of them would have been found in the streets as prostitutes or thieves.

With this confident claim, the Philanthropic gentlemen settled down to business by pointing out:

> That the expense attending the maintenance and instruction of these children of wretchedness has in the seven years amounted to upwards of twenty three thousand pounds, of which upwards of nineteen thousand pounds has been received by voluntary subscriptions and donations, and two thousand, five hundred pounds from the profits of the works in which the children have been employed–and the remainder is now a debt to the Society.

Further explaining how the City Corporation had supported their plan and mentioning how 'several of the trading companies of that opulent and lib-

---

6. At this time, Pitt held the positions of First Lord of the Treasury (Prime Minister) and Second Lord (Chancellor of the Exchequer).

eral Corporation contributed very generously' towards building costs, they were, nonetheless:

> sorry to add that the expence of these buildings has amounted to upwards of nine thousand pounds, and the sum contributed to that purpose have but little exceeded five thousand pounds, so that the Society has incurred a debt upon that account of near four thousand pounds–which, with what remains unpaid of the exceedings of their annual expenses beyond the amount of their annual income, leaves the Institution indebted to the amount of five thousand pounds.

Calamity would then ensue. As was argued, while they 'flatter themselves that they can now receive all the wretched children of either sex ... which the judges of assize or the magistrates of the several counties and cities of the Kingdom may think fit to transmit to their Reform':

> If they are not otherwise enabled to discharge their present debt, they must be driven to the distressing necessity of relinquishing their plan entirely, dissolving their Society and disposing of the buildings and ground in order to do justice to the creditors of the Institution, and this at the very time they have carried it to the wished for perfection and rendered it of the greatest publick utility.
> They therefore think it their duty to submit the present circumstances of the Institution to the consideration of His Majesty's Ministers, in the earnest hope that they will judge the Institution deserving publick support and worthy to receive from the liberality of Parliament the grant of a sum of money, sufficient to discharge the debt with which the Institution is now encumbered.[7]

Alas, no government aid was forthcoming. The Philanthropists' appeal may have failed on account of memories of the way grants given to the Foundling Hospital, earlier in the century, led to a rapid escalation in the commitment of Treasury funds. It is, however, just as likely that the society's threatened demise assumed low priority in the minds of Ministers who were preoccupied with wartime threats to national security, the precarious state of the economy and the rise of political radicalism. Indeed, even if the society was correct in detecting a 'mild spirit' of humanity residing within the heart of

---

7. The society seems to have been soliciting a sum of between £300,000 and £400,000–or, possibly as much as £ ½ million–at today's prices.

government, the Philanthropic mode of crime prevention was not at the top of its agenda.

Despite this determined display of government disinterest, the society was not deterred from vigorously raising funds by means of anniversary dinners and charity sermons. Its trading account also benefited from the support of the Philanthropic network. To keep the profits ticking over, vice-president Sir James Sanderson put business its way by ordering shoes for the Emanuel Hospital which was administered from the Guildhall. Philanthropic committee member, Mr. Henry Hoare, likewise ordered shoes destined for the Foundling Hospital. This banker and supporter of the SBCP as well as the SPCK also placed a large order for printing work to be done at the Philanthropic press.

The society's printing trade was similarly aided by another banker and SPCK supporter, Philanthropic vice-president James Martin MP, who requested that the master printer 'might attend the Treasurer of the Foundling Hospital to receive an order for some printing by his recommendation'. Word of mouth in SPCK circles perhaps drew the Reverend Rowland Hill to support the society's enterprise in the same way. A prison visitor, promoter of Sunday Schools and an advocate of the preventive benefits of small-pox vaccination, he is noted as having procured for the Institution 'the printing of books for the Society for Promoting Christian Knowledge'. He also recommended children for Philanthropic care.

Besides being aided by this network of enterprise, the Philanthropic Society did not neglect to advertise its wares in the public papers and proactively sought orders from firms and churches around the town. The search also extended into the confines of the Board of Agriculture. Established by Royal Charter in 1793, this can be regarded as another Enlightenment project in that it aimed to spread useful knowledge on agricultural improvements that would increase domestic food production. Funded by an annual Parliamentary grant of £3,000, its secretary was Arthur Young. As the superintendent relates:

> having desired Mr Russell to wait on Mr Arthur Young of the Board of Agriculture respecting the printing of their intended publications at the Reform–Mr Russell was favoured with the following answer–'That the Board of Agriculture have resolved

that the next book they print shall be done at the Reform'. At present they have several books in hand at other printers and their next publication will probably be fit for the Press in the course of a month.

Due care and attention was paid to other incidental matters arising. As this process of appealing against a Poor Law assessment on the matron's apartments at the former Female Reform in Bermondsey illustrates, the society would tenaciously pursue its charitable interests through the courts. The first appeal was granted in the Philanthropic Society's favour in April 1793, when four out of the five judges, sitting at the Quarter Sessions in Reigate, found that 'it was not a beneficial holding, but a holding in trust for the benefit of a charitable Institution'. In February the next year, the Parish of St Mary Magdalen, Bermondsey, brought the case to be re-heard at the New Sessions House in Southwark where the previous judgement was overturned on the opinion of 17 out of the 18 justices.

The matter did not rest there. The society's counsel then 'prayed the Bench to permit a Case to be made, for the opinion of the Court of King's Bench, which the Chairman reluctantly granted'. On the 24th May 1794, the case of 'The King against Susanna Field, Matron of the Philanthropic Society' was argued before Lord Kenyon, Mr. Justice Buller and Mr. Justice Grose. This resulted in an opinion in favour of the society for it was decided that Mrs. Field:

> was not an occupier of the premises subject to the payment of the poor rate, either within the general poor laws, or of the private Act of Parliament passed in favour of that Parish on that subject and therefore allowed the said appeal.

Establishing this principle in law hardly made an overwhelming impact on the state of the society's finances. As we saw in the memorial to Pitt, Philanthropic fortunes depended heavily on private benevolence. In view of this, there was a continuing quest for public subscriptions and donations, with congratulations offered when a committee member's personal approach was successful. Amounts such as £100 from the Duke of Bedford would be garnered this way and were supplemented by the casual gifts of visitors to the Institution's premises. Appropriating such revenue could, however, place the superintendent in some difficulty. Being aware of the rules drawn up in the aftermath of Mr. Young's misdemeanours, he was obliged to mention that:

> The Right Honourable Lord Melbourne visited with a gentleman and having enquired what sum constituted a Governor for life, and being informed, gave your Superintendent a bank note for £10, which has been paid to Mr Boldero [the Treasurer] for this purpose. He was desirous of accepting it lest any foolish idea might arise and prevent this gift–and requests the opinion of the committee whether in future he has their permission to receive any donation which may be offered to him–instead of referring the donor to Mr Decy, the Secretary.

Paradoxically, the carefully constructed rules did not regulate the rate at which funds were harvested. This oversight almost cut-off supply when the collectors' over-enthusiastic pursuit of subscriptions provoked a complaint. It had come from the evangelical Mr. Barclay, MP, a banker and long-standing annual subscriber who wrote to say he had been 'several times waited on for his subscription before it came due & that some Collectors had behaved very improperly on the occasion'. As Mr. Barclay was renowned for his benevolence and therefore not a funding source to be offended, the superintendent was asked to investigate. Regrettably, he had to confirm to the committee that:

> Mr Brook called twice in the month of February, and Mr Browne in April; Mr Stiff waited on Mr Barclay at his Counting House in Town in May–when that gentleman paid him a life subscription, to prevent his being so frequently importuned for his three guineas.

At 'War' with Mr Robert Young

Such difficulties paled in comparison to another problem which threatened the society's well-being. This was: What to do about Robert Young?

Young had not departed quietly from the scene of his disgrace (see generally *Chapter 1*). Having been disowned by the society and with the result of his examination before the Philanthropic committee circulated in the press, he promptly responded by applying to the society for a conference on the matter. This was refused as were a request for the return of his personal papers and an invitation for committee members to attend a public meeting on the affair.

Faced with this intransigence, Robert Young did not hesitate to broadcast his views on the 'treachery' of the Philanthropists who had cast calumnies upon his head. With the intention of resuscitating his reputation, he swiftly framed and published *An Introduction to an Account of the Foundation of the London Philanthropic Society and the Author's relations, thereto*. Outlining how the moral reform of the poor had exercised his attention since before he was twenty, this revealed that Mr. Young had spent at least 15 years systematically preparing his preventive policing plan by way of 'enquiries into the fruitful field of the universe'. Having 'found with delight, everywhere, a perfect analogy between physics and politics; between society and the natural world' — and after writing 'above forty essays and treatises' — he arrived in London, in 1786, 'from abroad'. He then published two other works.[8]

Hopeful of putting the principles of his design for moral reform into execution, Robert Young meanwhile made himself 'acquainted with many haunts of thieves; visited every prison and bridewell in the metropolis; solicited information and aid from the Bow-street and other magistrates'. He also engaged 'the constables, runners, and turnkeys' in his interests. Thus prepared and with a fund started among his 'private friends' in the early months of 1788, the plan was put into action by 'placing six young children, taken from criminal parents, at nurse'.

His perspective on his ensuing predicament raises some sympathy. As he declared, 'The system of moral Reform was my own, and it was entirely new; on it the success of all my hopes depended'. Yet the enterprise, which had 'arisen so rapidly to celebrity and consequence', had been taken-over by gentlemen interested in their own public 'glorification'. To this end he had been 'sacrificed' at the 'shrine of faction'. Admittedly, there were 'irregularities' in his books concerning the omission of charges for 'expences'. He had, however, provided a statement which took these into account. Also included were the sums paid out of his own pocket to get the enterprise started and to entertain society members when meeting at his house, in Warwick Court,

---

8. An examination of the third and fourth definition of the first book of Sir Isaac Newton's *Principia* (1787) and *An Essay on the powers and Mechanisms of Nature* (1788).

Holborn. These supplementary items he had 'purposefully' excluded, having thought it unnecessary to charge 'every minute expence, as an agent to his employer'. When they were taken into consideration, they demonstrated that it was he, in fact, who was at a loss.

The statement of expenditure had been ignored. What was more, little weight had been given to his 'incessant labours'. These had embraced:

> WRITING of plans, descriptions, advertisements, and paragraphs; books of accounts, letters of solicitation, explanations, and thanks; answers to enquiries, and applications of every kind, the First and Second Reports, which were honoured with much approbation ... VISITS and JOURNIES amounting to some thousands, for personal solicitations of patronage and support ... The CARE of inserting advertisements, distributing letters and bills ... SEEKING out criminal and vagrant children and youth, and inspecting their circumstances previous to admission ... SEEKING for a fit situation, hiring of houses and furnishing them, and the many etcaeteras of founding a new and extensive establishment ... attention to the morals of the children, initiating the matrons and mistresses in their duty ... [and] ... the establishment of trades.

Those time-consuming exertions, he explained, not only accounted for his being in 'arrears' with some financial details, but also had led to a 'long and severe illness, the effects probably of mental and bodily fatigue'. This illness had, furthermore, threatened his life at a time when his wife 'laboured under a very alarming indisposition; and an amiable child, the idol of both our hearts, we saw, daily and painfully lingering to her dissolution'.

By April 1793, Robert Young was again demonstrating that he had not been subdued by public naming and shaming. As was stated in the Philanthropic minutes:

> The Committee of this Society having very strong reasons to believe that considerable sums of money, as subscriptions intended to be paid for the use of this Charity by many benevolent subscribers, are collected by, and paid to persons who assume to be Collectors of this Committee–but are in fact under such imposition, collecting for the Reform instituted by Mr Young after his dismission from this Society.
>
> In order to prevent as much as possible a repetition of such gross frauds, the Committee judge it highly expedient again to notify and entreat the public and all present and future subscribers to the Society not to pay their subscriptions to any person calling himself a Collector of this Society until such Collector shall produce his authority and Certificate which is signed by the Committee appointing him to such office.

With an advertisement to this effect then 'placed in the publick papers', Young again sought an audience. Before any business could be conducted at a sub-committee meeting held at St. George's Fields in June, the superintendent arrived to inform the assembled gentlemen that Mr. Young was in the Reform and desired to be admitted. Being granted the request, he presented the following propositions:

> First, that a Committee of six persons chosen, not of the Committee, but three chosen respectively by Mr Young's opponents and by the Committee of the 'Society for a General Reform in the Criminal and Destitute Poor' be appointed to investigate and finally adjust all matters and questions in dispute between them and Mr Young.
> Second, that the same Committee be authorised to enquire into the causes, manner of procedure, and, object of the opposition made by them to the 'Society for a General Reform in the Morals and Condition of the Criminal and Destitute Poor'.

Upon this demand for arbitration and with Young also asking to be informed 'who was the Chairman of the Committee when the advertisement which he had read and of which he complains' was composed, the meeting swiftly adjourned. A Special Committee was then called to consider his requests and a reply was drawn up. This carefully avoided exposing any individual member to the wrath of Mr. Young.[9] The only thing of issue, it was decided, was 'the balance of £1,811.1s.7¼d unaccounted for by him as Treasurer and Collector of the Society of which he acknowledges the sum of £1.075. 10s. 1d to be due' and they had 'no other answer to give respecting the advertisement he complains of than it was … not intended to oppose any other Society or Charitable Institution whatsoever'. Directions were also given to the porter, steward and superintendent to ban Mr. Young from the grounds 'in case he should in future attempt to intrude himself into any of the meetings of the Society or Committee'.

An *Address* was also sent to Earl Grosvenor. He, we may recall, had given his support to Robert Young's projected British Settlement. He was also president of the Asylum of Industry which Young already had established on the Philanthropic door-step at Newington Butts. Attempting to disabuse

---

9. Whilst the danger of libel proceedings may have been in mind, this was a time when honour and reputation might be defended by a duel.

his Lordship of any offence which misrepresentation about their dealings with Mr. Young might have caused, the communication commenced thus:

> My Lord–the benevolent purpose of a Society for the Reform of the Criminal Poor, to which your Lordship has given your sanction by accepting the Office of President, so entirely corresponds with the views of the Philanthropic Society that it could not fail of receiving our most hearty approbation and sincere wishes for its success, as soon as we became acquainted with the nature of the Institution–for as the utmost stretch of our ability can only extend to snatch the forlorn and impending Youth from the precipice of guilt–we rejoiced to find that another Society was formed under your Lordship's patronage, for the recovery of the already fallen wretch and the reformation of the repenting criminal.

Stating it was only from 'anxious wishes for its success', as well as in 'justice to their own', that they felt incumbent to appraise his Lordship of how the pecuniary trust placed in Mr. Young had been abused, the Philanthropic gentlemen then described how that 'injury' had been 'aggravated' by:

> the depredations he committed upon our friends, [and] by the most impudent calumnies on those of our Society who had investigated his conduct and discovered his defalcations ... [As well] ... the similarity of the names and objects of the two Societies has led the public in several instances to mistake the one for the other, and subscriptions have in consequence been received by persons appointed by Mr Young–which were intended for our Society, the Philanthropic Society.

They also stated that:

> we have no intent of pursuing him further, for his late misconduct does not make us forget his former services, and we are still willing to acknowledge that to his assiduity the original Institution of the Philanthropic Society is greatly indebted.

This missive appears to have assuaged his Lordship's concerns. As was reported by committee member William Knox, who had presented the society's letter to his friend Earl Grosvenor:

> His Lordship expressed himself much pleased with the distinction made between their Society and Mr Young, which had not been so marked previously, insomuch as

our attacks upon him had been considered as opposition to their Society ... they had entered into nothing of Mr Young's case but thought it hard we would not hear him.

As a 'union' of voluntary effort will come under serious Philanthropic consideration in the next century, it is of interest to note here that Earl Grosvenor 'thought the two Societies ought to co-operate with and assist each other, as having the same object'. Nothing would come of this suggestion. His Lordship's hope that matters were 'now so far cleared up and settled, that neither Society would have any more trouble with them' was also confounded. Instead, aggravations would soon accumulate and wend their way to the Court of Chancery. The relatively private matter of a letter 'containing several charges against and many imputations on the Society' was considered 'unworthy of further notice' and only a small amount of umbrage was taken upon it 'appearing from Messrs. Coutts Banking Book' that the audacious Mr. Young had 'paid in to them one guinea, as an annual subscriber to the Philanthropic Society'. Matters precipitated, however, when that founder's side of the dispute was again presented to the public gaze. In July, a Special Meeting was summoned:

> in order to consider whether any and what proceedings are to be taken in consequence of an advertisement in the True Briton, of the 5th instant, respecting this Institution, one of which newspapers, sent by Mr Young, was this day delivered to the Chairman by Mr Piper of Atkinson's Coffee House.

Upon this information, the Philanthropic gentlemen decided to publish a rebuttal. They also resolved that a deputation should wait on their own presidents and vice-presidents to get their 'support and countenance' on the handling of the affair. Philanthropic president (the former Marquis of Carmarthen, lately Secretary of State for Foreign Affairs and now Duke of Leeds) conveyed his approval by letter. This concluded:

> So strange a conduct, originating either from a disturbed imagination, or that degree of resentment so commonly derived from disappointment in a favourite object (no matter whether laudable or base) could not, however, be passed over unnoticed by the Philanthropic Society and I think the Committee have acted upon the occasion with the strictest propriety. They may depend upon the utmost sanction and support it can be in my power to bestow throughout this business.

The impetus for taking legal action then wavered until May of the next year, when another Special Meeting decided that:

> having used every lenient measure in their power respecting Mr Young and finding that their expectations have been disappointed by his continuing to take advantage of their forbearance, they are reluctantly compelled to advise some more rigorous measures and as such, they beg leave to recommend to the General Committee the propriety of proceeding in law against Robert Young, as a defaulter.

The delay in taking proceedings may have been coloured by considerations of the costs that would be incurred. It is also possible that some argument had arisen over whether to proceed with a civil or criminal action. We can note, nonetheless, that the society's resolution was 'grounded on an opinion given by the late Attorney General on the case laid before him'. This had been sought at an early stage of the affair and was stated as follows:

> I think an action at law might be tried and a Bill of Equity filed for an account: the former is so much more expeditious and so much less expensive that I should recommend the experiment.
>
> (Signed) A. MacDonald
>
> 6th March 1791

Whether this opinion was delivered on the basis of friendship or payment, it again indicates that the Philanthropic Society had access to influential quarters. Archibald MacDonald had succeeded Richard Pepper Arden as Solicitor General in Pitt's administration of 1784. He then succeeded him as Attorney General in 1788, the year that Pepper Arden became Master of the Rolls and one of the first subscribers to the Philanthropic Society. In 1790, MacDonald was appointed Lord Chief Baron.[10]

It is, perhaps, no coincidence that legal action to prevent further harm to the Philanthropic's reputation and fortune was undertaken just at the moment when the government grant was applied for. Both were being threat-

---

10. It was thus Sir Archibald to whom the society petitioned for a conditional pardon in the case of Stephen Lee, in 1796.

ened by Mr. Young's imputations and debt due to the society. As the Duke of Leeds observed on hearing a suit would be instituted:

> I think the Society are not only justified but consistently with every principle of public justice bound to proceed against Mr Young to the fullest extent of legal prosecution, in which object they may depend on my particular support and the more general support, I should trust, not only of the Society but the public at large, in obtaining satisfaction to an Institution of such national importance as the Philanthropic Society for injuries sustained from any quarter–still more if from that whence its institution had perhaps derived its origin and from whence at a subsequent period it received the first determined insult and material injury.

Robert Young was undeterred by impending legal action. More rumours of his collecting activities were relayed to the society and, later that year, he was spotted by vice-president Dr. Sims who reported to the superintendent:

> that a person the size of Mr Young, and by his manner he imagined it was him, alighted from a chariot yesterday and went to several houses in Hackney. He was so very importunate to a lady, the mistress of one of them, and in so urgent a manner, solicited even the smallest donation for the Philanthropic Institution. To get rid of so importunate and troublesome a guest, she gave him a crown–it is reported that he collected nearly £20.

With such persistent solicitations being, no doubt, assiduously conducted elsewhere, we may not be too startled to discover that Young had found the means of putting his British Settlement scheme into progress by 1795. Not, however, in the 'waste-lands of Derbyshire' as originally envisaged. Extraordinarily, its foundations were instead set on a tract of land near Crawley, in Sussex, where the 'ground had an abundance of stone, brick-clay, rich loam, and fine sand' and where a 'rill of excellent water' could be harnessed 'to make at once a fine reservoir for domestic purposes and an excellent fish-pond which may afford a valuable and cheap supply of provisions'. Its Founder was, nonetheless, still being 'persecuted'. So much, it would seem, as to justify the publication of:

> Mr. Young's REPORT on the attempts made by the USURPERS OF THE PHILANTHROPIC SOCIETY, to DESTROY the BRITISH SETTLEMENT, founded on Tilgate Forest, Sussex, for the Self-support and Reform of the destitute and criminal Poor.[11]

The bold Robert Young had, indeed, rushed into print to allege that the 'invaders' of his first foundation not only ousted him in order to 'monopolize' his plan but had then set out to destroy his Asylum of Industry and succeeded in bringing about its downfall. On hearing about his renewed labours in getting the British Settlement established, their 'hostilities' had been resumed and signalled the start of 'what may be called the second Philanthropic War'. This was a contemptible turn of events for the 'war' was being waged by the very men who had 'raised a Wall' and turned his original Philanthropic 'Asylum' into a 'Prison' — a 'sort of mill for grinding children good'. Not content with invading his first scheme and vanquishing his second, their attention was now directed to subverting the new project.

As he scathingly related, with the British Settlement's superintendent and workmen 'on the foot, and proceeding rapidly' to fence the land and build a cottage:

> The *Philanthropists* sent down a *spy*: as he had to pass through the village of Crawley, he spread there the calumny against me. He stopped at the Swan, at Pease-Pottage Gate, a public house opposite the land, where the Superintendent lodged. Rather unfortunately, almost as soon as he sate down, and began his enquiries, the Superintendent came in to his dinner; and the *spy*, guessing who he was, instantly got up, left his liquor and the money on the table, went out at the *back door*, got into a chaise from which he had alighted, and drove off. This *spy* I took, by the description, to be Mr William Houlston, of Chancery-lane; and here we found that the enemy could not even look a *servant* of the British Settlement in the face.

The Philanthropists had, furthermore, sought to ensure he remained '*in terrorum*' by circulating 'myriads' of pamphlets which were 'crammed down the throat of the public' by a multitude of messengers and 'covered the land like the plagues of Egypt'. For the production of this torrent of 'libels' which assailed his reputation with 'falsehood, innuendo and equivoque':

---

11. This book and other pamphlets were sold from the British Settlement's Office at No. 12 Bow-Street, Covent Garden.

the *Philanthropic* Press in St. George's Fields, was made permanent, like the guillotines of Robespierre, and groaned under the work of death.

Particularly reprehensible was the allegation that the money collected on the British Settlement's behalf 'was all a swindling business'. So too was the circulation of a caution, in the 'style, evidently' of 'a police advertisement'. This had been printed 'under the pretence' that he was being prosecuted, at the Philanthropists' instigation, for defrauding the public. But, Young added:

> That I was in the Fleet Prison is the only truth it contained; and I much question if any unfortunate prisoner those walls ever surrounded, has before been honoured with so general and assiduous a notification of his confinement to the world.

If his enemies neglected to mention that this unfortunate sojourn in The Fleet was due to heavy debts incurred in executing his original scheme, Mr. Young had faced-up to their onslaught by placing bills 'all over London, as companions to their own'. In 'fear' of having to account for their actions, the Philanthropists then had applied to the Court of Chancery for 'protection'. This move afforded him some comfort for:

> It was an ample triumph to me to see them run crying to the Court of Chancery, to prevent a meeting of their own subscribers, on the subject of their dispute with me.

Was Robert Young correct in asserting that the 'Magistrates of Police' had 'been assailed to induce them to break the peace, in aid of this confederacy'? Had the 'clerks to the Police Offices' been 'bribed' to 'interrupt' his collectors? While we remain wondering about these allegations, he was convinced, nonetheless, that the Philanthropists had ensured 'the law' was biased against him in ensuing proceedings and that:

> Every art of the black-legged practitioner was tried: my attorney was bought, and my Counsel left without briefs when they came to plead.

Little additional information on these matters can be gleaned from a pamphlet published in March 1796, entitled *Mr Robert Young's Address to the*

General Body of Subscribers of the Philanthropic Society and to the Nation on the unparalleled Abuses, and Atrocious Delinquency of the Usurpers of the Philanthropic Reform. Neither does the affair get mentioned again in the Philanthropic *Minutes* until a 'Statement of the Proceedings, in Chancery — The Attorney General against Robert Young' was inserted in the spring of 1797. Outlining the complexities in the case, this highlights the high status of the legal figures involved and conveys something of the seriousness of the matter. Overall, it gives us further insight on the character and circumstances of the defendant.

Not unexpectedly, Young had confidently claimed that the information filed against him, on the 12th December 1794, 'did not contain any matter of Equity sufficient to raise or establish any right or demand against him, or to draw him into a Suit with the said Court'. Nevertheless:

> This demurer came to be agreed before the Lord Chancellor on the 31st January 1795 when his Lordship, being clearly of opinion that the same was inadmissible, would not suffer the Attorney General to reply to Mr Mansfield who argued for the demurer, and ordered it to be over-ruled.[12]

Then, on the 6th June:

> the defendant put in an answer to the information, to which answer exceptions were filed on 2nd July following and which exceptions were, by order dated 20th July 1795, referred to Master Popham, to enquire whether said answer was sufficient or not.

This Master Popham was an author of the Gaol Acts of 1774 and had been an MP for Taunton and chairman of its Quarter Sessions.[13] In 1786 he was appointed a master of the Court of Chancery. There, in a report dated August 1795, he 'allowed all the exceptions taken to the defendant's answer'. Subpoenas for a 'better answer' were then issued and afterwards 'attachments with proclamations both in London and Middlesex'. But, with Robert Young 'absconding' these could not be served:

---

12. The Attorney General of the time was Sir John Scott, later Lord Eldon. Mr. Young's counsel was, probably, James Mansfield who had twice been Solicitor General.
13. As such, he had seen an outbreak of gaol fever kill 8 out of the 19 prisoners in Taunton gaol.

Whereupon, on 17th January 1796, a Commission of Rebellion was issued against him, and he still absconding, the same was on 3rd February returned *non est inventus*, upon which return an order was obtained, dated 4th February 1796, for the Sergeant–at–Arms to apprehend the defendant–but it appears by the Certificate of the Sergeant–at–Arms, dated February 19th, that the defendant could not be found.

Robert Young, had, however:

> found means to put in another answer on the 18th February, which together with the former answer was by order dated 27th February, referred to the said Master Popham, on the former exceptions. The said Master, after much delay on the part of the defendant–and many attendances on the part of the Relators–and hearing counsel on both sides, made his Report dated 4th May 1796, allowing the first, second and third exceptions.

An order was afterwards obtained on the certificate of the sergeant-at-arms for a 'Commission of Sequestration' against Mr. Young. This was issued on the 13th May and returned on the 27th — 'no estate or objects of the Defendant having been found'.

The Philanthropic pursuit of Mr. Young did not end there. On the 28th June:

> an Order was obtained on Petition for that purpose, that the Case should be set down to be heard before his Honor, the Master of the Rolls, in order that the Information might be taken *pro confesso*. And the Relators' Clerk in Court was also ordered to attend at the hearing, with the record of the Information.

The matter continued on 14th July when the now knighted Philanthropic subscriber, Sir Richard Pepper Arden, Master of the Rolls, allowed the case to be heard on those terms. He also ordered that the proceedings be referred to another Master in Chancery. This was Mr. Wilmot who was advised to take account of all the sums of money received by Young as intendant and treasurer of the Society from 19th September 1788 to the 'the time he resigned the said offices' and since that time 'by him and any other person or persons by his order'. Mr. Wilmot was also directed to compute the interest due on the debt. And, as for Robert Young? He was ordered to pay the costs of the suit and an injunction was awarded to 'restrain' him 'from interfering in or interrupting the Management of the said Charity or the receipt of subscriptions for the same in any manner whatsoever'.

The society delayed putting this decree into execution. That was, until Robert Young had:

> by certain injurious letters and declarations, directed to his Grace the Duke of Leeds … and lately made public by the said Robert Young, at Brecon, again attempted to disturb the interests of the Society.

This location was possibly carefully chosen by Young as a new pasture in which to defiantly perpetrate further mischief. In the *First Report* he had noted that 'it will be learned, with pleasure, that the example of this society has been already followed in other places. A similar Institution bids fair to be established in Wales, by the exertions of George Hardinge, Esq., MP, one of the judges there, and a Vice-President of this Society'. As this Welsh Philanthropic Society was probably still operating, reports of his re-emergence—along with news that Master Wilmot had calculated that the sum of £2,289.9s.6d was due—prompted the committee to agree 'that the necessary steps be taken for enforcing obedience' to the terms of the decree, in December 1798.

Did the fearless founder immediately bow to the law? Hardly so. Robert Young most likely was already on his way to France, where he resided from December 1798 to April 1800—as a Government spy! Re-surfacing to publish *Gnomia; or the Science of Society* in 1801, we find him therein soliciting subscriptions to cover future editions of a *Gnomian Review* and accounting for the circumstance which had led to an 'interval of suspension of the work'. As he intriguingly confides:

> The first and second Numbers of this work appeared eighteen months gone, the preparations of France for invading this country, was the circumstance that immediately gave rise to the choice of that part of the work being first published; at that very juncture, whilst he was arranging his ideas, such as they were … the Author, unexpectedly received an order to repair to France, in the employ of the British Government, he gladly embraced this opportunity of enquiring in the enemies country, all the information possible, relative to their hostile views, and resolved to have applied for an early leave to return, had their projects continued; but the affairs

of France taking another course, he was happy to remain there, with the occasion of visiting and residing, accredited by both governments, in several distant provinces as well as in Paris, as long as the service on which he was sent required.[14]

Whilst we can appreciate why Robert Young had 'gladly embraced' the opportunity to remove himself to France at that particular juncture, we are left wondering whether he ever would — or could — willingly have paid his dues to the 'usurpers' of his design for moral reform. Although we might also remain convinced that he was treated rather unfairly by the society, being vigilant in pursuit of the Philanthropic interest was of fundamental importance in the governance of its affairs. Not reluctant to seek government aid for an enterprise perceived to have national utility and applying the principle of frugality to its domestic economy, the Philanthropists had endeavoured to enhance the Philanthropic Society's public credibility in a period when there was no Charity Commission to call such voluntary operations into account. They thus played a crucial role in establishing the sound foundations on which their Institution entered the 19th-century. There remained, however, much to adjust in the light of experience.

---

14. Young networked extensively in pursuit of the latest Enlightenment discoveries. Having received 'from a brother in law at Christiana, Dr Muller, a gentleman who ranks amongst the first, in Europe, as a physician, as a chemist, and as a mineralogist', an introduction to citizen 'formerly Count' de la Cépède, director of the [previously Royal] Botanical Gardens and of the National Museums, Young then met with several members of the Council of Mines as well as Monsieur Guyton, Director of the French Polytechnic School. That 'establishment to which we have no parallel in this country' was much admired by Young. It provided free education to even pauper children 'of genius' with the purpose of forming 'statesmen and warriors, ministers and generals, for the future service of the nation'. It was also from where 'Bonaparte selected a number of students to accompany him on his expeditions to Egypt'.

CHAPTER 4

REFORMATORY REFINEMENTS

By 1810, Philanthropic fortunes were on the ascendant. Increasing numbers of subscribers were investing in the enterprise designed as an Introduction to Police in all civilised countries and the society's petition for an Act of Incorporation had received the sanction of Parliament. As well, a chapel had been built at the St. George's Fields site and the society's operations were being conducted in three distinct departments: a 'Reform' for criminal and delinquent boys, a 'Manufactory' for other boys taken under its protection and the 'Female School'. An expanding network of talented Philanthropic gentlemen would spend a great deal of time and trouble on forging these new arrangements.

Network Expansion
The society had continued to attract the support of men of rank and influence. Following the death of the Duke of Leeds, the position of Philanthropic president had been accepted by the Duke of York and Albany in 1799. His Royal Highness shared the improving concerns of many Philanthropic associates. After being blamed for a disastrous military campaign in the Low Countries in 1794, he had embarked on a reform of the army's organization when appointed commander-in-chief in 1795. This task involved devising a system of periodic reports on officers, standardising procedures for recruitment and discipline as well as bringing the internal management of regiments under centralised control.[1] Also ensuring that the troops were inoculated against small-pox and establishing a school for the orphans of soldiers at Chelsea Barracks, he had, in addition, placed Thomas Trimbath in the Philanthropic Reform and taken an interest in that lad's welfare.

The Philanthropic patronage of this Grand Old Duke of York proved profitable to the society. On his first attendance at an Anniversary Dinner, the Duke's gift of one hundred guineas 'so powerfully affected the feelings and

---
1. Barnett (1970).

liberality of the company' that voluntary donations amounted to £1004.15s.7d on the night. His royal brand of presidential patronage might also have plumped-up donations to the Refuge for the Destitute on similar fund-raising occasions. That society was founded in 1804 and had taken premises at Cupar's Bridge, Lambeth, for the purpose of providing:

> places of refuge for persons discharged from prisons, the hulks–unfortunate and destitute females, and others, who, from loss of character or extreme indigence, cannot procure an honest maintenance, *though willing to work.*[2]

Closely replicating many objectives of Robert Young's Asylum of Industry, the refuge had on-board Edward Forster (junior) as treasurer and the Reverend John Grindlay, LLD as its chaplain, superintendent and secretary. Both gentlemen were early supporters of the Philanthropic venture. The Reverend Dr. Grindlay is noted on the Philanthropic Committee list in 1792 and Forster's name enters in 1794. A botanist and future vice-president of the Linnean Society, Forster was acting as a Philanthropic auditor by 1806. This responsibility was shared by Colonel Henry Harnage. In his retirement from active duty he had become inspecting field officer of the London Yeomanry and Volunteer Corps[3] and was also treasurer to St. George's Hospital. Charles Bosanquet was yet another Philanthropic auditor in 1806, the year his father, Philanthropic vice-president Samuel Bosanquet (senior), died. Other vice-presidents of the time included the evangelical Earl of Aylesford, Viscount Cremorne and the Hon. Philip Pusey.

Swelling the Philanthropic complement of vice-presidential power and prestige were Earl Spencer, the Marquis of Salisbury and Earl Grosvenor, who had succeeded to the title on the death of his father in 1802. These names may well have haunted Jeremy Bentham as he reflected on the problems that had beleaguered his panopticon ambitions. The Penitentiary Act of 1794 had not included a suitable clause for the compulsory purchase of land and his

---

2. The Refuge's *Short Account* (1806).
3. A letter from George Washington, dated 11th of June 1779, to (the then) Major Henry Harnage in Cambridge, Massachusetts, relative to an exchange of sick prisoners-of-war, indicates that Mrs. Harnage accompanied her husband on campaign during the American Revolutionary War (University of Virginia Library).

proposal to build on a site at Battersea Rise had been tenaciously opposed by its holder, Earl Spencer. After failing to get another plot up-stream from Woolwich and with a view to building at Tothill Fields, Bentham then met resistance from 'old' Earl Grosvenor on whose adjacent estate resided his son, Viscount Belgrave. This soon to be 'new' Earl Grosvenor, was an MP from 1790-1802 and commissioner of the Board of Control of India from 1793-1801. His charitable activities included support for the Bible Society to which Earl Spencer, a member of the SBCP and a vice-president of the Marine Society, was also attached.

The Marquis of Salisbury, however, was owner of the site subsequently acquired nearby at Millbank on which a penitentiary eventually appeared. This was not the one designed by Bentham. Although his hopes for executing the panopticon design were revived after Sir Samuel Romilly urged Parliament to implement provisions of existing Penitentiary Acts, they were finally dashed by a House of Commons Select Committee set-up under the chairmanship of George Peter Holford. Son of an immensely wealthy Master in Chancery, Holford was called to the Bar in 1791 and elected an MP in 1802. Succeeding his father as a director of the East India Company in 1804 and appointed Secretary of the Board of Control for India by Pitt that same year, it was upon going out of the latter office, in 1810, that Holford was invited to chair the Select Committee by his friend, Home Secretary Richard Ryder.

Charged with taking evidence on the efficacy of existing penal measures and briefed to consider the expediency of erecting a national system of penitentiary houses funded by government, the Holford Committee delivered a report which encouraged the administration to proceed with building a model penitentiary on the Millbank site. It also ruthlessly rejected Bentham's arguments on the utility of operating the penitentiary by way of contract management. Under such a system it concluded, a pecuniary advantage would be made the most prominent object of attention, rather than the reformation of prisoners through seclusion, employment and religious instruction. Instead, it recommended that the penitentiary should be managed by a committee of gentlemen whose rank and position in society would induce them to employ a portion of their time for the benefit of the prisoners and the public.[4]

When Millbank's first Committee of Management was appointed by the Prince Regent on the 12th February 1816, at its head was the Rt. Hon. Charles Abbott, Speaker of the House of Commons, step-brother to Bentham and an early subscriber to the Philanthropic Society. Holford too was on Millbank's Management Committee. As he also had been one of the three supervisors appointed by government to deal with the penitentiary's construction, these outcomes probably drew some wrath from Bentham who suspected Holford of 'packing' the committee with like-minded friends in order to destroy the panopticon scheme and get himself a position.[5]

Holford had, however, already served a Philanthropic apprenticeship in the trust-management of reform. As he would be a key-player who contributed both time and ideas to advancing the society's interests, we can note that his active involvement formally began with his election to the General Committee in March 1800. Perhaps drawn into the Philanthropic fold through a family relationship (his sister, Charlotte Ann, having married Charles Bosanquet in 1796), Holford's Philanthropic career began at a time when the expediency of obtaining an Act of Incorporation began to loom higher on the society's agenda.

An Act of Incorporation and the Chapel Affair

> An Act for establishing and well-governing the charitable Institution commonly called *The Philanthropic Society*, formed for the protection of poor Children, the Offspring of convicted Felons, and for the Reformation of Children who have themselves

---

4. Romilly had begun a campaign for a reduction in the use of the death penalty in 1806. His motion urging the government to implement the Penitentiary Acts of 1779 and 1794 was debated in the House of Commons in June 1810. The Committee on Laws relating to Penitentiary Houses was appointed on the 4th of March 1811 and Holford presented the Committee with his own report on the 17th of May. After a sparse discussion by committee members (including Bentham's friend William Wilberforce), the Holford Committee's First Report was ordered to be printed on the 31st of May, the Second Report on the 10th of June and the Third Report on the 27th of June 1811. A Penitentiary Bill was then introduced by Holford in the House of Commons in January 1812 and passed in April. Bentham's compensation of £23,000 was eventually agreed by the Treasury Commissioners in June 1813.
5. McConville (1981:132 ftn.).

Shows why we should never give up on the capacity of people to change

Jim Hopkinson, Bradford Children's Services

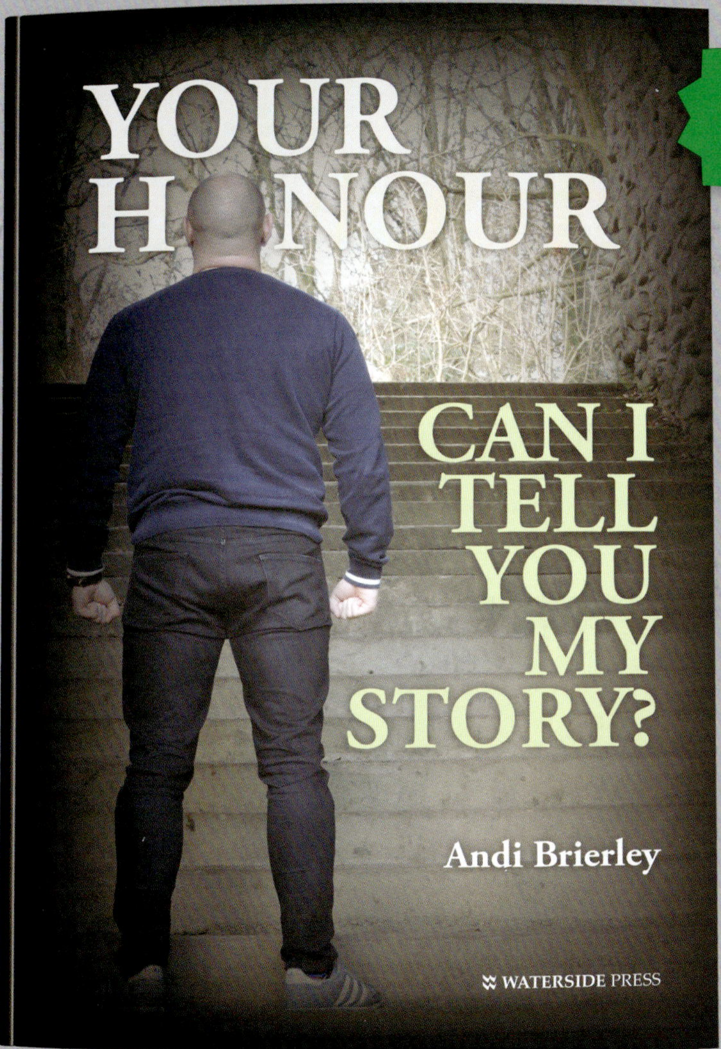

YOUR HONOUR
CAN I TELL YOU MY STORY?

Andi Brierley

Waterside Press

NEW

Free UK Delivery

WatersidePress.co.uk

Your Honour Can I Tell You My Story?
by Andi Brierley

Andi Brierley's story of his progress through care, prison and social rejection to youth justice manager in Leeds contains countless clues for those who work with troubled young people. It begins with failures to deal with his chaotic early life moving from place to place, fragmented parenting and poor role models. In a family home encircled by criminality, drugs, violence and baffling adults he ended up first in a young offender institution then in prison.

There he learned how to act and think as a prisoner for his own survival, something that only made matters worse when trying to re-adapt to the world outside on his release. Caught in a downward spiral, hooked on drugs, partying, not strong enough to resist negative influences and his well-being deteriorating, the book shows how small things made a difference.

Until he regained self-worth and rescued his life. Important for the messages it contains for professionals and young people in trouble with whom he has forged a remarkable connection.

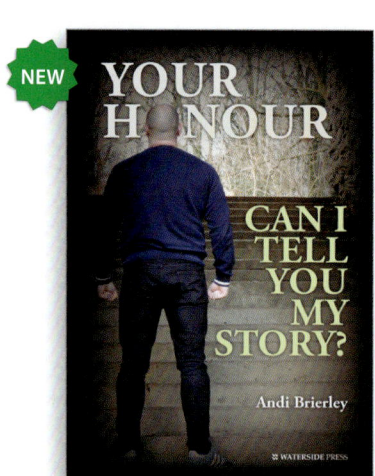

As featured in the *Yorkshire Post* and the Association of YOT Managers *Bulletin*

Available in paperback & ebook
(inc Kindle, Apple and Google)
258 pages | Published in April 2019
ISBN 978-1-909976-64-1
Price £19.95

More details at www.WatersidePress.co.uk

WATERSIDE PRESS

Turn around stories
Writing as a route out of crime and towards a better life

Prison writing is a valuable two-way process. Education aside many prisoners have changed their lives using writing as a bridge to a new life and career. Our first book in this genre was Bob Turney's acclaimed *I'm Still Standing* back in 2002. Recommended personally by Lord Longford, Bob the one-time prolific burglar turned author actually went on to become a probation officer! Ex-offenders who followed his lead include Alan Weaver (who became a social worker, *So You Think You Know Me?*), Ben Ashcroft (young offender to youth worker, *Fifty-one Moves*) who tells of his constant changes whilst in care and Justin Rollins (ex-graffiti artist and now motivational speaker, *The Lost Boyz* and *Street Crhymes*) whose books have been adopted as set texts on degree courses in Birmingham and elsewhere.

Another ex-prisoner turned author whose book has been widely used in education is Frankie Owens whose *Little Book of Prison* also made the final of the People's Book Prize. There is also a book, *Recovery Stories*, about those who have survived addiction.

Actor Stephen Fry's turn around story was included in a collection called *Going Straight* along with that of the train robber Bruce Reynolds whose life changed after being released from his 25 year sentence. Andi Brierley (opposite) who went from prisoner and heroin addict to manager of a youth justice unit in Leeds is the latest in this considerable line-up. Each of these books centres on identifying the changes, choices and threads that led from being an offender to law-abiding citizen.

  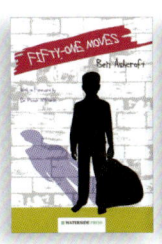   

Further details, information and reviews of these and other key texts are available at our website.

WatersidePress.co.uk

Free UK Standard Delivery on Every Order

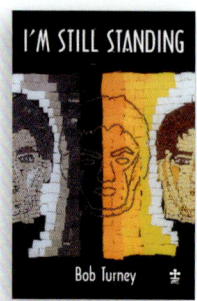 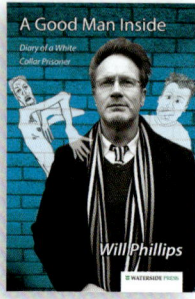

Bob Turney's *I'm Still Standing* is the book that established the turn around genre with Waterside Press. Will Phillip's *A Good Man Inside* is a diary of the impact of imprisonment on a white collar offender telling how he survived it before returning to normal life.

Order Online
WatersidePress.co.uk
Call +44 (0)1256 882250
or ask at all good bookshops

Payment by invoice — for multiple copy orders only, we may invoice your firm/institution (at our discretion). Please place an order via our website and select "Invoice With Order" as your payment method.

Free UK Delivery

- UK Standard Delivery is **FREE** for all orders and takes 2–5 working days.
- First Class starts at £2.00 rising by £1 per additional book to a maximum of £5.95 for 5+ books.
- **In stock items are typically despatched within 24 hours.**

International Delivery

- For rates see www.WatersidePress.co.uk/delivery

   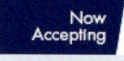 

Ebooks

Most Waterside Press titles are also available as ebooks. These can be read on a variety of devices, including **Kindle**, **iPhone/iPad**, **Android**, **Nook** (and many more). You can buy them through online retailers, including **Amazon**, **Apple** and **Google Play**. Search the web, or see our website for details and links. Our ebooks are also available to institutions via **library agreements** — ask your supplier or contact us for more details.

Available on

Amazon, Kindle and all related logos are trademarks of Amazon.com, Inc. or its affiliates. The Apple logo is a trademark of Apple Inc., registered in the U.S. and other countries. Apple Books is a service mark of Apple Inc. Google Play and the Google Play logo are trademarks of Google LLC.

Waterside Press
Sherfield Gables, Sherfield-on-Loddon,
Hook, Hampshire, RG27 0JG. Tel. **01256 882 250**

been engaged in criminal Practices; and for incorporating the Subscribers thereto, and for better empowering and enabling them to carry on their charitable and useful Designs.[6]

Incorporation was not a new idea in the realm of charitable activity. The Foundling Hospital and the Magdalen Asylum, for instance, already had employed this legislative device for regulating their affairs. It also had been mooted at an early stage in Philanthropic proceedings. During a meeting held to consider the progress of work on the St. George's Fields site in 1794, the Building Committee resolved to 'recommend to the General Committee to take into consideration the expediency of applying for an Act to incorporate this Society'. Possibly some difficulties associated with obtaining building leases from the City Corporation had been encountered and then overcome by placing the matter in the trust of the society's men of substance. Such circumstances may have been the background to the 'indenture', obtained in 1793, which struck an agreement:

> between the MAYOR and COMMONALITY and Citizens of the City of London of the one part and James Sanderson, Knight, one of the Aldermen of the City of London, John Harman of Frederick Place in the said City, Esquire and James Sims of Lawrence Lane in the said City, Doctor in Physic …, vice presidents of the Charitable Institution or Society called the Philanthropic Society and Edward Gale Boldero of Cornhill.[7]

This form of contract was still being used when Philanthropic John Julius Angerstein, of Pall Mall, also underwrote the liability in 1805.

Problems concerning legal liability clearly arose when the matter of 'who is or are the proper person or persons to be made plaintiff in the case' against Robert Young (see generally *Chapter 3*) was considered. At the end of this episode, the issue was still causing difficulty, for:

> Mr Rooke, the Solicitor employed to carry into effect the decree of the Court of Chancery against Mr Robert Young, having reported that he had taken the necessary proceedings for that purpose and that in order to facilitate the effect thereof he had

---

6. Act of Incorporation (1806).
7. John Harman, a banker, had been a committee member alongside Jeremiah Bentham in 1790 and soon became a Philanthropic vice-president.

applied to Mr Boldero, the Society's Treasurer, for a letter of Attorney to authorise him to demand of the said Mr Young the sum found to be due by him to the Society and that Mr Boldero had executed such letter of Attorney, desiring when he did so that this Committee would consider of Indemnifying him against any damage which might happen to him for doing so.

The Poor Laws also laid the Philanthropic trustees open to claims. In this regard, the idea of an Act of Incorporation had been raised in 1793 when it was resolved that:

> A bond with sufficient penalty be given by the Treasurer and Trustees of the Society to the Church Wardens of the Parish of St. George the Martyr's, Southwark, in the County of Surry to indemnify the said parish and parishioners from all such costs, charges, damages and expenses which they may be put to on account of the apprentices or any such persons belonging to the said Society gaining settlements in the said Parish until an Act of Parliament can be obtained to prevent the same and that the funds of this Society be subject to such damages, viz. if any should happen.

Claims did occur. In 1803, on an 'application by Parish Officers of St. George for payment of a bill of £1.5s.3d for the maintenance of a boy in the workhouse of that Parish belonging to this Society', the committee 'ordered that the same be paid'. It may be imagined that this was not paid with alacrity. Indeed, the matter of a 'disclaimer of settlement' was already under investigation. As the society's solicitor, Mr Rooke, reported in 1801, he had:

> advised with Mr. Randal Jackson thereon, who thought it desirable to get a clause introduced into some private Act to relieve the Trustees from their present liability.

Randle Jackson,[8] a barrister and Parliamentary counsel for the East India Company and the Corporation of London, was another useful member of the Philanthropic legal network. He had attended the society's meetings from May 1794 and was elected a committee member in 1797. While he later became chairman of the Surrey Quarter Sessions and found time to set down his *Considerations on the Increase in Crime and the Degree of its Extent*

---

8. His name is variously spelt Randal or Randell but more frequently Randle in the records.

in 1828, his advice now led the society to consider 'the expediency and practicability of such an application'.

Urgency was lent to the matter when additional legal irritations began to emanate from the Philanthropic chapel building project. At first glance, this seems a surprising undertaking. In early publicity pamphlets, the society had pledged to subscribers that only such buildings as were 'absolutely necessary' to accommodate the children would appear in the grounds at St. George's Fields. It also had promised that the 'erection of an edifice, and all unnecessary expences for magnificence, would be avoided'. Nonetheless, the prospect of conferring a religious resonance on the enterprise seems to have inspired proposals for this embellishment of the Philanthropic Plan. More pragmatic considerations also brought the item to the fore. The society was certainly satisfied to hear from the Reverend Dr. Grindlay that:

> twenty five young men and eleven young women of the Institution were confirmed at St Saviour's Church, Southwark, by the Bishop of Winchester, when his Lordship, the attendant clergy and several respectable inhabitants of the neighbouring Parishes expressed themselves much pleased with the proper behaviour of the young persons of this Society on this solemn occasion.

But, from time to time, the Philanthropists had been perturbed to discover that the children's regular Sunday processions to Divine Service in Churches nearby, provided a host of opportunities for creating mischief. One such escapade involved the boys Pearce and Moone who:

> absconded and overtook the girls on their way to Church and insulted the Matron by the appearance of taking stones to throw at her – Pearce went on to Bermondsey Church and therein made signs to the girls – both he and Moone returned to St. George's Church and came back with the other boys – these boys have before insulted the girls by climbing from the Pigsty upon the wall of the Female Reform and improperly speaking to them.

Girls too could seize the opportunity to escape. Frances Cooke absconded on the return journey from St. Mary Magdalen Church in Bermondsey and sped-off to her grandmother who lived in York Street, Westminster. She then required to be fetched back by the matron. Frances had been admitted in 1794 and was the daughter of:

Thomas otherwise William Cooke otherwise George Bailey convicted at the December 1793 Sessions at the Old Bailey and ordered for Transportation the Second Time being a very Old Offender. This girl was recommended to the notice of the Society by Mr. Kirby, Keeper of Newgate, who says of the father that he is a well known and Old Tenant of Newgate, but very orderly while under confinement there, as well as during the time he was working out his former Sentence at Cumberland Fort – so much as to be discharged from that place, at the expiration of his Time, with the Bounty, as it is called, usually given to those who behave well.

For a society intent on presenting the mellow fruits of reformation to potential subscribers, the children's public displays of naughty behaviour were worrying. By the turn of the century, they had provoked the Philanthropists into declaring it necessary to 'procure two additional persons' to accompany them to and from church 'in order to prevent their absconding, or improper communication'.

These 'inconveniences' were compounded by those met when arranging Benefit Sermons. Since this important aspect of Philanthropic business took place in a climate of competition with Parishes and other charities, gaining access to that conduit of benevolence would be another of Superintendent Durand's travails. As his *Journal* for March 1796 discloses, in pursuit of a venue for the Anniversary Sermon and in 'obedience to the Committee's orders', he had waited on committee member Mr. Knox:

> who intends visiting the Reverend Dr. Eaton but considers that were the Doctor to grant this Society the use of the Church [St. Anne's] for the Anniversary Sermon it would by no means be beneficial to the Charity, there being frequently charity sermons for the benefit of the Parish Children.

The superintendent was then sent to wait on the Reverend Dr. Hamilton to request the use of St. Martin's. Regrettably, Mr. Durand was advised that it was out of that gentleman's power to grant the request having already given 'permission for a sermon to be preached for the Freemasons' children'. Afterwards desired to 'wait on Mr. Baker to request the favour of his intent to procure the Pulpit of Saint Clement's Church', this committee member 'very obligingly accompanied him to visit the church wardens'. Alas, the superintendent had to report that, as a sermon was to be 'preached there for the benefit of the Lying-In Hospital, shortly, and another for their own parish', the request could not be granted'. Within a few weeks, however, the society was able to transmit 'particular thanks' to:

> the Reverend Dr. Layard, Prebendary of Worcester and Chaplain in Ordinary to His Majesty, for the excellent discourse delivered by him on Sunday the 17th April Inst. at King Street Chapel, Golden Square, for the benefit of this Institution.

Clouds of charitable rivalry could also be unwittingly provoked. During the previous year, the superintendent had relayed to the committee the Aldersgate Church Wardens' suggestion that 'as a further inducement to have a full congregation' it would beneficial 'to procure Mr. Printer of the Foundling to use his vocal powers in a hymn suited for the occasion'. Mr. Printer, as a blind child, had been taken under the protection of the Foundling and trained-up as an organist. By this time he was 'Singer' in their chapel and a star attraction. He was not an asset willingly shared. As Philanthropic (and Foundling) committee member Mr. Ballard reported:

> he had made an application to the Committee of the Foundling Hospital and was extremely disappointed by receiving from them a disapproval of Mr Printer's favouring this Society with his attendance on Sunday the 14th instant, which Mr Printer very obligingly was willing to do.

Elements of charity fatigue also emerged to blight Philanthropic prospects. With the Aldersgate church wardens additionally hinting that 'it would be very beneficial to the society' to secure the attendance of the Lord Mayor and a sheriff at the sermon, the superintendent was dispatched on this mission. Not only would he find that the Lord Mayor 'wished to have some temporary retirement' from charitable activity, but, waiting upon sheriff Burnett he was:

> informed by this gentleman that in his official situation he had been under the necessity of lately attending several charity sermons and likewise other duties of his office so very much attached his time he was really desirous of some little relaxation and Sunday being the only day which offered him an opportunity he trusted the Committee would excuse him.

Whilst other similarly inauspicious responses likely coloured the decision to build their own chapel, the Philanthropists had approached the proposition with caution. Even though a fortuitous legacy had allowed the society to discharge its building debt in 1798 and request an estimate of 'the expence that might attend building a Chapel with 800 seats', by March 1800 matters had progressed only to the extent of considering erecting:

> a temporary building of board and canvas for the purpose of performing Divine Service.

Making his Philanthropic entrance at this point, Holford drove the chapel plan forward by donating £21 towards a permanent building. At this expression of faith in the venture, the society resolved that any similar donations would be kept in a separate 'Chapel Fund'. Afterwards installed on the Chapel Committee, Holford lost no time in preparing an *Address from the Philanthropic Society to the Public on the Subject of Erecting a Chapel*. One thousand copies of the same were ordered to be printed:

> under the direction of Mr Holford and that one copy be sent to each life governor residing within the reach of the Penny Post and that each Collector be furnished with 50 copies for distribution.

Now expressing a 'conviction of the infinite importance of giving the children, as soon as possible, the advantage of attending Divine Service within their own walls' and, moreover, finding the City Corporation amenable to a proposal for building on vacant land adjoining the Female School, the society began erecting the 'shell' of a chapel with 1,200 seats. As this edifice was not expected to exceed £8,000 and with the time-scale for raising the money carefully calculated, all seemed set fair.

Ecclesiastical discord loomed into view. The first intimation of trouble came in a letter from the Rector of the Parish of St. George's, to whom the society had applied for 'approbation' of the chapel. Sufficiently moved by the contents to request its solicitor 'to prepare a draft of a case on the subject of the Rector's answer for Counsel's opinion', the society was then nonplussed to hear that the Bishop of Winchester thought 'it would be irregular to open the Chapel without some arrangement putting it under ecclesiastical authority'. Grateful for receiving this 'caution', the Philanthropists strove to 'assure him that it had never been in contemplation to open the Chapel without his sanction or to have any person to officiate therein without his license'. Stressing that 'the contract now made is only for the shell of the building', they asked him to allow a 'deputation of their body to wait upon him when he comes to town'. After all:

> The Philanthropic Society has always had the children under its care instructed in the faith and principles of the Church of England and that it would be contrary to the wishes of the Society that any person should officiate who should be considered by the Bishop of the Diocese as unfit to give such instruction.

The chapel affair continued to aggravate and perplex. It may well be that ecclesiastical suspicions were aroused by the inter-denominational composition of the Philanthropic body of trustees. At this time, the Established Church was feeling its authority threatened by the growth of dissent and by the emphasis placed on Bible-based Christianity by Evangelicals within the Anglican Communion. So far as this encompassed wariness about the dangerous influence of lay-authority, these apprehensions were shared by the Philanthropic cohort that met to consider a complaint made against one of the master-tradesmen in 1804. This was Mr. Morgan whose:

> conduct in putting a Hymn composed by himself into the hands of the boys without the sanction of the Chaplain was extremely reprehensible as was also his encouraging them to sing it at Bailey's funeral after the Superintendent's letter of the 29th July last and that he be ordered to attend the Committee on Friday next to make and apology to Mr. Durand for his disobedience to his authority and receive a censure from the Chair. And that he be informed that any interference with the boys on religious subjects in future will be followed with his immediate dismissal from the Society's service.[9]

Chapel negotiations dragged on. The Philanthropists were at a loss to understand why this should be so. Theirs was an Institution whose 'utility' was 'so

---

9. Bailey had just received the balance of his apprenticeship awards but 'was soon after unfortunately drowned as he was bathing'.

universally confessed' that its 'prescribed limits' in admitting children had been 'frequently made the subject of regret by some of the first characters in the legal administration of this country'. What was more, their chapel plan had been undertaken to avoid the necessity of substituting 'Domestic Prayer' for 'Public Worship' and was thus intended to give the children 'early habits of attending Divine Service with their neighbours'. In addition, the society was:

> not aware that any right of interference in the appointment of the persons officiating has ever been exercised in any of the Chapels belonging to the different charities in the metropolis and that the Society is apprehensive of great inconvenience and injury to the Charity from such interference (especially as the living of Saint George's is of small value).

The society's 'future happiness and welfare' continued to be threatened by a particularly obdurate rector. This was the Reverend Brand who published pamphlets on political economy and opposed the Philanthropic chapel by way of another. His 'small' living from the nearby Church of St. George the Martyr was, nevertheless, in the gift of a powerful patron. Of this the society was appraised when, after persistently attempting to cultivate the Rector's consent, they were informed that the Reverend Brand:

> cannot on any point give legal validity to the arrangements you may lay before me respecting your intended Chapel, without the concurrence of the Bishop and of the Patron.
> That high officer of the Crown in whom the patronage is vested is the Lord Chancellor. He must therefore be contacted by you before any proper answer can be given by me to anything which relates to these arrangements.

At mention of this patron, the society dispatched a deputation of Philanthropic gentlemen to confer with the Lord Chancellor. They were unsuccessful in claiming his attention. Despite frequent attempts to gain personal audience — or a reply by letter — the legality of the chapel administration failed to capture his interest. Considering the magnitude of his lordship's workload, the low priority given to Philanthropic concerns is not so surprising. We last encountered him as the Attorney General involved in the case against Robert Young. Then Sir John Scott, he had been created Baron Eldon and Lord Chief

Justice of the Common Pleas in 1799 and in 1801 became Lord Chancellor. Indeed, the society's entreaties would scarcely have merited his attention at this time. After a lull, hostilities with France had resumed in 1803 and, as a member of Pitt's War Cabinet, he was most likely pressed by rather more weighty affairs of State.

With the chapel building almost finished but no prospect of a settlement in sight, the society prepared a Petition for an Act of Parliament to 'incorporate the Society and legalise [their] chapel'. It also resolved 'that the Bill be prepared under the direction of Mr. Holford and Mr. Bosanquet jun. and that they be desired to attend its progress through Parliament'. This duty was accomplished in the House of Commons. Equally attentive to the society's interests in the House of Lords was the Rt. Hon. Lord Hawkesbury (Home Secretary, 1804-06) along with Philanthropic vice-president, the Rt. Hon. Earl Spencer (Home Secretary, 1806-7). Their Lordships were duly thanked when the Act of Incorporation was passed on the 22nd of July 1806.

A chapel keeper was then appointed to sleep on the premises on a 'moveable bedstead' and a 'Constable or Peace Officer' was requested to 'attend at the chapel every Sunday' from the time the doors opened. Quite what local threats to order were envisaged are not mentioned, but, dangers from abroad were addressed by ensuring 'that a copy of the occasional prayer in case of Invasion' was placed in the Reader's Book. With Mr. Hatchard, 'Bookseller in Piccadilly', directed to furnish the chapel with a range of religious books, the society prepared to attract a substantial — and generously disposed — congregation to its chapel in November.

What Might Work Better?

While Holford's elevation to the position of Philanthropic vice-president, in July 1806, probably recognised his chapel building exertions, he had also applied himself to a wider agenda of governance.[10] As he was at the heart of developments leading to a significant refinement of the society's system of reformation, it seems pertinent to return to the time he was first elected to the committee in March 1800. Soon installed as a Philanthropic visitor and thus provided with ample proofs of defects in discipline, his interest in

---

10. Holford filled the vacancy caused by the death of Samuel Bosanquet (senior).

finding solutions may have been kindled by the case of Edward Lion. The following month, having 'broken open the Porter's box and stolen a variety of articles thereout', Edward was ordered to be:

> publicly and severely flogged round the inside of the Reform, in the presence of all the boys, with a label on his forehead with the word 'Thief' inscribed thereon, his master attending and directing the punishment ... and that all the earnings which may be due to the boy be given to the Porter, towards reimbursing his loss, any deficiency whereof is to be ascertained and paid by the Steward on the Society's account.

There is no record of Holford's thoughts on this punishment. Nor about that which was inflicted on the boys who would be flogged for:

> concealing themselves in the vaults under the Chapel in order to converse with the girls in the Female Reform having stolen the keys of the vaults for that purpose.

Even so, Holford was well positioned to gather evidence on how other important Philanthropic business was conducted. Within a week of being elected on to the General Committee, he was appointed chairman of the Committee of Trades and Finance. By December, he was ready to present a paper on his 'Considerations on the Expediency of putting out the boys &c'. This led to him being nominated chairman of a Special Committee set-up:

> to enquire into all matters relating to trade now carried on within the Reform for the purpose of ascertaining to what extent it is expedient for the Society to embark its Capital in Trade.

Its deliberations sowed the seeds for a radical separation of the Philanthropic boys. Although finding it difficult to 'distinguish as far as possible what portion of the profit of each trade arises from the labour of the apprentices' with 'sufficient exactness', the gentlemen of this sub-committee had deduced the following:

Produced Profit in 1800	£		Employs Boys	
Shoemaking	172	20	12 little boys	32
Taylor	108	6	& 3 botchers	9
Ropemaker	444	10	Spinners: 2 Dressers, 10 Wheelboys	22
Printer	478	3	3 Errand boys	6
Copper Plate Printer	17	3		3
Bookbinder	28	2	Boys in Warehouse	2
Deduct Errand Porter & loss on stocking goods	36		The rest of the boys are not so employed as to produce profit	
Total	1211			

Holford and his companions were then charged with devising a scheme to apprentice-out some more boys. When this was delivered in March 1801, the first of its many regulations was that:

> Two lists shall be kept in future of the boys within the Reform—all boys hereafter to be admitted on account of their own misconduct shall be entered on list No. 1 and such as shall be admitted in consequence of the viciousness of their parents on list No. 2.

With the classification procedure thus clarified, the visitors were asked to determine which boys should be apprenticed out 'forthwith'. Holford then laid a paper on the committee table regarding the form of 'indenture' to be adopted. This matter had been settled by himself and James Allen Park. Yet another member of the society's legal network and a future Philanthropic vice-president, Park would be promoted to the Bench of Common Pleas in 1816 and was afterwards knighted. Besides being a Fellow of the Society of Antiquaries he found time to be a trustee of the Marine Society and Magdalen Asylum as well as a member of the SPCK and Humane Society. He would also be a vice-president of the Church Building Society—along with future Philanthropic vice-president William Wilberforce—and had displayed an early interest in such endeavours by serving on the Philanthropic Chapel Committee.

Holford, meanwhile, prepared a further 'paper of instruction and advice to the boys as shall be apprenticed out of the Reform'. He then presented to his fellow Philanthropists:

> several copies of a printed paper relative to a plan for adding to the present establishment of this Society a vessel upon the river, for the reception of some of the boys.

This proposal is intriguing. As an economic expedient, resort to ships would not have been unusual. Many charitable enterprises in this period recruited ships as floating chapels or hospitals and the Marine Society used one as an initial training school for its boys. The hulks also provided the government with a pragmatic solution to a prison numbers crisis. Nevertheless, Holford's Philanthropic innovation was specifically designed for boys on the 'No. 1 List'. As such, it can be considered an early expression of ideas on the importance of separate provision for criminal boys. This would only be realised by the State in 1823, when the *Bellerophon* hulk was designated for that specific purpose.

While Holford, in his *Statements and Observations Concerning the Hulks* (1826), would endorse that initiative on the grounds of its separating 'convict boys, under 14, who used to be distributed indifferently with those of maturer age', his Philanthropic proposal of 1801 was not adopted. The society was, indeed, swayed to the opinion that it was 'absolutely necessary to separate the two classes of boys under the care of the Society'. But, another paper on the subject, prepared by the still very active vice-president Dr. Sims, was then swiftly laid on the committee table. The records, unfortunately, do not reveal whether this gentleman criticised or supported Holford's suggestion. What we do know is that, in 1792, Dr. Sims presided at a Building Committee meeting which had considered a 'probationary house' to be 'absolutely necessary for the purpose of separating the disorderly and diseased from the rest of the boys'. Yet, although the society then was:

> now and more convinced of the necessity of erecting a probationary house for the reception of the boys taken immediately from the gaols to prevent the danger of contamination not only of body but of the morals of those who have made a progress in improvement.

it simply had resolved that when 'any new objects' were admitted:

> a plain coarse canvas frock be provided which they shall wear at all times whilst they remain in a state of probation, the period of which to be at the will of the Committee.

We can surmise that Nathaniel Banner wore such a frock when received in April 1793. Nathaniel was born in Dean Street, Soho and had been convicted at the Old Bailey for stealing 12 yards of cotton out of a shop. His father, a lawyer, had died three years before and his mother, a washerwoman, was living in King Street, Seven Dials. Within a few weeks, Superintendent Durand respectfully reported to the committee that Nathaniel had:

> hitherto behaved with decency and propriety and that he at present appears ... likely to answer the Intent of this Institution and to prove he is not insensible to the feelings of affection the Superintendent begs permission to relate the following circumstance which he was a watchful observer of. Last Sunday his mother and sisters – one of who is very near his own age – came to visit him. I sent for him ... when at sight of his sister he eagerly flew and caught her in his arms and carried her to his mother where he wept most bitterly. This is the youth whose brother received capital punishment for having transgressed the laws of this country – and who very near his awful exit gave this youth very serious and pathetic advice.

By August, Nathaniel's repeated elopements from the Institution had led Superintendent Durand to comment that, 'if this boy should again run away after the confinements and scourging with advice he has received ... there can be little hopes of his reforming'.

The Philanthropists were even less successful in dealing with Richard Jackson's moral diseases. When Richard was admitted in 1796, the committee ordered that he 'be carefully watched and attended to for a month, during which period the visitors are requested to make a constant report to the several committees of his conduct'. Richard did not await the Philanthropists' opinion. Instead:

> this hypocritical and hardened offender by means of tying his sheets which he had torn in slips, as likewise his probationary jacket together–by the assistance of which he dropped from the window and made his escape.

Used also to denote 'degradations' for misconduct, the probationary jacket was still being employed when the subject of separating the boys re-emerged in 1801. This time, a Special Committee was appointed to consider the 'best means' to the end and Holford was invited to 'revise the rules and orders of the Society'. The 'most proper place and the necessary arrangements respecting the situation of the boys' was also considered and the Special Committee then reported — with some urgency — that:

> it had seen a house situate near Bermondsey which appeared to them to be remarkably well calculated for the purposes of the plan approved of ... to be had on lease for 21 years at the low rent of 30gns per. annum–and that there were several other persons desirous of taking the said house.

The Bermondsey house was taken 'without loss of time'. To signal the new arrangements, the words 'Philanthropic Society's Manufactory' were painted on the gates of the existing premises at St. George's Fields. The purpose of the new 'Philanthropic Reform' was similarly distinguished and, with 'necessary' alterations made to the premises, the first boys were admitted.

That is, Reform boys entered once the rules and regulations for this new department were agreed. Presented in a copious report, they reveal the development of a more rigorous reformatory regime: one still revolving around work and religion but with a heightened emphasis on constant surveillance. Priority was given to the task of engaging a clergyman of the Church of England as chaplain and the Reform's 'resident establishment' was to be comprised of a 'Master with his wife as a housekeeper' along with a servant 'called a Porter' who was to 'occasionally assist in instructing the boys in their work'. This was envisaged as being:

slop work, a trade which is thought business may be easily procured; which is attended but with little waste materials; and which may be taught by the Master and his assistant.

As the society's steward was then asked to supply a 'small quantity of junk' to employ the boys 'until other work can be obtained', it is feasible that in referring to 'slop work' the practice of chopping-up old rag material (junk), ready for converting it into paper, was what the Philanthropists had in mind. Although 'slop work', at this time, could also refer to sewing low-quality, cheap clothing for sailors, it is rather more likely that society commenced the initiative by training Reform boys in the oakum-picking craft. This involved the re-cycling of old and tarred ship's rope by way of teasing the fibres apart into piles of hemp that could be stuffed between ships' planks and again waterproofed. Indeed, while details of the work produced by the Bermondsey boys remain rather cloudy, the committee soon felt obliged to order that a 'bason be erected within the Reform for draining water from the oakum'. It also noted that:

> Mr Huffman who has lately supplied the Reform with Junk and Rope to untwist or pick into oakum and also Hair-rope to be picked for the use of Plaisterers; having visited the premises has informed the Master that he cannot continue to send any more materials unless there is a proper shed or warehouse to keep these articles perfectly dry both before and after they are manufactured.

While oakum-picking would become associated with humiliations suffered by workhouse and prison inmates, there is no suggestion of the primary design in selecting this occupation being the imposition of degrading and hard labour. Rather, it was viewed as an expedient means for instilling useful habits of work in the boys within a regime which paid attention to the 'distribution of their time with respect to instruction'. A tightened programme of 'Rules for the Internal Management of the Reform' was also applied. To prevent contamination from external sources, only committee members and the chaplain—or magistrates from the counties of Middlesex, Kent and Surrey—were allowed unrestricted access. Parents had to be accompanied by the chaplain or visitors during visits for which written authority had previously been obtained. Needless to say, 'no person' from the Female School or Manufactory was permitted to enter.

Although the Manufactory boys would continue to enjoy a degree of laxity in being allowed to go out on errands and were no longer guarded by their masters at night, the new rules now decreed that at the Reform:

> The boys must not be left without some person to watch over them, either by day or by night–nor be permitted on any account to go out.

The Reform boys' potential for creating ingenious 'inconveniences' had also been addressed. The rules further specified:

> They must not be allowed to have money in their pockets–pens, ink, pencils, writing paper and all books (except such as have been seen and approved of by the Chaplain) must be kept out of their reach and great vigilance must be used to prevent them from having in their possession any kind of rope or twine or any knives or other sharp instruments.

Considering that nails or metal spikes strapped to legs were normally used to tease rope fibres apart (and were still being employed by boys in the oakum-picking room at the house of correction, in Tothill Fields, later in the century[11]) we must assume that a particularly close watch was kept on the boys engaged in this craft within the Bermondsey Reform.

Strikingly, these new arrangements also allowed an innovative two-way stage-system of punishments and rewards to be introduced. On one hand, the rules prescribed that the chaplain 'make a report to the Committee, once in every two months on the state of the Reform', with particular mention of 'what boys are sufficiently reformed to be removed to the Manufactory'. The rules also decreed that boys placed in the Reform could not only be:

> such as are admitted by the Society on account of their own delinquency–but that boys guilty of such vices or immoralities in the Manufactory as shall render them unfit to associate with the other boys there, may on a representation in writing to that effect, made by two Visitors to the General Committee, be transferred by order of such Committee to the Reform.

---

11. Mayhew and Binney (1862:400).

Having thus diligently explored what might work better to effect successful reformation, the authors of these refinements carefully captured the essence of their approach. As they explained:

> The foregoing regulations are submitted by the Special Committee as the best which have occurred to them, but they cannot conclude without observing that in forming an Establishment of this kind we must depend as much upon the information to be collected in the progress of the undertaking as upon the knowledge with which we set out on it–and that the Committee must therefore expect to be called upon to make alterations from time to time in any plan which can now be adopted as experience shall point out defects or suggest improvements.

Shades of this evidence-based ethos would inform an even more radical revision of Philanthropic reformatory arrangements in the 1840s.

Education, Health and Morals

So, without further ado — and having recruited Thomas Urchin and Matthew Walker as 'suitable Objects' — the new Philanthropic Reform opened. These boys were not the most felonious of criminals. Thomas had been found 'guilty of many petty thefts' and Matthew had been 'expelled by the Trustees of Tower Ward School for picking pockets and also the receiving of some shoes stolen by other boys'. Their time in the Reform was distributed thus:

On Sunday

Rise at 7 o'clock – Prayers – Breakfast at 8 – Morning Service by the Chaplain or Master at 9, without a Sermon – the Master to read a discourse to them at 12 – Dinner at one – Evening Service by the Chaplain or Master at 3 – boys to read to the Master at half-past 4 – Supper at 6 – Prayers at ½ past 7 – in bed at 8

On Weekdays

Boys to rise at 6 – Prayers – work till 9 – Breakfast – first lesson of the day to be read at 10 – work or other instruction till 2 – Dinner, 2 till 3 – work till 6 – Supper at 7 – Prayers at ½ past 7 – in bed at 8

At mealtimes they enjoyed the following diet:

Breakfast

Milk & water & dry bread – butter to be allowed on Sunday

Supper

Bread & cheese & beer, or for those with whom
cheese may disagree, the same as breakfast

Dinner

Sun. Beef boiled or baked with potatoes
Mon. Broth & bread
Tue. Rice puddings boiled
Wed. Leg of beef stewed with vegetables
Thu. Pease soup made thick with vegetables but without meat
Fri. Stewed mutton and potatoes
Sat. Rice puddings boiled

Mr Fallowfield (the master), his wife (the cook-housekeeper) and the porter were allowed an additional two small joints every week as well as an allowance of butter and cheese. No mention is made of whether former committee member, the Reverend Dr. Grindlay, enjoyed any meals on the premises, but, he had been appointed chaplain of the Reform, on a salary of £100, commencing from the 3rd of September 1802. By February 1803, he was able to report that two boys were 'now sufficiently reformed' to be removed to the Manufactory. Of the others:

- 10 are very much reformed and can read well
- 4 are extremely ignorant, and their general conduct not quite satisfactory

The following year, his assessment of the Reform boys was, that:

- 8 behave extremely well, can read distinctly, appearing to understand their religious duties

5   behave correctly and can read well
2   behave correctly and can read a little
1   behaves quietly but appears to be dull and at present ignorant

It is difficult to determine the rate of successful reformation as the chaplain's reports are not systematically recorded. It would seem, nevertheless, that while some cases of rapid transformation did occur, most boys spent two years in the Reform before transferring to the Manufactory. Paying attention to details of previous education was, however, an increasingly important consideration in assessing the children's condition on admission. As George Brookham's case-history reveals, he was 12 years old when admitted into the Reform in September 1803, having been found to be:

> the natural son of a woman who lives in Kent, and was married to a person last Michaelmas who turned the boy out of doors soon after, when he wandered about the country for some time with two different parties of vagrants till through their artful persuasions he broke into a house and stole several articles for which he was tried and capitally convicted last Oxford Assizes–he received sentence of death but was recommended to mercy by the judge through the humane interposition of Stephen Lushington Esq. In consequence of being ordered to be admitted into the Reform, His Majesty was pleased to grant him a pardon, and he was received under the protection of this Society–he is extremely illiterate but seems of a mild & tractable temper.

As for Benjamin Downes, aged 13 when admitted in January 1803:

> This boy was convicted at the Stafford Assizes of stealing a Fowl and recommended by the magistrates of that county. He is of a soft disposition–very stupid and does not know his ABC.

The virtue of Benjamin's case was transmitted to the society by the Honourable Dudley Ryder. Brother to Home Secretary Richard Ryder who would appoint Holford to the Penitentiary Committee, he became Under-Secretary of State for Foreign Affairs in 1804. In 1809 he was created Earl of Harrowby and, by the 1820s, had been elected a Philanthropic vice-president.

Also destined for the 'No.1 List' was Samuel White. Aged ten when admitted into the Reform in January 1806, Samuel's reception was in consequence of an application made by Surrey magistrates who:

> Stated that this boy had been deserted by his mother who absconded after committing an inhuman murder on one of her children. The father is stated to be a black sailor and the mother a gipsy-woman of very bad character, having six or seven children of various complexions and it was thought the boy had been too often a witness of many of her barbarous acts. This boy cannot read or say his prayers—and is in a state of most deplorable ignorance of all religious or moral duties, although of an active vigorous body & lively capacity.

As Samuel behaved well in the Reform, he was removed to the Manufactory in August 1807. In May 1810, he was apprenticed to Mr. Moore, the Master Taylor.

Despite parental neglect of the children's moral education proving a resilient concern, the society also attempted to ensure that all the children learnt their ABCs, could read *The Bible* and repeat the catechism by ordering:

> 3 dozen of Bishop Wilson's Instructions to the Indians
> 2 dozen of Sellon's Abridgement of the Bible
> 1 dozen of the English Instructor
> 4 dozen Catechism Books
> 3 dozen Mrs Trimmer [morally edifying tales]
> 6 dozen Bibles
> 3 dozen Prayer Books
> 2 books of Tutors Assistant
> 24 slates[12]

This educational provision may hardly have extended beyond that available in many other schools of industry. At the outset, the public had been assured that the society would avoid breeding discontent in the children, through 'forming' them only to their 'humble station' as labourers. It was now operating amidst a rising debate on whether seditious practices might stem from

---

12. One dozen spelling books were included in a similar order of 1807.

teaching the children of the poor to read and write. Indeed, in the aftermath of the French Revolution, even Sunday Schools which delivered a curriculum of reading and writing without the benefit of being regulated under established church principles, were feared to have the potential of inculcating seeds of insubordination and discontent. Traces of such sentiments—as well as an endorsement of the crime preventive value of the Philanthropic curriculum—can be glimpsed in the case-history of Maria and Elhanan Jewell. This girl aged ten and boy aged eight were 'immediately admitted' in December 1802 under these 'very particular circumstances':

> The father now lies under sentence of death at Chelmsford–he stated to the court that he had lived honestly and industriously till that pernicious publication (Payne's *Right's of Man*) by chance fell into his hands and on this ground made it his dying request that the court would endeavour to procure admission for his children, or some of them, to the Philanthropic Reform where he trusted their morals and principles would be secured.

In this atmosphere of apprehension, Whitbread's Bill seeking rate-subsidised education for poor children, failed to capture majority support in 1807. Delivery of educational provision based on the Philanthropic Plan might, however, have found rather more favour on the grounds of its economy. That factor was certainly emphasised by Patrick Colquhoun when seeking the Legislature's sanction for his *New and Appropriate System of Education for children of the labouring poor* in 1806. Echoing many of the preventive policing ideas paraded in early Philanthropic texts, he advocated that, as one means of achieving 'the greatest possible good at the least possible expense', the mode of dispensing moral and religious instruction should be set upon the Anglican Dr. Bell's monitorial system. This, he explained, already had been adopted in the Free School, Westminster, as a 'means of preventing criminal offences by [instilling] habits of temperance, industry, subordination and loyalty'. Just as importantly, economy had been derived from this system by making it the 'province' of the master and mistress 'to direct the whole machine in all its parts … from their respective chairs [and] overlook every part of the school, and give life and motion to the whole'. Monitors, appointed from amongst the pupils as 'superior teachers', then ensured that 'learning' was passed down to the others.

Whether Colquhoun's utilitarian recommendations were particularly in mind, in 1808 the Philanthropists sent two boys to learn from the methods of 'Mr. Reynolds of Lambeth Charity School who is fully instructed in Dr. Bell's plan of instructing young people in reading'.[13] By 1812, Dr. Bell's system had also been adapted for use in the Female School. Therein, the 41 girls were divided into four classes. As the Reverend Dr. Grindlay's *Register of the Conduct and Improvement of the Girls* reveals, the pupils who excelled in the daily examination of their progress in reading and spelling—as well as in their knowledge of scripture and the catechism—became monitors of the class below.

By this time, the Philanthropists had also built a new schoolroom and revised the time-table for the Manufactory boys. These initiatives stemmed from yet another enquiry into the state of Philanthropic trades. This was conducted by the Manufactory Committee which then recommended that the boys in that department:

> of the ages of nine, ten and eleven be placed under a schoolmaster and taught reading, writing and arithmetic in the present working hours with the exception of such a number as may be employed in turning the wheel of the Rope-spinners or as may be engaged usefully in any of the workshops but that the Boys so occupied shall be taken in rotation from the Schoolclass who will not therefore become permanently attached to any particular trade in consequence of such employment.

Perhaps here attempting to strike a compromise between fostering trading profits and shadowing the educational requirements embraced in the Act for the Preservation of the Health and Morals of Apprentices (which Sir Robert Peel, the elder, had introduced in 1802), the society had, nonetheless, conscientiously cared for the health of its children. The level of attention paid to this matter may, indeed, have exceeded that displayed not only in factories and mills but in many prisons and houses of correction of the period. Although the medical trio of Dr. Sims (physician), Mr. Houlston (surgeon) and Mr. Hooper (apothecary) had no precise medical duties prescribed in

---

13. As the dissenting Mr Lancaster's educational establishment was equally convenient in Borough Road, the Philanthropic prior commitment to Anglican-based instruction may account for this preference.

the Philanthropic Regulations, they performed amputations, dealt with assorted disorders (including toothache, head lice, fever[14] and 'the Itch'), dispensed medicines and directed how the children were to be protected against smallpox.

Sometimes supervising the infliction of floggings, these medical gentlemen also reported on the state of the cells and their inmates. The conditions discovered therein were variable. Whereas they might report that it was 'dangerous' to keep some children in the cells for too long on account of their feet swelling from 'excessive cold', concerns would also be expressed when 'exceptionally warm' weather rendered these places of confinement 'rather offensive'. Dr. Sims would also:

> submit the idea of having a dormer window in the stocking manufactory room as he conceives it will be prejudicial to the boys health, not being now sufficiently ventilated, and he likewise is desirous that an aperture be made in the wainscot in the room intended for the sick for the same purpose.

As Dr. Sims would soon depart from the scene, a reprise of his Philanthropic career is due. He had visited the premises—almost on a daily basis—as the Institution settled into St. George's Fields. Besides offering probationary proposals, he inspected the quality of the small beer provision and recommended where milk could be purchased in a less adulterated state than previously obtained. Taking pains to seek 'permission to have Dr. Lettsom and his son to officiate for him in his absence—in the country—in the case of those indisposed at the Reform', Dr. Sims even found time to deliberate on:

> the propriety of having thin walls erected at certain distances in the range of shops to prevent any accident by fire spreading and consuming the whole. Likewise having Hartley's prevention Plates on the doors where necessary.

At the age of almost 70, he retired to Bath. Before doing so, this stalwart vice-president gave forewarning that he might no longer be so assiduous in

---

14. George Cornelius Sharpless who had been sentenced to death at Nottingham in 1796 before being admitted into the Institution, was taken ill with a fever on the 13th of November 1802 and died on the 21st. Eight of the 'senior boys' were permitted to attend his funeral and 'behaved with the utmost propriety'.

its interests. He also sought approval from the 'Committee Gentlemen of the Philanthropic Society' to be assisted by Dr. Rees:

> who has been educated regularly, is a member of the College of Physicians, is a member of the College of London and Physician to the London Dispensary; he is besides the medical friend to whom I at present entrust the care of my own health and that of my family–He is a married man and the father of seven children ... had I applied for this assistance fifteen months ago, I might probably have escaped a severe illness, brought on by over exertion, part of it in your service.

Probably also disappointed by his recent ousting from the presidency of the London Medical Society, Dr. Sims eventually tendered his resignation from Philanthropic duties in January 1810. At this, Dr. Rees applied to be Physician to the society. He too was disappointed. Upon the Committee receiving a letter from 'Dr. George Birkbeck, 25 Cateaton Street, offering himself as a candidate for the office of Physician to this Institution', that gentleman was 'unanimously elected'.

Dr. Birkbeck would not be quite so immersed in the Philanthropic cause as Dr. Sims. A Quaker friend of Dr. Lettsom and active in the work of the General Dispensary, Birkbeck had been a Professor of natural philosophy in Glasgow and was committed to advancing the spread of education for the working classes. Helping set-up the London Mechanics' Institution in 1823, he joined with Lord Brougham in establishing the Society for Disseminating Useful Knowledge (SDUK) and in founding University College. Birkbeck's approach to medical duties would, nevertheless, create some Philanthropic consternation. So much so, that the society's secretary was requested to write:

> expressing the regret of this Committee that the case of Mary Ann Worlock in the Female School had been neglected by him and requesting that he would pay immediate attention to her care.[15]

Considering that the Philanthropic gentlemen 'recollected' a former instance of a lapse in Birkbeck's attention, we can appreciate why this reprimand was

---

15. Mary Ann was admitted in 1820. Her mother had been 'convicted at Gloucester Assizes of poisoning her husband, and executed for the same'.

issued. It elicited a somewhat caustic reply. As this illuminates Birkbeck's conception of voluntary medical duty and affords a glimpse inside the Female School, it is worth reading his letter in full. It is dated 30th November 1823 and was sent to the society's secretary from 50 Broad Street:

> I had yesterday the honor of receiving a letter from you, conveying a resolution of the General Committee and today I have obeyed the mandate of that Committee.
>
> I found Mary Ann Worlock who has been the subject of visceral disease with consequent abdominal dropsy, in the Day Room of the Female Pupils, and both by her own account and my observations, improved in her health-
>
> By what stretch of description her situation had been so represented to the Committee as to induce them to say she was 'suffering under severe illness' I am unable to ascertain: and the expression is not only now inapplicable, but could not have been justly applied at any time since I first saw her for she has never been confined to her bed, and three out of the four visits I paid her, took place in the Matron's room-
>
> That my visits have been as frequent as necessary, I have reason to believe; at least I know that many private patients circumstanced as she is, and under the care of a respectable Apothecary, have not required more attention than she has received. In such cases medical interference is not called for as it is in those which are acute. By careful management in time, and the time will not be short, this girl may I hope recover; and to that recovery I shall be ready as I have already been to contribute what is due to from me-
>
> In what manner she has been 'neglected' by me, my knowledge of the matter, which I presume is almost as accurate as that of the Committee, does not enable me to discover and I am quite at a loss to comprehend by what temper or mis-statement a resolution could have been dictated which conveys the most unwarrantable and offensive accusations to which I was ever subjected.
>
> I have the honor to remain
>   Sir
>   Very faithfully yours
>   George Birkbeck

Although feeling that his 'explanation does not appear completely satisfactory', the committee's 'investigation of this subject' was dropped. Dr. Birkbeck then continued as the Philanthropic's 'Consulting Physician' until his death, in 1841.

In January 1810 (the very same month in which Dr. Sims abandoned the society) vice-president Holford's Philanthropic exertions also began to wane. Not yet diminished by demands flowing from his Millbank Penitentiary avocations, the decline was generated by a dispute revolving around the appointment of a reader for the Philanthropic Chapel.[16] Holford had just led a Special Committee appointed to 'look into the qualification of candidates for vacant Offices in the Society', and encountered a rapid rejection of its recommendations. He then wrote to express 'his intention to withdraw himself from the active management of the affairs of the Society'.

This jolted the society. It already had suffered a turbulent time in the staffing realm of its affairs. Following the death of 'the worthy Superintendent John Durand' at the beginning of the previous year, his daughter Marian had been employed as matron of the Female School and a Mr. Napier appointed as his replacement. But the latter, although seemingly a 'fit person', had not lived up to expectations. In September, he was dismissed for having 'shewn great inattention to the interests of the Society' by refurbishing his apartments 'without authority' and at 'much unnecessary and unjustifiable expense'. In November, Mr Richard Collier was appointed his successor.

Soon afterwards, Matron Durand departed from the scene. Her exit was not the result of conflict with the new superintendent. Instead, it was somehow associated with the disgrace of the Reverend Mr. Forth. In December, that clerical gentleman had been summoned to a 'trial' before the committee who found the 'charges' brought against him 'fully proved' and:

> that so much Indiscretion, and such Impropriety of conduct on his part, have appeared in evidence and have been admitted by Mr Forth as to make it impossible for him to hold the Office of Reader in the Society's Chapel or that of Chaplain to the Manufactory.[17]

One of these clerical vacancies was at the root of Holford's upset. Although prevailed upon to 'retain some share' in the society's 'direction', his involve-

---

16. Clerical appointments were taken very seriously by the Philanthropic Society and summoned a particularly splendid vice-presidential turnout in 1826. This included Earl Spencer, Earl Grosvenor, the Earls of Hardwick and Harrowby and William Wilberforce who had been elected a Philanthropic vice-president in March 1822.
17. The Reverend Forth immediately objected to the 'verdict' in a rather intemperate manner. Although later apologising, he was not reinstated. A sub-committee was afterwards appointed to enquire into the conduct of the matron and servants of the Female Reform and the resignation of Marian Durand and the under-matron followed.

ment thereafter was extremely restricted. He still served Philanthropic interests, nonetheless, and the next year communicated that:

> he had received an intimation from the Secretary of State for the Home Department, the Right Honourable Richard Ryder, that there were now in Newgate three boys under sentence of death and whom it would be necessary to transport unless they could be taken by this Society, in which case they would on account of their youth … be recommended to His Majesty for Pardon.

Even though finding a Home Secretary willing to refer cases was something of a novelty for the society at this time, only two of these boys were admitted. One, William Mann, had been sentenced to death on account of a burglary and, like his companion, received a pardon from the Prince Regent on His Majesty's behalf. Aged 17 on entering the Reform department in March 1811, William was found to be:

> of an indolent disposition, can read very little and has received few [religious] instructions … he had been at work for some time with Mr. Snooke, 5 King's Head, Drury Lane, previous to his imprisonment who gives him a good character.

In June, it was reported that William 'was of mild temper & behaves very quietly & improves in reading'. With his conduct continuing to be 'uniformly correct' he was permitted to enter the Navy in July 1812; Lord Sidmouth, the new 'Home Secretary of State, having consented to the same'.

From May of that year, the Reform department's criminal and delinquent boys had been accommodated at the St. George's Fields site. Considerations of economy and efficiency again underpinned this new arrangement. Besides providing a 'material saving' on rent and staffing costs, it was beheld to afford 'greater efficacy with which this important branch of the Society's establishment can be controlled by the Committee'. The relocation was also considered 'indispensably necessary' for, by enabling the Reform boys to attend Divine Service in the Philanthropic Chapel, it would, expediently, allow the society 'to consolidate the Offices of Chaplain to the Reform and Chaplain to the Manufactory'.

Orchestrated to refrains on the low state of finances, such rationalising retrenchments had become a familiar feature of Philanthropic governance.

The society's men of business had also negotiated their way through a world ordered by deference and patronage to resolve a range of legal difficulties that threatened their socially useful enterprise. This Philanthropic fellowship was comprised of particularly zealous medical, legal, political as well as religiously inclined gentlemen who self-consciously attached importance to testing and adjusting in the light of experience. Finding considerable scope to innovate around the existing statutory framework, they had devised new rules and regulations for effecting institutional improvements. In consequence, a classified structure of departments appeared on the scene and a more systematic stage-system of reformation had been developed.

As future Philanthropic cohorts guided the society into the Age of Reform, their journey would be attended by an increasing clamour of public concern about juvenile crime and delinquency. It also, as we shall see, was accompanied by an internal chorus of rising alarm about the Philanthropic Society's well-being.

CHAPTER 5

A THINNING MESH OF SUPPORT

Highs and Lows

Having seen the effort expended on garnering friends and funds we might expect to find the society's fortunes flourishing over the next two decades. That was not to be. Little financial advantage flowed from having carved a niche in providing for children of the dangerous classes. This is somewhat surprising considering that Luddite agitations and other insurrections would wrap around the issues of unemployment and ever increasing Poor Law rates to concentrate minds on matters of law and order. The problem of juvenile crime and delinquency would, indeed, be brought into sharper relief and occupy the attention of a succession of Parliamentary Select Committees and government enquiries. Yet, by the time the State's response to juvenile offenders took shape in the Parkhurst Prison Act of 1838, the society was not enjoying a prosperous maturity. Instead, it was teetering on the brink of a terminal crisis.

The Philanthropists could scarcely have anticipated the society's slide from pre-eminence. After all, their Institution had become such a show case of innovation that, over the period 1814-19, it attracted an extraordinarily grand parade of visitors from home and abroad. Not only were the Philanthropic premises at St. George's Fields graced by the attentions of Her Imperial Highness, the Grand Dutchess of Oldenburgh (with a large party of ladies and gentlemen) but Sir Robert Peel (with three ladies) also found the enterprise worthy of a visit. So too did the Archduke of Austria in the company of Sir William Congreve, MP, Comptroller of the Royal Laboratory and superintendent of military machines. The Institution also received the attention of His Imperial Highness the Archduke Michael as well as the Grand Duke Nicholas of Russia who already had inspected Millbank Penitentiary within a month of its opening. This Grand Duke was accompanied on his Philanthropic visit by vice-president George Holford.

As one of the focal points in a Grand Tour of enterprise and improvement, the Philanthropic Institution was likewise not ignored by John Griscom on his journey around Europe in 1818-19. A Quaker and professor of chemistry and natural philosophy at Columbia College in New York, he had embarked on his travels in a spirit of enquiry to see what ideas from the Old World could be applied with advantage to the New.[1] Arriving in London supplied with introductions, his first days were occupied in attending a meeting of the British and Foreign Bible Society and one of Sir Joseph Banks's scientific lévees where he conversed with the 'illustrious' Sir Humphrey Davy. He then dined with his 'worthy friend' and fellow Quaker, William Allen. The wealthy proprietor of a chemical business, Allen was active in the campaign against slavery, involved in the Lancastrian School movement and vigorously pursued the cause of criminal law reform. He also escorted Griscom on a visit to Parliament where the gallery was 'so entirely full, that, after remaining some time, crowded and squeezed most uncomfortably' they thought it 'best to retreat'.

Griscom's visit to Parliament the following day was more gratifying for he heard the 'distinguished philanthropist' William Wilberforce speak 'in a style of great animation' on the 'cause of suffering humanity'. This was just after Sir Samuel Romilly had 'moved for further enquiries into some cruelties that had been practised' on slaves in a West India plantation. It was also before Lord Brougham spoke on a 'motion relative to a Parliamentary inquiry into abuses upon charities, chiefly devoted to education'. Much impressed with Brougham's 'masterly display of popular talent; abounding with keen invective against the House of Lords, for having stripped the Bill of all its best features', Griscom declared that he 'could scarcely have chosen a day more favourable to the wish of hearing the best speakers of Parliament upon subjects of general interest'. This more than made up for his visit, earlier that day, to the Court of Chancery where he heard 'some dull pleadings before the Lord Chancellor by lawyers with large powdered wigs hanging

---

1. The following account draws upon Griscom's *A Year in Europe* (1823). Like many members of the Philanthropic Network, Griscom's interests were multi-faceted. He was a member of the Literary and Philosophical Society of New York, and amongst his other publications are: *Hints relative to the most eligible method of conducting meterological observations* (1815), *Monitorial Instruction* (1825) and *School Discipline* (1832).

down to their shoulders'. Of their compliance with that 'ancient custom', this Enlightened gentleman of a new republic remarked:

> To my unpractised eye there is a stiff formality in their appearance, which closely borders on the ridiculous.

Griscom's investigations soon took him south of the Thames where, after spending time at the Asylum for the Deaf and Dumb and the School for the Indigent Blind, his attention was 'next directed' to the buildings and workshops of the Philanthropic Institution. William Allen, who subscribed one guinea annually to the society, most likely accompanied him on this visit.

On his return to New York, Griscom's tale of the Philanthropists' aims and approach impressed associates in the Society for the Prevention of Pauperism. Perceiving juvenile crime to be a major indicator of social and moral decay and believing—like the Philanthropic founders—that poor parental guidance and association with adults in prison were at the heart of the problem, they engaged in a campaign to reclaim vagrant, depraved and criminal children from contaminating environmental circumstances. By 1824—and with the Philanthropic establishment held up as a model which came 'nearest in its general system' to that which they would recommend—their subsidiary Society for the Reform of Juvenile Delinquents had acquired the sanction of the City Corporation, approval from the State Legislature and enough funds to open a House of Refuge. This was publicised as 'the first of the kind in the United States, by which the experiment of juvenile reformation has been fairly attempted'. With modifications made to the Philanthropic Plan 'requisite to adapt it to the local circumstances', this New York City House of Refuge took root on the site of an old arsenal 'near the head of Broadway and the Bowery'. But, with the children's frequent escapes indicating a need for purpose-built accommodation, a new Institution was soon erected. This was based on a plan 'somewhat similar to the state prison at Auburn' with clanking doors to the separate cells in which the children were locked each night.[2]

---

2. Hart (1832).

As for local Philanthropic circumstances? Some cells there were, heavy doors indeed, and many windows undoubtedly barred. Like their New York counterparts, the children at St. George's Fields also attended to their duties within a regime regulated by the ringing of bells. Even so, the New York configuration of penitentiary features was not introduced as a solution to problems that erupted in the Female School in 1817. At that time, about 111 boys resided in the Manufactory department, 19 were in the Reform and around 35 girls were sheltered in their separate building.

It is unclear what precise mixture of criminal and non-criminal girls resided in the Female School, or, whether attempts were made to calculate what proportion of each category should be admitted. If there was such a policy in place, it is hard to detect beneath the inconsistencies betrayed in the *Admission Registers*. In 1811, for instance, the society had no difficulty in admitting Jane Dampier, aged eleven, who was recommended by William Morton Pitt. A Philanthropic committee member in 1804, Morton Pitt afterwards served on the Holford Committee and was one of the magistrates who had placed Jane in confinement in Dorchester Goal for 'setting fire to her master's house'. Nor had the society experienced any problem in receiving minor offender Jane Dent, aged ten and a half, who had stolen several articles and 'frequently absented herself from her mother for some days altogether', when recommended by Patrick Colquhoun. Likewise Eleanor Henry aged ten, who had been found 'guilty of pilfering' was admitted when recommended to the society's care by Lady Wellington in 1812.

Yet, in February the following year, Sarah Plumb, 'stated to be 12 years old next April' and who also had been 'guilty of pilfering', was refused admission. Sarah had been recommended to the society by Sir Thomas Plumer, the Attorney General and one of the society's first subscribers. As to why the society's rejected the request of this future vice-chancellor of England and soon to be Philanthropic vice-president,[3] it was:

> on account of her mature age, appearance, and the apprehension that her being mixed with the other girls may be attended with mischievous consequences.

---

3. Plumer was a trustee of the British Museum and, like Philanthropic vice-president James Allen Park, was also a fellow of the Society of Antiquaries.

Mischievous consequences were certainly in flow by the 5th of February 1817. The matron of the Female School then had to report that 'at a little after seven in the morning' eight girls 'made their escape at the street door by artfully contriving to take the keys from the place where they were deposited'. This was not the first sign of disturbing breaches in the Philanthropic system of protective surveillance. The previous year, some 'communication' with Manufactory boys had required the external wall of the garden to be raised and topped 'with glass set in the cement' along with the following 'requisite' fortifications:

> That a latticed door be placed at the foot of the stairs next the school room; that sun blinds should be fixed to the windows of the matron and sub-matron's bedrooms, to be provided with padlocks and staples at the bottom, and that a positive injunction be given to the matron and sub-matron never to allow any girls to go into those rooms, until the blinds are locked down.

Although most of the truants were quickly returned by parents or friends, Zylpha Williams's account of her escapade reminded the society that it had no legal powers to retain the children inside the Institution's walls. This was a festering worry. In the earliest years, the Philanthropic gentlemen had been particularly disconcerted by the case of Charlotte Murrell. Aged 13 when admitted in 1790, Charlotte had been found in a state of vagrancy and her mother was dead. But in 1794, when her 'father in law' removed her from where she had been placed in service, the superintendent received orders to take her away from that individual's house 'his character by no means being such as to intrust a girl of this age to his care'. Charlotte was re-admitted but later absconded from another placement with the 'determined resolution never to return to the Nunnery as she termed the Reform'.

The society's fears for Charlotte's moral welfare deepened when Superintendent Durand discovered that she was again living in the residence of her 'father in law'. This person, however, posed other threats for he had boldly informed the superintendent that:

> if I attempted to force the lock, or proceed further into his house ... as he was now up to me—having had proper advice, he should make the Society pay for it.

The society's benevolent intentions were still being resisted in 1817. As the matron informed the committee, the 15 year old Zylpha:

> says she went with Mary French to her grandmother who lives by Shadwell Church and slept with Mary French at the grandmother's and also adds that when the person sent by the Superintendent came to the door to make enquiry the grandmother hid them under the bed–in the morning when Zylpha Williams came away, Mary French tried to come with her but the grandmother would not let her, but said she would get her a place herself.[4]

If the thought of leaving Mary under the grandmother's care caused the society to fret, more worries followed. A flight of thirteen girls occurred in the evening of the 3rd of May. They had made-off through the laundry window 'having previously unfastened it by taking out the rails and also forcing the padlock of the garden gate'.

Further pandemonium ensued on the 5th of September when 17 girls came down from their dormitories and daringly 'made their escape by forcing back the lock of the street door'. Although three were 'recovered immediately' and some captured by the 'several persons sent off in search of the others', at this mass exit of nearly half the girls in the Female School, an immediate enquiry was launched.

Some suspicion of at least one cause of the problem already had been aroused. The Special Committee set-up to prevent further escapes was specifically enjoined to consider 'whether the confinement of the girls in the Female School has not been more severe than absolute necessity requires'. With this guidance before them, the investigators found that the escape had 'not arisen from any vicious motive' but from the 'general restlessness at the close confinement to which the females were subject and from a desire to see their relations and friends'. The recommended remedy was to reward the girls' good behaviour by permitting home visits 'provided their friends undertake to fetch them in the morning and return them by six o'clock in the evening'. It was also advised that 'once in every week' the matron, with proper attendants, should:

---

4. Zylpha (sometimes Zelpha) had been admitted in 1813 on the recommendation of the overseers of St. Saviours Parish, having been 'guilty of pilfering'.

take out such a portion of the girls as they can conveniently manage, and to accompany them in a walk for reasonable recreation; so that the girls may go out in turn, unless the matron should think it necessary to confine them at home as a punishment.

Striking a balance between protection and over-control of their charges was a long-standing and fraught Philanthropic task. It had not, however, deterred the society from allowing Manufactory boys the freedom to run errands and take advantage of an established system of tickets-of-leave.

But, astoundingly, as a further remedy for the disorder reigning amongst the girls, it was now decreed that 'no criminal girl shall in future be received into the Female School'. This decision is understandable in view of the Special Committee's investigation also confirming that the 'restless conduct' had:

> been much fermented by a few of the older girls who had been criminal before they were received into the Institution, and who have repeatedly disturbed the harmony which formerly subsisted in the Female School.

Nonetheless, even though the female inmate-mix had proved hard to handle, it is surprising to find the society deciding to exclude all criminal girls rather than creating a Female Reform along the lines of that established for criminal boys. It is particularly strange considering the lack of specialised provision elsewhere in the Metropolis. Although the Refuge for the Destitute would soon establish a separate department into which criminal girls were received and Elizabeth Fry helped institute a 'House of Discipline and School of Reform for viciously disposed and neglected Female Children' in 1825, the latter initiative was deemed necessary because 'As yet no Institution has been formed for the specific object of arresting the progress of Vice in the minds of Female Children, already contaminated by actual Guilt'. Indeed, in evidence given to a Select Committee in 1835, its members also pointed out that:

> On Application to the Committee of the Philanthropic Society they stated that they had no Power of receiving into their Female department Children guilty of stealing, or any similar misconduct; the Girls in their School being the Children of Criminals, but not themselves Transgressors.[5]

---

5. Report of the Select Committee on Gaols and Houses of Correction (1835), Part IV, Appendix

Reluctance to stretch scarce resources probably played a great part in reducing Philanthropic endeavour in this sphere. The society had, indeed, referred 'the practicability of erecting a Reform for the reception of female criminals' to a Special Committee in 1813. But, in the wake of having just expended funds on building a new Reform Department for boys at St. George's Fields, nothing came of the matter.

Economic considerations likewise coloured the society's unwillingness to establish a department for the 'infant offspring of convicts' and concede to 'the immediate admission of a child of two years old of that description' in May 1812. This had been proposed by William Garrow Esq., another early subscriber to the society who had visited the Philanthropic Institution at St. George's Fields in May 1798. This soon to be Solicitor General and then Attorney General in the footsteps of Sir Thomas Plumer was, nonetheless, informed that:

> the Society is neither provided with habitations for such an addition of children, nor suitable servants, nor friends adequate to such an undertaking, the present state of the Society's finances having induced them to make recent application for the increase of them for the purposes of their present undertaking.[6]

When William Withering Esq., a Birmingham magistrate, enquired the next year whether some arrangement could be made for occasionally receiving 'criminal infants' on 'condition of the parish making an adequate allowance for them', his proposition also was rejected. Not, this time, for the aforementioned reasons. Instead it was on the grounds of being 'not consistent with the rules of the Institution which require personal examination of each object previous to admission'. Perhaps underpinned by a reluctance to have its autonomy in the choice of objects eroded, this rhetoric was nevertheless

---

to Evidence (p.547). This School of Reform was for girls 'not under Seven Years of Age nor above Thirteen, who have been found guilty of stealing, or any other Offence causing Loss of Character or Danger of Imprisonment'.

6. Although these infants would have been considered 'mere nurse children' and therefore not proper Philanthropic 'Objects', the society had received James Randall, aged three, in July 1792. His father and mother had been transported after a 'daring robbery'. James was placed under the care of the matron at the girl's branch of the Institution until he was seven.

belied by the society's readiness to welcome other children who were sent, unseen, from far-off places.

Such erratic exercises in discretion exasperated the Philanthropic visitors of 1819. In an *Account* of 1814, the society had taken pains to inform the public that its interest was confined 'to cases of grave delinquency' and:

> that Objects are not admitted on account of mere youthful irregularities; of the effects of a truant disposition, or of such acts as bear the complexion of vagrancy rather than of fraud or felony.

Despite this declaration of intent — and with the offspring of criminals still being admitted — the visitors found 'much of their time taken up in explaining who are the proper Objects of their Institution'. This, they believed, had grave implications for the wellbeing of the society. Noting the lack of rules to guide them 'other than are expressed in very general terms in the printed reports', they felt bound to warn that:

> it has not infrequently happened that some Visitors have not had the same opinion on this subject as their predecessors–cases that have been rejected by one have been thought eligible by another; and there have been serious instances of offence given to valuable friends of the Institution who have had the Objects they recommended refused as ineligible, when similar cases have at other times been received.

Such inconsistency was not the visitors' only anxiety. Whilst retaining Philanthropic wards within the walls often posed problems, the society was also prey to wily parents who sought to off-load responsibilities by claiming their children had committed crimes or delinquencies. Protecting the society from accusations of relieving the 'burthens of the bad members of the community' had been close to the hearts of the Philanthropic founders. As they also recognised that charities could 'create clients for their benefits', weeding-out undeserving applications had been made an early visitorial duty. It was, however, an on-going concern. This, vice-president Holford well knew and highlighted when publishing his *Thoughts on the Criminal Prisons of this Country* in 1821. Tussling with the question of 'whether imprisonment, in any shape or form, can be effectual to stop the growing evil of youthful iniquity', he reflected that, as offences 'proceed in a great measure from the conduct of [their] parents, sometimes from their direct encouragement, oftener, from their neglect':

> To be effectual therefore for the purpose of lessening the number of youthful criminals, the punishment should apply in some measure to the minds of the parents, and should carry with it some terror to their feelings ... although the confinement and the discipline of the prison may be irksome to the boy, yet the parents may be apt to congratulate themselves on having got him off their hands ... and may be considered by other parents as having a draw prize in the lottery of human life by their son's conviction.
>
> This reasoning is not only theoretical, but is founded in some degree upon experience. Those who have been in the habit of attending the committee of the Philanthropic Society know, that parents have often accused their children of crimes falsely, or have exaggerated their real offences, for the sake of inducing that Society to take them; and so frequent has been this practice, that it is a rule with those who manage that Institution, never to receive an object upon the representation of its parents, unless supported by strong testimony.

To avoid being victims of such deceitful practices—and with the hope of standardising admissions procedure—the exasperated visitors applied themselves to formulating a list of 'precise rules' that would answer 'all questions upon the nature of the Institution in whatever concerns the admission of Objects'. In focus were the 'Offspring of convicted Felons' under 14 and 'Criminal Boys' between nine and 13 years of age. For the latter category, it was specified that the parents had to be 'in destitute Circumstance and unable to take proper Care of him; or of Characters so vicious, as to have been the Cause of his Delinquency'. Additionally, if the boy had not been imprisoned but was charged with an offence on the oath of a 'creditable' person (not a relative), magistrates who then declined to proceed with the case, in the hope of his future 'amendment', were required to complete a specially devised form. In this, they had to certify the circumstances under which the boy was recommended 'to the Protection of the Philanthropic Society'.

Remarkably, a copy of this magistrate's certificate was inspected by a House of Lords Select Committee on Gaols and Houses of Correction to which the society's steward was called to give evidence in 1835.[7] This was not

---

7. SC on Gaols and Houses of Correction, PP (1835), Vol. XII., Appendix to Evidence, Part IV. p.538.

Mr. Thomas Russell's first Parliamentary appearance. In 1817 he had entered centre stage before a House of Commons Select Committee of Enquiry into the State of Police in the Metropolis. On that occasion Steward Russell was sandwiched, as it were, between former Philanthropic committee member Edward Forster junior (who was appearing before the Select Committee as treasurer of the Refuge for the Destitute) and 'William Crauford'. Crawford was another Quaker. He also was the 'gratuitous secretary' of a society which had been set up in 1815:

> [to] ascertain the extent and causes of the alarming increase of juvenile delinquency in the metropolis, or rather the circumstances in the character and situation of the juvenile delinquent that might be justly considered as excitements to the commission of crime.[8]

Established in the year that brought peace with France and the end of the Anglo-American War, this society would find the 'principal causes' to be the 'improper conduct of parents; the want of education; the want of employment; the violation of the Sabbath, and habits of gambling in the public streets'. To these were added the 'auxiliary causes' of the severity of the criminal code, the defective state of the police and the existing system of prison discipline.

These findings would scarcely have startled the Philanthropic founders. What lent this society a novel credibility, however, was the scale of evidence it presented and the method of its collection. Its committee had divided the Metropolis into districts in which sub-committees — armed with questionnaires 'calculated to obtain the necessary information' — interviewed 'some thousand boys' in confinement and also their friends and relations.[9] These ambitious and systematic enquiries undoubtedly outshone anything hitherto attempted by the Philanthropists. Even so, the 'facts' which Steward Russell delivered on his society's preventive policing performance were sufficient to impress the Select Committee of 1817. Not only did its members believe that the Philanthropic had 'fully answered the views of its benevolent founders'

---

8. SC on the Police, PP (1817), Vol. VII., Minutes of Evidence, pp. 428-9.
9. SC on the Police, PP (1817), Vol. VII., Minutes of Evidence, pp. 428-441. This society's membership has many overlaps with the Society for the Improvement of Prison Discipline and the Reformation of Juvenile Offenders (SIPD). The SIPD acted as a pressure group for reform and was supported heavily by members of the Refuge as well as the Philanthropic Society.

for 'much the greater proportion of those who have been there brought up, turn out well', it also wished:

> [to] direct the attention of the Public to this excellent Institution, which is well deserving a more extended patronage, not only for the end which the Establishment has in view, but also for the success which has attended its labours, arising from the excellence of its regulations, and the frugal manner in which its funds are administered.[10]

Fickle Funding

Unfortunately, this glowing testimonial did not swell the Philanthropic coffers. Despite memories of riot and sedition that culminated in the Peterloo Massacre of 1819 and the Cato Street Conspiracy to assassinate the Cabinet in 1820, hopes of monetary recognition for the society's part in nipping crime and disorder in the bud would deflate over the next decade. It may well have taken under its wing Caroline Harrison, aged nine, whose father John 'was convicted of High Treason and transported for life' for being involved in the conspiracy.[11] But, instead of a steady replenishment of revenue, the period brought large clouds of financial gloom lowering overhead. Such a depressing forecast would hardly have seemed credible when, in 1817:

> Jeremiah Harman, Governor of the Bank of England, attended the Committee and communicated to them that the Court of Directors having frequent occasion to prosecute for forgery and as the Philanthropic Society appears to be the most eligible Asylum for many children who are hereby left in a destitute state, they had it in their intention to make occasional application on their behalf. The Governors also communicated that tho' the Court of Directors are aware that no subscription to this Institution entitles the subscribers to a preference in the reception of Objects–they had voted a donation of one thousand guineas.

This was a spectacular donation: whether stemming from humanitarian concern for the children or as a means of salving consciences over the consequences

---

10. SC on the Police, PP (1817), Vol. VII., Second Report, Part VII, p. 332.
11. The plan was to blow-up the Cabinet as it sat at dinner in the house of the Lord President of the Council. This personage was Philanthropic vice-president, the Earl of Harrowby. Caroline's father had hired the house in Cato Street which the conspirators used as a base.

of prosecuting parents in pursuit of the Bank of England's interest. Forgery was of particular concern to the bank at this time and was one of the felonies for which reprieves were rarely given. In this context, it may not be so coincidental to find that, at the same meeting, the committee's attention was also brought to:

> the case of the eight infant children of Ann Woodman who was now under sentence of death in Newgate for issuing forged notes of the Bank of England at whose suit she has been prosecuted–the father of these children having been executed for the same offence.

Only two of these children, Hannah aged 13 and Charlotte aged 11, were received into the Female School, 'the remaining six children being too young for admission'. While the fate of these infant offspring is unknown,[12] we can, perhaps, be more certain that Jeremiah Harman had exercised his influence to benefit the society. Joining the Philanthropic Committee in 1792, he was a Director of the Bank of England from 1794, became its deputy governor (1814-16) and governor (1816-18). At the committee meeting during which the case of the Woodman children was discussed, he was nominated a vice-president of the society; a 'vacancy having occurred' on the death of his father John. That gentleman was considered one of the society's 'most zealous and liberal friends and benefactors' and had helped underwrite the Indenture which enabled the society to obtain building leases from the City Corporation in 1793. Jeremiah, who continued as a director of the Bank of England, likely maintained the Harman family's reputation by playing no small part in seeing that a further 'munificent donation' of £1,000 came the society's way in 1820.

This largess was no doubt welcome. Faced with a 'considerable drop' in income over the past few years, the society had appointed a Special Committee to investigate its causes. Having 'taken into account the amounts of subscriptions, life donations, the produce of several trades, chapel collections and pew rents', the 'diminution' was found to have:

---

12. Acres (1931) notes that the mother was later pardoned.

arisen from there being less employment in some branches of the trades in time of peace than in time of war, the pressure of the times upon individuals of limited income, and the opportunities which other charitable institutes have of coming more fully before the public by an election of the Objects taken under their care, which this Society is unable to adopt and also from the very trifling contributions which are made at the Chapel doors.

These conclusions do not seem untoward. Peace had not brought prosperity to the nation but, instead, economic depression and a growing burden of taxes. With government orders for new ships ceasing and with many vessels laid-up after hostilities ceased, the society probably had experienced a rapidly falling demand for the products of its rope-making department. The slump in Philanthropic business may also have been compounded by competition from manufacturers who could afford to apply the latest technological advances to production and thus under-cut prices in this and other trades.[13]

As to being hampered from raising the Philanthropic profile and funds by way of 'electing' children? A customary abhorrence was most likely at the root of the trouble. This method of admission (by which subscribers voted to sponsor children brought to their notice) was already a proficiently publicised practice of the Foundling Hospital. The society, however, was in something of a bind on the matter. Although it had not scrupled to publish lists of named children 'together with the most striking circumstances that constituted their qualification for its benefits' in the *First Report*, this tool for soliciting funds had been swiftly discontinued in 'tenderness to distant relatives, upon whom the details might bring an unmerited disgrace'. The censorship was soon extended to cover the identities of 'immediate kindred and friends'.

Subsequent experience had shown that the society's wards could also be disadvantaged by the stigma of their Philanthropic background. In reply to the 1817 Select Committee's questioning on why contact had been lost with the 'better part' of the girls who had left Philanthropic care, Steward Russell stated there could be 'no doubt' that:

13. Although Henry Maudsley's innovative machinery had been employed in some stages of production at the ropery at Chatham Dockyards from 1811, the society does not appear to have switched from using labour intensive, craft-based methods in the long rope walk at its Manufactory.

they endeavour as much as possible to conceal their place of education, and with many persons it would be a great obstruction to their advancement in service if it was known that they have been educated in our establishment ... on account of their having been the children of convicts, they are more particularly liable to reproach from fellow servants than from masters and mistresses, who would of course be more liberal; instances have come to the knowledge of the committee of girls having lost their situations in consequence of representations of their fellow servants, that they could not live with them in consequence of their having been thieves, or the children of thieves.[14]

As for the diminishing returns on the Philanthropic Chapel investment? Very 'trifling' contributions continued to be received. By 1827, its under-performance in this sphere had become even more marked. In consequence of the impetus given to church building through government subsidies (aimed at promoting the moral welfare of the nation in turbulent times[15]), the pomp in which the Philanthropic Chapel once gloried had been punctured by new rival attractions in the neighbourhood. Realising it was engaged in a somewhat 'Holy War' of market forces and discovering that:

> Many of the pew renters having complained of the high price at which the seats in the Society's Chapel are let–and having expressed a wish for a reduction, and the seats in the neighbourhood churches and chapels now let at £1.0s.0d per seat.

the society resolved 'that for the future the annual rent of each seat be reduced to five shillings'.

Strangely, although a considerable 'falling-off of the company at the Anniversary Dinners' meant that donations from this formerly fertile source had also declined, the Philanthropists decided to buy the freehold of the land at St. George's Fields. Ostensibly, this venture was driven by the necessity of reducing expenditure on the rates. As the society reminded the Bridge House Estates Committee when attempting to negotiate a reduction in the purchase price of £8,980:

---

14. SC on the Police, PP (1817), Vol. VII., Minutes of Evidence, p.445.
15. £1 million was given in 1818 and a further £500,000 in 1824. Briggs (1959/1979:213) suggests this government strategy was adopted in preference to creating an efficient professional police body or repressing by force all signs of unrest.

> That your Committee was sensible of the benefits likely to arise from the Philanthropic Society at a time when there was no existing Establishment for preventing Juvenile crimes and therefore encouraged the Institution in its infancy by fixing a small rent for the interior ground–
>
> Your memorialists have however at great expense become tenants of much additional frontage ground and have also by their buildings added a large and permanent value both to the property they occupy and that of its neighbourhood by which means the valuation now made has been greatly increased.

Quite what was said by treasurer Samuel Bosanquet, who headed the deputation 'specially summoned' before the City's Court of Common Council, is not mentioned.[16] But, having reached an accommodation on the matter and taking the caution of addressing 'a respectful letter to HRH the President and to such of the Vice-President's as are Peers, apprising them of the Bill for the Society before the House of Lords, for the purchase of the freehold', the requisite Act passed on the 17th of June 1823.

Dipping into Philanthropic capital to complete the deal brought less than pleasurable returns in the short-term. Admittedly a measure thought 'on the whole highly expedient and conducive to the permanent interests of the Society', it was shortly recognised to have 'involved its finances in increased embarrassments'. Even so, the society does not appear to have rued giving the appearance of possessing a chest of Philanthropic silver on the one hand and pleading poverty on the other. At a committee meeting, held under the chairmanship of vice-president Mr. Justice Stephen Gaselee in January 1825, the Philanthropic gentlemen came to the following audacious resolution:

> That it is desirable to make an application to his Majesty's Secretary of State for the Home Department for a grant of the sum of £10,000 which the Society have been compelled to expend on the purchase of the freehold.

Mr. Justice Gaselee had been a Philanthropic committee member since 1803 and was also president of the Royal Humane Society. Recently installed as a justice of the Common Pleas and soon to be knighted, he would achieve long-lasting notoriety in being caricatured by Charles Dickens, in the *Pickwick*

---

16. The former Samuel Bosanquet 'junior' had succeeded Edward Gale Boldero as treasurer in 1812.

Papers, as the very short and comically pompous Mr. Justice Stareleigh who presided over a trial for breach of promise.

Rather more startlingly, in real-life the Philanthropic Mr. Justice Gaselee would play a prime-role in dispatching 14 year old John Any Bird Bell to the gallows from Maidstone Assizes on the 29th of July 1831. Ruling on the admissibility of the boy's voluntary confession to the murder of 13 year old Robert Taylor (as written down by the committing Rochester Magistrate's Court clerk and on which confession the illiterate John had made his mark), Mr. Justice Gaselee allowed the confession to be read in the third person 'and the prisoner was convicted and executed'.[17]

Still, although nothing had come of a previous entreaty to the Home Department in 1794, we might suppose that Gaselee and his fellow Philanthropists had high hopes riding on the persuasive powers of the deputation sent to 'Mr Secretary Peel' in 1825. Sir Robert Peel, the younger, had succeeded Lord Sidmouth as Home Secretary in 1822 and then sponsored the Gaol Act of 1823 which attempted to effect a more systematic regulation of prison conditions and discipline. In that year he had also ordered that the former war-ship *Bellerophon* should, under the superintendence of John Henry Capper, be used as a separate convict hulk for juvenile offenders sentenced to transportation. That division of the convict establishment was then transferred onto the specially fitted frigate *Euryalus* in 1825, by which time, Peel had begun to drive through legislation which reduced the number of capital offences held on the Statute Book.

Regrettably, although Home Secretary Peel 'promised' to take the committee's representations 'into his consideration', the society waited in vain for a favourable reply. Philanthropic aspirations had, no doubt, been underpinned by awareness of the government grant of £1,500 received by the Refuge for

---

17. Home Summer Circuit (Crown Side), *Rex v. Bell* before Mr Justice Gaselee and Lord Tenterden, C.J. (in Carrington and Payne, 1833: 162-4). Although the name on the confession is given as John Heneker Bell, this otherwise appears to be the case of John Any Bird Bell which nowadays is extensively cited to highlight the boy's youth, his hanging and his body's dissection afterwards. John's younger brother James (aged eleven), was not committed for trial, though present when the victim was robbed of nine shillings and had his throat slit. Instead, James was called as a witness for the prosecution. When commenting on *The Times*'s report on the case, Gatrell (1994:3) notes that Gaselee over-rode the jury's recommendation for mercy, saying that 'he had never before tried so atrocious a crime'.

the Destitute in 1814 with the blessing of Home Secretary Sidmouth and increased by him to £5,000 per annum in 1819.[18] Information on this government generosity most likely circulated within the Philanthropic network. George Holford had been a vice-president of the Refuge since 1806 and other Philanthropists also served on its committee. By 1828, however, the superintendent of the Refuge's Male Department could inform another Select Committee on the Police of the Metropolis that, in addition to the Treasury grant, financial arrangements for maintaining its inmates were as follows:

> Thirty four are paid for by individuals; there is an association at Guildford that sends lads; there is one at Maidstone; there is the Sheriffs Fund and the City Bridewell Committee; and there is one gentleman who pays for eight himself always.[19]

The vice of envy could well have been in the Philanthropic air. The society's declining income was assuming such melancholy proportions that an *Address* was prepared for circulation. This was issued in the particular hope that members would do all in their 'power to prevent so painful a result as the decay or extinction of what has long been deemed one of the most useful and meritorious charities which adorn this Metropolis'. As the predicament was summarised:

> the expenditure, notwithstanding the utmost frugality in every department has for some years past greatly exceeded the income; and within the last year to the extent of £1,200. The deficiencies have hitherto been supplied by occasional legacies; but upon these no prudent dependence can be placed. Very many of the early friends of the Charity have been removed by death; the Chapel, from the numerous Parochial Churches erected in the neighbourhood, has ceased to be a source of any considerable revenue, and amongst so many other appeals to the charitable Public, more novel indeed and speculative, the Annual Subscriptions to the Philanthropic have very seriously declined.

It was a worrying situation for the Philanthropic gentlemen to consider. Theirs was a charity whose crime prevention endeavours, they believed, could 'never want the charm of novelty to recommend' and whose 'happy experience

---

18. Sidmouth was elected a Refuge vice-president in 1818.
19. SC on the Police, PP (1828), Vol. VI., Minutes of Evidence, p. 182.

of nearly forty years' had placed 'its success beyond speculation'. Yet, resources had not kept pace with needs. This was somewhat untoward at a time when the Legislature had 'noticed with alarm' the 'fearful growth' of juvenile crime and had taken the subject 'under their anxious enquiry' and when:

> [as] Magistrates and Jurors especially we are called to view almost with hearts thuddering the ordering from session to session, the thronging groups of youth of both sexes at the bar of public justice waiting often with hardened indifference the sentence of the laws.

A slight shift in funding policy now occurred. This possibly was triggered by thoughts of adopting the Refuge's more varied arrangements. These were certainly different in kind to those of the Philanthropic Society whose Superintendent Collier informed the Select Committee of 1828 that its expenses were 'wholly defrayed by voluntary contributions'.[20] Soon afterwards, a proposal was received from 'the Governor of Newgate on behalf of the Sheriffs Fund for the admission of two boys now in Newgate, upon terms similar to those upon which such boys are admitted into the Refuge for the Destitute'. At this, the society resolved to admit them and decreed:

> That in future it be made a Regulation for the government of the Committee that upon the payment of every hundred pounds by any Body Corporate or individual, the criminal boy recommended ... shall be admitted into the Institution provided the case shall appear to the Committee upon inquiry to be within the spirit and regulations of the Establishment, and free from any special objection.[21]

Uncertainty still loomed over the society's future. Although the arrival of a magnificent legacy of £9,000 did much to stave-off extinction, there were few signs that a steady flow of new subscription revenue could be so fortuitously secured. The Philanthropic auditors of 1831 painted a gloomy picture. Donations and subscriptions had continued to decline from £1,645 in 1824 to £1,224 by 1830. This was of dramatic contrast to the hey-day year of 1813 when the total income derived from these sources amounted to £2,438.14s.6d.

---

20. SC on the Police, PP (1828), Vol. VI., Minutes of Evidence, p.163.
21. The Sheriff's Fund for discharged prisoners had been founded in 1808 and was dispensed from the Sessions House at the Old Bailey.

The society was undeniably still wealthy in terms of capital assets and would remain buoyant enough to celebrate its fiftieth birthday. Even so, the downward spiral in revenue had become a worrying font of decay in Philanthropic foundations. This worry would combine with other problems of governance and create acute anxiety.

Diminishing Returns

Meanwhile, in the world outside the Philanthropic walls, a degree of Parliamentary reform took shape in the *Representation of the People Act* of 1832. The next year, a government grant of £22,000 came the way of voluntary schools that could match-fund a proportion of this State aid from their own subscriptions. That Treasury bounty was increased in 1839 and thereafter administered by a Privy Council Committee with the aid of an inspectorate set-up to supervise the standard of educational work conducted under the scheme.[22] The Philanthropic Society did not receive any portion of this money. Nor did it remain untouched by the political sensitivities which fermented during the long passage of the Reform Act through Parliament. As the Committee heard with 'deep regret':

> on Sunday 28th August 1831 the gentleman engaged as a substitute for Mr Price gave great offence to the congregation by strong political allusions in his sermon so much so as to occasion great numbers to withdraw during the time of Divine Service.

No doubt dismayed at the prospect of having the chapel collections further diminished by clerical subversion, the Philanthropists were no less concerned to hear that 'upon many occasions of Anniversary Sermons, demonstrations have appeared among the elder boys of strong feelings excited by the allusions to the former criminal state of the Objects of this charity or their connections'.

Demonstrations of misconduct by Manufactory boys had also brought the matter of internal discipline into heightened focus once more. With an

---

22. Although this committee had no statutory existence and so no statutory powers, Roberts (1969:115) notes that it 'possessed the most effective power of all, that of the purse'.

urgent investigation into its causes conducted and the means of dealing with the offenders considered, a Special Committee ordered:

-that George Robinson who had been intoxicated and riotous on Sunday afternoon and again on Monday evening and placed in confinement on Tuesday the 15th Inst. by the Chaplain and the Superintendent, be confined in the same upon bread and water another week, and pay out of his rewards the amount of damages done by him, and be kept from going out during the pleasure of the Committee.

-that George Armitage who was intoxicated on Sunday and Monday evening, be fined one guinea from his rewards, and kept from going out until further orders.

-that James Warwick who was intoxicated on Monday evening be fined 10s/6d. and not allowed to go out without the leave of the Committee.

-that Walter Willis, who was seen smoking on Sunday afternoon and in the evening guilty of very unruly behaviour and endeavouring to get out by deceiving the watchman, and yesterday going out for the day contrary to orders, be deprived of his monitorship and the coloured clothes for one month.

-that William Lacey, who returned intoxicated the last time he visited his friends, and was seen smoking on Sunday, be confined for one week upon bread and water.

-that the boy guilty of reading improper books in the Chapel … be presented to and admonished by the Chaplain.

This display of intemperance, along with an interest in amending the rules 'respecting the forfeiture of the Boy's earnings in cases of absconding, as established in 1809', enticed vice-president George Holford into action. Having continued to attend committee meetings from time to time and occasionally discussing matters of chapel business, he now presided over a meeting which decided to 'draw up some Rules and Regulations for the better government of the pupils'. This was, however, the twilight of Holford's Philanthropic career. Although nominated to head a Special Committee appointed for the purpose, he was not deeply engaged in this task. Nor does he appear to have investigated what was at the root of the misbehaviour which prompted the society to place *chevaux de frise* upon the walls and give a gratuity to:

William Bates, the Society's Beadle as a mark of the Committee's approbation of his conduct in reference to the late attack made upon him by the Boys.

If the society's 'existing force' was now deemed 'insufficient to keep order' at St. George's Fields, the appointment of an additional beadle did not provide an adequate solution. Next year, the 'breakage' of a chimney pot attracted the watchman and beadles 'to the spot' where they found themselves 'too late' to prevent some boys escaping over the newly spiked walls 'with great danger to themselves'. More disturbingly, when Superintendent Collier attempted to place a returning absconder, William Smith, in confinement 'according to rule', he found his mission frustrated when:

> [William] commenced a most furious resistance. Mad with liquor–the noise he made and the horrible language he uttered, are altogether in-describable. Various efforts were made to seize him which were defeated by his great strength and activity. At this time a large portion of the older boys left their shops and united in exciting Smith to further opposition. The monitors were called down and appeared well disposed, but shrunk from the menaced violence of the other lads. The Superintendent endeavoured to mark some names, but could not succeed to any extent from their continued motion. He also tried to expostulate with them, but to no purpose.

While this incident rekindles memories of Philanthropic boys 'in riot' at the end of the 18th-century, a new supplementary force could now be summoned to disturbances. Discerning that the society's private policing system was ineffective and:

> Conceiving it necessary to use strong measures, the Superintendent sent for a Police Officer, who, finding upon his arrival, that he was likely to be overpowered, went back for others and returned with a force of seven men, when the boys, after a slight contest, were subdued with the assistance of the monitors, and Smith apprehended.

If, as seems probable, this account provides an illustration of the 'Peelers' in action, we may wonder at quite how many officers of this new professional corps of police were required to restore order within the Philanthropic walls.[23]

---

23. This police body had been created by Peel's Act for Improving the Police in and near the Metropolis (1829).

We might also be amazed to find another well-known figure from the annals of criminal justice appearing on the scene. This was John Henry Capper, superintendent of the convict hulks. Soon after the turbulence was quelled:

> the Chaplain and Mr Capper (Visitor) arrived. The latter gentleman took much time and pains in investigating the circumstances, and the former in reasoning with the boys–
>
> By Mr Capper's orders, Smith was taken to the Police Station, until the evening, and Dinard, Childs and Abell, as most prominent in the outrage, were placed in the cells. Jones, a boy lately from the Reform, having been found prepared with a quantity of stones, was by consent of the Chaplain and Visitor returned to the Reform for the present.
>
> The cells being nearly all previously occupied, Mr Capper was under the necessity of liberating Wright and Newton a few hours before their time to make room for others. In the evening, Mr Capper revisited, and remained nearly two hours–Smith was brought in after nine o'clock, and placed in one of the cells under Mr Capper's direction.

As clerk for criminal business at the Home Department, Capper had been in communication with the society at least as early as 1813 when it resolved 'that Ann Bowman Toft be delivered to her mother on the production of a certificate from Mr Capper of the Secretary of State's office that she is permitted to take this girl with her other children to her husband, now at Botany Bay'. Listed amongst the subscribers in the Philanthropic *Account* of 1814, Capper was elected to the committee in March 1830 and lived nearby in Sidmouth Cottage, Lambeth Terrace.[24] This was a convenient residence from which to sally-forth and meet with other Philanthropic gentlemen who would ponder on how the scale of punishments and rewards, 'so defective and injurious, in several points', could be altered to better effect.

Capper and Holford are fleetingly entwined in the Philanthropic tapestry. Both visited the Institution on the day after the 'riot' and attended the meeting which decided to punish William Smith with a dose of solitary confinement. While there is no mention of these gentlemen holding conflicting opinions on William's just deserts, we might suspect they may not

---

24. From 1815, Capper combined the superintendence of the hulk establishment with his work as clerk at the Home Department.

have worked together in entirely easy harmony on the matter of improving the Philanthropic system of discipline. Capper would, no doubt, have been very much aware of how Holford, in his *Observations Concerning the Hulks* (1826), had claimed that the hulk establishment's continuing 'evils' were the result of a 'defective system of management' which required 'the interference of Parliament' for its correction.[25] Carefully adding that he did not intend 'to charge misconduct on any of those who have the care or custody of the convicts in the Hulks' and was not inclined 'to pursue a course which would probably lead to controversy in writing between me and Mr Capper', Holford conceded, nonetheless, that the 'appropriation of a separate vessel for the confinement of convict boys' had been a 'material improvement'. He was also convinced that:

> if these youths are sent out of prison at the expiration of their confinement without further care or thought concerning them on the part of the public, they must in general, for want of better friends and connections, and from the ignorance of the world, fall again into the arms of their former acquaintance, and be drawn back into their old pursuits. I am much inclined to think, that an enquiry into this subject would shew the expediency of some arrangement respecting criminal boys, founded upon the principle of sending such as are friendless here, out of the country.[26]

Capper was likewise interested in the matter of after-care provision. When called before the Select Committee on Police in 1828, he candidly admitted that on release from the hulks 'eight out of ten that have been liberated, have returned to their old courses; and those very boys are mostly boys who have had parents to receive them, which is a thing I have always studied, in recommending them for pardon'. He further confided that, with the difficulty of providing employment for boys on their discharge in mind, he had been induced to:

---

25. The hulk establishment was a long-standing subject of Holford's interest. When chairman of the Penitentiary Committee, he had been asked (probably by his friend, Home Secretary Ryder) to investigate the state of the hulks and had worked with the Philanthropic William Morton Pitt on the matter. In 1812, they presented a paper on suggested improvements to the new Home Secretary, Lord Sidmouth, but their advice was ignored.
26. Holford retired as an MP in 1826 after having been a member of the Poor Law Committee as well as the Committee on London Prisons. His farewell appearance in the Philanthropic ledgers is noted on 22nd April 1831. Holford died in 1839.

recommend to the Secretary of State that after a certain period of their sentence, when they grow into a state of manhood, they should be actually transported to New South Wales where there is occupation and there they may begin the world anew.[27]

These sentiments on the benefits of exile would be echoed by Philanthropic Steward Russell when appearing before a House of Lords investigation into the state and management of gaols and houses of correction in 1835. Conducted under the chairmanship of the Duke of Richmond, this enquiry was set-up in the context of an escalating number of committals for serious offences which, by feeding into a rapidly rising prison population, did little to foster confidence in existing penal policy. With an even greater prison numbers crisis looming on the horizon,[28] many of the Richmond Committee's recommendations would swiftly be taken-up by government and embodied in the Act for Effecting Greater Uniformity in Practice in the Government of Several Prisons in England and Wales and for appointing Inspectors of Prisons in Great Britain (1835). And, as for Steward Russell's contribution to the rigorous enquiry underpinning this legislative feat? When asked whether it would 'be advisable instead of committing juvenile offenders for trifling offences, that they should be sent to reformatory asylums', he had replied:

> Undoubtedly, if after a few years they were brought up and sent to the colonies it would be a wonderful benefit both to the Public and to the Boys themselves because if that were done they would never relapse into their former habits.[29]

Sending boys to sea for such purposes had formed an important part of the early Philanthropic repertoire. It had become rather challenging to put into practice. As Superintendent Collier explained to the Select Committee of 1828, the society had 'occasionally during the war sent boys to sea, but that is now very difficult'.[30]

---

27. SC on the Police, PP (1828), Vol. VI., Minutes of Evidence, p.106.
28. McGowan (1995:90) notes that in 1820 there were 13,700 committals for serious offences and by 1840 the number had increased to 27,000. Over the corresponding period, the prison population doubled.
29. SC on Gaols, PP (1835), Vol. XII., Minutes of Evidence, pp.523-4.
30. SC on the Police, PP (1828), Vol. VI., Minutes of Evidence, pp.163-4.

A fresh disposal route now appeared on the scene. Just as the society was deliberating over how to provide for Thomas Brown outside the Institution in 1833, an offer from the Society for the Suppression of Juvenile Vagrancy was received. With it appearing 'that the said Society will send this, or any other boy of suitable age, to the Cape of Good Hope and apprentice him there, upon payment of ten pounds, the consent of the boy and his friends being first obtained', Thomas was dispatched into its care. Subsequently renamed the Children's Friend Society, this voluntary enterprise had been established by Captain Brenton in 1830 and trained destitute and delinquent children for employment in the colonies.[31] Possessing a novelty value which the Philanthropic now lacked, it attracted a flush of subscribers and was invited to trumpet its merits before the Richmond Committee. Likewise proclaimed in that forum were the reformatory achievements of the Refuge for the Destitute and those of the Warwickshire Asylum which had been founded by Magistrates at Stretton-on-Dunsmore in 1818.

Encouraged by these tales of success, yet dismayed by evidence on the alarming plight of 'the hordes of boys congregated on the Hulks', the Richmond Committee roundly endorsed the virtues of a 'system of Reformatory Schools established by private individuals for the reception of juvenile offenders'. It also recommended 'that the practice of confining them on the Hulks should be altogether abandoned with the least possible delay'. Although this would not be achieved until 1843, an *Act for establishing a Prison for Young Offenders* passed in August 1838. This Act was a fruit of the Richmond Committee's suggestion that 'some unoccupied barracks or forts connected with the neighbourhood of places of embarkation' might be found for:

> [the] accomplishment of an object so important as the due Custody, the effective Punishment, and the timely Reformation of that large Class of Juvenile Offenders whom the Ingenuity of more mature and experienced Delinquents renders the instruments of so much increasing criminality.[32]

---

31. In Brenton's *Account* (1837), he claimed for his society a 'tendency to prevent crime and poverty and eventually dispense with capital punishment'.
32. SC on Gaols, PP (1835), Vol. XII., Report.

The story of the development and demise of the State's resulting Parkhurst experiment is well documented. What has not been so remarked upon is the importance of Clause XI of the Parkhurst Prison Act. As this would provide a crucial strand of legislative tracery surrounding future Philanthropic developments, we can note that it declared:

> And whereas Her Majesty has lately exercised Her Royal Prerogative of Mercy in granting Pardons to young Offenders who have been sentenced to Transportation or Imprisonment, upon the Condition of placing himself or herself under the Care of some charitable Institution for the Reception and Reformation of young Offenders named in such Pardon, and conforming to and abiding by the Orders and Rules thereof ... it is expedient that some Provision should be made for carrying the same more fully into effect.

Intriguingly, Home Secretary Lord John Russell appears to have explored the likelihood of implementing this clause in Philanthropic partnership just before the Act was passed. At least, this seems to be at the nub of the communication sent from Whitehall to the Philanthropic Society, dated the 16th of June 1838:

> I am directed by Lord John Russell to request you to inform his Lordship, whether in case he should think it advisable to recommend in certain cases Juvenile Offenders for admission into the Establishment of the Philanthropic Society they can be received. If you can allow them to be received I am to request information on the following points:
>
> –as to the number of children, boys and girls, that can be received into the Establishment
> –as to the probable cost of each child per annum
> –as to the employment provided for the children during their continuance in the Establishment
> –as to the manner in which the children may be disposed of by the Committee on their discharge
>
> I am
> Gentlemen
> Your Obedt. Servant
> S. M. Phillipps

Peculiarly, the Philanthropic rafters did not resound with jubilation. Although this letter expresses the Home Department's interest in calculating the amount of Treasury grant required to reform juvenile offenders though voluntary agency, that potential source of revenue was not tapped. The society did not follow precedent and organize a deputation to pursue its financial interests. Instead, the Home Secretary was speedily informed that, as criminal girls were not admitted and as the major portion of the accommodation was reserved for Manufactory boys, only the small Reform Department would be 'qualified' for the contemplated objectives. What was more, while the society was 'most anxious to attend to the recommendation of the Government, Judges, and Magistrates as heretofore, in the admission of criminal boys' and:

> However desirous the Committee might be of rendering their Institution available to the fulfilment of any wishes of the Government, they feel it necessary to point out that their buildings are not capable of being increased to such an extent as to render the admission of more than a very small additional number of children possible.

This response seems rather timid. Still, memories of past government rebuffs may well have lessened the Philanthropic drive to bid for Treasury funds on this occasion. Nevertheless, it is surprising to find the society not leaping at the opportunity to advance even an estimate of the cost of maintaining juvenile offenders. This seems even more so in light of the views recently expressed by Steward Russell. His final observation to the Richmond Committee had been that:

> If the government would grant the Society a moderate sum per Annum for each of the criminal Boys that should be maintained and instructed in the Reform Establishment of the Institution, and if after their Two Years Probation the Government would then afford the Society pecuniary means for sending them to the Northern Colonies, to be there apprenticed to agriculturalists, they would very much assist the declining Funds of the Institution, and greatly increase its Benefits to the Public, by enabling the Society to extend its Protection to a far greater Number.[33]

Whilst we must await to see how this proved a prescient vision of things to come, it seems apt to note here that Steward Russell's Philanthropic service

---

33. SC on Gaols, PP (1835), Vol. XII., Minutes of Evidence, p.524.

of around 50 years was drawing to a close. His death was announced at the beginning of 1837 and was followed by that of Richard Collier, Superintendent for nearly 30 years. The vacancy caused by Russell's demise was filled by James Dingle. Previously appointed resident schoolmaster (having satisfied the society's preference for 'a man about 30 years of age ... who must be well acquainted with accounts'), Mr. Dingle found the society's finances so alarmingly in ebb that he felt bound to place on the committee table:

> a statement of debt owing by the Society in the respective quarters of March, June and September amounting to £2,570.10s.10¾d besides the £1,000 borrowed of Messrs. Bosanquet and Co. in September ... and with no apparent means of paying even the Christmas salaries, the balance in the bankers hands being this day only £217.14s.0d.

Not all was well in the Philanthropic household. With resource flows steadfastly refusing to turn in the society's favour by the end of the 1830s, another Special Committee was appointed to deliberate on what could be done to diminish expenses and increase the Philanthropic funds. The resulting report marks something of a turning-point in affairs for its conclusions began to shake the society out of the doldrums. It also displays how the Philanthropic evidence-gathering tradition was followed by this generation of gentlemen. As they related:

> Your Committee have carefully enquired into the present affairs and arrangements of the Institution; and have also perused the various reports of former committees. They have visited and enquired into the constitution and success of other establishments corresponding in some degree with the objects of the Philanthropic Society.

These Philanthropic investigators had, indeed, ranged widely under the leadership of Samuel Richard Bosanquet. Following his brother, committee member James Whatman Bosanquet, into the Philanthropic fold in 1838, Samuel Richard was one of the revising barristers appointed on the passing of the Reform Act in 1832. A son of the Philanthropic Society's treasurer—and thus having Charles Bosanquet as his uncle—Samuel Richard also was the nephew of John Bernard Bosanquet who had been one of the commissioners appointed to enquire into the practice of the Common Law Courts in 1828.

Afterwards made a judge of the Court of Common Pleas and then knighted, John Bernard had consented to be a Philanthropic vice-president in 1836.[34]

By March 1840, however, this Special Committee had examined all previous Philanthropic Committee reports and the trade accounts for 1832, 1835 and 1838. It had also taken evidence from:

> Mr Dingle, the Steward, on the class of work and class of customers
>
> Mr Kettle, the new Superintendent, on the education, training and discipline of the boys
>
> Mr Barnes, the Beadle, on the state of order and discipline in the Institution
>
> W.J. Kent, the Warehouseman, on the state of the order book
>
> The Chaplain, on which boys were given religious instruction
>
> persons who had been brought up in the Philanthropic Society'[35] as to the effectiveness of Philanthropic training in providing a means to earn a honest living
>
> Mr Searle, Superintendent of the Refuge for the Destitute regarding how long the Refuge kept its inmates, what work they were set to and how much was paid to apprentice them out of that Institution
>
> Mr Robinson, Vestry Clerk, respecting the children apprenticed out of St Giles's Workhouse, and
>
> the City of London Union and the Parish of Newington regarding their apprenticeship schemes

The Special Committee also explained why investigations had extended beyond the original financial remit. Although a 'necessary enquiry into the finances of the society which the decreasing state of the funds rendered

---

34. In a reworking of ideas that circulated when Samuel (senior) had joined the Philanthropic founders at the end of the 18th-century, the Charity Organisation Society – with a Charles and Bernard Bosanquet as leading lights – would seek to banish the ill-consequences of 'indiscriminate charity' later in the 19th-century.
35. Such as G. W. 'now an old man' who had left the society in 1811.

urgent' was undertaken 'in the first instance', an examination of the trade accounts had uncovered that:

> taking into account the expences of clothing and maintenance of the apprentices, and omitting all charges which are not strictly personal, the trades taken altogether yield no profits, but occasion a loss to the Institution.
>
> Having arrived at this result, it became necessary to ascertain what was the comparative benefit to the inmates themselves from their being apprenticed and taught their trades within the Institution.

Thus inspired to obtain evidence from the aforementioned sources, the members of this Special Committee were 'brought to the irresistible conclusion that the apprentices are not benefited by being bound to masters within the walls, and being kept in the Institution till their apprenticeship is completed'. It was furthermore observed that:

> The restraint also of an Establishment surrounded with walls, upon young men till the age of 21, gives it the character of a prison, and renders it irksome, and almost insupportable to them. This produces discontent among the apprentices, and this discontent extends itself to the younger boys; among whom from the age of 15 to 17 the chief symptoms of insubordination are manifest ... there is also some impropriety in many young men of 20 and 21, undressing themselves in the presence of one another, and sleeping together in the same apartment.

If this condemnation of the existing state of affairs was confounding, the suggested remedy was surprising. Going on to consider the economic advantages a quicker turn-over of the inmates would bring, members proposed:

> That in future, no boys be apprenticed within the walls of the Institution, but, that they be apprenticed to respectable masters in various trades and callings out of the Institution, at between the age of 14 and 16; according to their characters, and their advance in education. This will increase the number of trades and occupations to which the young men may apply themselves to an indefinite extent; which the Committee consider to be a great advantage. As they will remain in the Institution only four years on an average, instead of 10 years, a much larger number will receive the benefit of it.[36]

---

36. In this recommendation, they may have been mindful of the shift towards shorter apprenticeships which had been recognised in the Poor Law Act of 1834.

There was no great rush to amend existing practice, even though the Special Committee had 'considered all their recommendations with a view to their practicability' and had 'reason to believe that none of the detail will present any great difficulty in the execution'. Nor did the society take on-board the suggestion that, as 'your present committee have not sufficient data before them to bring them to a full conclusion upon this subject', it would be for future investigators:

> to consider whether the space of ground occupied by the Society might not be somewhat diminished, and a profitable use made of the ground economised.

This hesitancy is not altogether unusual. As with proposals for creating a separate 'probationary' Reform Department and building the Philanthropic Chapel, new ideas took time to gain hold and their realisation often rested on the drive of energetic members. The present tardiness may, nevertheless, indicate that the society was not fully persuaded by the Special Committee's analysis of the situation. There is also the likelihood that other governance issues clouded the picture. Although some movement was made towards accommodating a recommendation on 'electing' the children of criminals,[37] the chapel prospects were about to dim further. As the Reverend Dr. Rice, the society's chaplain warned, collections were 'likely to be seriously afflicted more or less by four additional churches ... in the neighbourhood, and one of which will be within two or three hundred yards of the Chapel itself'.[38]

Disarray was also reigning within the walls. Indeed, further disorders had signalled such an increased 'sense of rebellion which has appeared in the Institution' that, once the inmate leaders were punished, the society was driven to:

> censure deeply all the officers, masters, journeymen, porters and other servants of the Institution who were present, or had any intelligence of it, for not immediately assist-

---

37. Five such children were elected in December 1841, at the Quarterly Court held at the London Coffee House, Ludgate Hill.
38. The Rev. Dr. Rice was acting 'gratuitously' as the society's chaplain. He would be appointed headmaster of Christ's Hospital School by 1850.

ing to quell the disturbance and for not on this, and all other occasions supporting the officers of the Establishment.

Disconcertingly, continuing rifts in the higher staff regions did not mend matters. By May 1840, the Philanthropic gentlemen had been impelled to conclude that:

> much of the present difficulty in the present management of the Institution, arises from the want of cordial cooperation in the two chief officers which extends its influence over subordinate attendants, and to the boys who are well acquainted to the circumstance.

Not all was bad news. The Philanthropic enterprise now received the personal endorsement of one of the most influential figures in the field of criminal justice reform. This personage was no less than the Duke of Richmond who consented to become Philanthropic president at the beginning of 1841.

By then, the society had made a momentous decision. Even though the appointment of a chaplain-superintendent had previously been resisted for, in having to intervene in 'acts of riot and insubordination' he would be called upon to 'perform duties which a clergyman would justly deem offensive and degrading',[39] the Philanthropists now decided it was imperative to place their Institution in the hands of:

> one zealous, clever, active, and in every other respect qualified officer ... [and] ... That a resident Chaplain, anxious for the well doing of the Institution, and having the Superintendence of the Institution would be the most essential benefit in a variety of ways and would much lessen the labours of the Committee.

With this in view, yet another Special Committee was asked to search for a suitable candidate. The quest was rewarded. By March 1841, having 'carefully informed themselves' on the matter, the gentlemen reported to the General Committee that they were:

---

39. Such an appointment had been proposed by a Special Committee in 1827.

assured of the full competency of the Reverend Sydney Turner, to discharge with great and signal advantage to the Institution the duties which they have proposed … [and] … recommend him to your favourable notice.

Their confidence in the Reverend Sydney Turner's abilities was not misplaced. As we shall see, Turner would assiduously attend to his prescribed duties and 'constantly endeavour, in every way in which he may be able to promote the prosperity of the Institution'.

The society's governance was also in the hands of Philanthropists who were determined that their enterprise would not remain moribund. They may not have leapt at the opportunity for engaging in partnership with government to provide for the reformation of juvenile offenders. Nor did they have a clearly defined survival strategy in mind. They were, however, prepared to explore exciting new avenues for turning-around Philanthropic fortunes. Somewhat unexpectedly, the society's revival would entail travelling from St. George's Fields and into fresh pastures at a Reformatory Farm School, in Redhill.

CHAPTER 6

ENLIGHTENMENT

The journey to the Reformatory Farm School was far from uneventful. Nor were the changes wrought in the society's mode of operation by the end of the 1840s a straightforward result of the Reverend Sydney Turner's vision and energy. Even though he assumed a great deal of control on his appointment, a significant number of Philanthropic gentlemen would continue to take a very active interest in governing the society's affairs. They also discovered there would be many twists and turns along the road to Redhill.

Change or Decay?
As Turner did, nonetheless, play a key-role in revitalising and reshaping the Philanthropic enterprise, it seems apt to begin the journey by hearing him deliver his first *Report on the Education, Discipline and Employment of the Children under the Society's Care* at the end of 1841. This new chaplain-superintendent certainly made an impressive entrance onto the Philanthropic stage. Considering he was only twenty-six years old and addressing an audience that included one of the most influential penal reformers in the land — the Society's president, the Duke of Richmond — it is remarkable to find him not so overwhelmed as to inform the gathering that it was 'necessary' to occupy their attention 'at a greater length' than he 'would have wished to do'.[1]

Turner was not cast in the mould of recent superintendents. Rather, his mission statement is so strikingly confident in tone and steeped in the empirical tradition of observation and analysis that it is as though an Enlightenment gentleman was striding on-scene once more, imbued with a belief

---

1. At this point in his career, Sydney had received an MA from Cambridge (1836), was ordained (1838) by the Bishop of Winchester (a Philanthropic vice-president) and had 'held for some time the curacy of Christ's Church Southwark' (DNB). His father, Sharon Turner, was a historian, FSA., associate of the Royal Society of Literature, a solicitor and legal advisor to the Tory review. He had been a close friend of Isaac D'Israeli and acted as Benjamin's godfather when that future statesman was baptised in 1817.

in his ability to solve Philanthropic problems by a clear input of reason. He was, undeniably, a self-conscious moderniser who declared:

> On entering on the duties of Resident Chaplain I had laid it down as a fixed rule of my future agency to make in everything the utmost use of the means and materials already in existence—and while improving the plan and machinery of the Institution wherever according to modern principles of education and controul these might be defective to introduce no alteration suddenly or unless a clear and very evident advantage were likely to result from the change. I have therefore made few innovations in any part of the former system of the Institution—proposing to myself to wait and watch for opportunities to remodel silently and gradually those portions of its arrangements that still seem to me to require reform.

Doubtless reassured to find their new employee professing commitment to incremental—rather than revolutionary—change, the assembled gentlemen must also have been gratified to hear that he had already remodelled the society's educational provision. Although assessing that the Manufactory department's instruction in cyphering and writing required no improvement—being 'equally good for its method and practical efficiency'—Turner had been askance to discover that:

> The points on which interference were most clearly called for were, the Style and Tone of reading—the deficiency of general information—and the sameness of Religious Instruction—which last by long use of the same few books had become an exercise of the memory—much more than of the mind—a result which experience has shewn will almost inevitably follow under any system unless there be a constant variation of the Books to be studied and a continual novelty and unexpected change in the questions asked.

To remedy these deficiencies, SPCK publications entitled *Faith and Duty, The Miracles, Lessons on the Universe, Stories from History* and *The Second Class Reading Book* had been obtained. This literature was supplemented with books from the Library of Entertaining Knowledge, a subsidiary of the SDUK which had been set-up by Lord Brougham and Dr. Birkbeck amongst others. Believing that 'communicating a better knowledge of their own language' was a 'desideratum in the general education' of the children, Turner had also placed the elements and principles of English grammar on the curriculum and given prominence to 'the writing from Dictation which exercises the pupils in the correct spelling and arrangement of ... words'.

The Reform Department's educational arrangements had not required remedial measures. Its pupils displayed a:

> Remarkable quickness in progress in the elements of learning and for general good conduct ... much of it due to the diligence and patience of the Reform Master, [and] something of it may be also perhaps owing to the much smaller number and age of the Boys which the Reform contains.

Regrettably, little of merit had been detected within the Female School. Scarcely changed from when the Reverend Dr. Grindlay recorded its achievements earlier in the century, the cleverest girls were still employed as monitors and the 'essential feature' of their education remained a training in 'household and laundry employments'. This curriculum did not satisfy Turner. Its utility was limited:

> [for] it must not be overlooked that a knowledge of accounts, the writing a legible hand—and some acquaintance with the matters of most common use and interest in the world are essential to make them useful servants and especially to make them useful wives and managers of families—to enable them to do justice to those they be connected with and to have resources for making their homes comfortable and attractive.

While equipping the girls for these future duties soon placed them in the hands of a new matron with experience as an 'assistant school teacher', Turner does not mention whether they enjoyed the 'extended reading' advocated for the boys. That provision, Turner stressed, was no mere 'indulgence' which might arouse criticism from being viewed as a means of giving the Institution's boys 'actual knowledge'. Rather, it was:

> a means of exciting intelligence and giving occupation ... [for] ... I believe that usually in proportion as an interest is aroused in Mental and Intellectual things, the craving for sensual excitement is diminished and that a taste for reading and a desire for acquiring information is seldom found combined with very low and degrading habits.

This civilising philosophy had also brought Turner, 'as an experiment', to encourage a taste of music and set books of a 'superior class' aside for the use of older boys who had ceased to attend school.[2] These initiatives were firmly entwined with his strategy for correcting defects in discipline. Although feeling it 'hardly proper and certainly unpleasing' to allude to previous errors in that realm of governance, he had, nonetheless, concluded that:

> There appears to have been a very much too low estimation of the character and qualities of these young men and boys themselves–a mistake that produced a tone and manner or style of expression and too often a style of conduct to them which at once excited a spirit of distrust and dislike upon their part destroying all confidence or regard towards those who superintend them–& blunting too many of the better and kinder feelings that might else have been awakened ... this error appears to have been accompanied by another perhaps even more unfortunate–namely a habit of continual resort to measures of violence and personal chastisement.

That approach certainly had been counter-productive, for:

> Punishment lightly and hastily inflicted on uncertain and changeful rules has always the effect of making its power and moral influences less felt–the just and the unjust inflictions are mingled together–and the defender becomes in his own & his companions' estimation more or less a martyr ... to make the penalties effectual, they must be inflicted with discrimination as to the disposition and nature of the Criminal and must be inflicted with every possible appearance of firm and serious consideration and there must be kindness and personal attention given when the offence has been punished to make the distinction evident between the offender and his fault–on any other system the punishment especially if an act of personal violence must have the effect of multiplying the offences it would correct.

In this analysis we may recognise a tracery of the sentiments on 'just pain' which coloured reformative penitentiary strategies at the end of the 18th-century. It is also worth recalling that moulding young minds through the persuasion of kindly moral influences had been a thorny problem for Superintendent Durand. But, undaunted by past failures, Turner resolved:

---

2. The books included some from his own library and were placed in a closet in the dining-room with the 'custody' of them given 'to the chief elder'. The children's singing performance in the chapel was improved by 'introducing a knowledge of Mr Hullah's plan' and two boys learnt to play the flute after a committee member gave them the 'necessary elementary instruction'.

[to] study the individual Character of the Boys themselves. To give a fair and full hearing to every statement–whether in complaint against others or justification of themselves. To have as few laws and restrictions as possible and these simple and well known. To make the sentence and the reasons for it as public as possible and to excite as far as can be excited a spirit of self respect and in a certain degree pride and sense of dignity in all.

Some success had been achieved. Admittedly, at first 'as was natural there was a tendency to mistake liberty for licence and mildness for weakness'. This had lessened as a clearer understanding of the new system of 'mild government' gained ground. Furthermore, with the schoolmaster designated 'The Lieutenant and the Sub-director of the Institution — my representative in my absence, responsible to none but myself', Turner could claim that this improvement:

already had the good effect of decreasing the cases in which he had to resort to force to vindicate his authority for himself. He finds the Cane much less frequently required and there are often two or three days in the week in which he is able to let it remain shut up from view or is required only to bring it out and shew it without seriously using it.

Remodelling of the authority structure also involved appointing a 'person who had received a free discharge from the army' as 'second resident subordinate'. As Turner enthused, with this appointment 'and at the wish of the boys themselves', drill exercise had been introduced 'with a view to accustoming the boys to habits of regularity and subordination as well as to improve their general carriage and give them an additional object of attention and interest'. In addition, 'a more cheerful spirit' had been fostered through providing 'Hoops, Posts and Bars for swings and gymnastic exercises'. Turner also had ensured the 'grass plots which it was once punishable to be found upon' were 'left free to the use and enjoyment of all'. What was more, he intended to take measures, as spring advanced:

[to] encourage the taste and inclination for the Cultivation of Gardens, which have been always experienced to be useful instruments of moral formation.

The audience to Turner's next annual report may, nevertheless, have not been too surprised to hear him confessing a resort to corporal punishment, in four instances. These were for familiar species of fault—insubordination, correspondence with the girl's school and continued idleness.

The Philanthropic gentlemen may have been rather more astonished to find him requesting 'the enlargement and rebuilding of the Reform'. But experience—along with a close perusal of past Philanthropic ledgers—had 'confirmed and clarified' that the discipline in that branch of the enterprise was such as 'hardly deserves the name'. After all, the 'facts' showed:

> That the acts of disturbance, theft, misconduct &c. which have taken place in the Manufactory have in the great majority of cases–been suggested and committed by boys who have originally entered the Society as Reform boys.
> That in almost all the instances on which the boys expulsion, absconding or after criminality–the Society's effects have been partially or wholly disappointed–such individual will be found to be of this same class of Reform Boys i.e. Juvenile Offenders.
> That among the boys of this Reform class itself a further distinction may be drawn–the cases above referred to as those in which the Society's endeavours have been more or less frustrated–being almost uniformly those in which the boy was certified or ascertained to be not only guilty of one or two misdemeanours but of confirmed habits of depravity.[3]

Such boys had plagued Superintendent Durand. They had also been in vice-president Holford's sights when he recommended the creation of a separate Reform Department at the turn of the century. Turner now suggested a further refinement of the Philanthropic's 'probationary' arrangements. This was to place the more hardened rascals in a 'first division'. Boys 'of a better sort and guilty of lighter offences' could then be transferred into a 'second division' in which they would be allowed more liberty. Putting this new classifying system into practice was feasible, he argued. After all, the society had sufficient ground to build on at St. George's Fields and—if constructed to receive 60 boys—a new Reform would not amount to much more than £2,500. Moreover, the 'advertizing, discussing and writing about such a plan

---

3. As the society had lost track of its membership, a 'correct account' was called for and presented to the committee in March 1841. This review of Philanthropic affairs also found a sub-committee set on the task of tracing all previous *Journals* and *Minutes* and providing an *Abstract* of the latter.

of extension would be of most important service in keeping the Society's claims and operations before the public'. Indeed, if the Institution was thus enlarged in usefulness it would:

> be a weighty argument for the Government granting the Society an annual vote as is now done with reference to the Refuge for the Destitute.

His plea did not fall on entirely stony ground. Neither did it immediately flourish in the still unsettled Philanthropic climate. Although considered 'highly important and advantageous', as the society was continuing to fret over how to execute its existing plan within the bounds of reduced resources, the proposals were referred to a sub-committee for consideration. At this—and hopeful of not being considered 'troublesome or to be exceeding the proper limits' of his position—Turner requested one of the society's auditors to 'lend his powerful assistance' to the cause. As he declared:

> I am too great an admirer of established things to like change. But when the choice lies between change and decay I would rather have and carry out the change while there are yet resources to give it force and efficacy sufficient to avert the evil.

A startling change materialised. Astoundingly, while this sub-committee refrained from making any recommendation 'relative to the extension or alteration of the Reform premises', these gentlemen now discovered:

> several circumstances which combine to shew, that the Female School may be both judiciously and safely discontinued ... without serious diminution of the Society's resources or of the Public interest in its operations.

This seems a mystifying recommendation. The Philanthropic enquiry of 1840 had found that branch of the Institution 'most admirably conducted' and 'highly satisfactory in its results'. The reconfigured complement of investigating gentlemen concurred with that assessment. Nonetheless, having been 'compelled' to recognise the society's plan of operation was 'too extended, and the branches of its Establishment too numerous and costly for its resources', they had uncovered good economic grounds for banishing the girls. Not only had the average admissions dwindled from nine in 1839 to four in 1842, but also, no candidates were on the waiting list. Furthermore, as only 25 girls were expected to remain by the end of the year, the 'advantages' derived from this department would soon be 'wholly disproportionate to its expenses' of not 'less on the average than £850 per annum'.

Yet, it scarcely seems credible that so few girls had been found in need of Philanthropic protection. The country was shifting from recession into depression and even many honest and industrious citizens were sliding into poverty, despair and crime. These were very hard times. As Engels would discover during his investigations into *The Condition of the Working-Class in England in 1844*:

> On Monday, Jan. 15th, 1844, two boys were brought before the police magistrate because, being in a starved condition, they had stolen and immediately devoured a half-cooked calf's foot from a shop. The magistrate felt called upon to investigate the case further, and received the following details from the policeman: The mother of the two boys was the widow of an ex-soldier, afterwards policeman, and had had a very hard time since the death of her husband, to provide for her nine children. She lived at No. 2 Pool's Place, Quaker Court, Spitalfields, in the utmost poverty. When the policeman came to her, he found her with six of her children literally huddled together in a little back room, with no furniture but two old rush-bottomed chairs with the seats gone, a small table with two legs broken, a broken cup, and a small dish. On the hearth was scarcely a spark of fire and in one corner lay as many old rags as would fill a woman's apron, which served the whole family as a bed. For bed clothing they had only their scanty day clothing. The poor woman told him that she had been forced to sell her bedstead the year before to buy food. Her bedding she had pawned with the victualler for food. The magistrate ordered the woman a considerable provision from the poor-box.[4]

Amazingly, one of these boys was delivered into the Philanthropic Reform. Despite some discrepancies in details, an application was made on 2nd February 1844 for the admission of:

> John Hoscroft, born Jany. 3rd 1832–[Police Court Worship Street, charged with the offence of] Stealing a Cow-heel in company with his brother. There was no doubt of the crime being committed from Want & Hunger–[parents names and description] John Hoscroft of 'L' Divn. of Police–deceased & Mary, Charwoman. The family were

---

4. Engels (1892:30).

found by the Police Const^bl. in a most miserable state of Poverty–residing at 2 Coles Place, Quaker St., Spitalfields.[5]

So, why in these times of hardship—when contemporaries like Disraeli would fret over the prospect of a divided nation if not revolution—should the society's sub-committee consider abandoning its girls? True, admissions had been restricted to those of criminal parentage since 1817. But, as this potentially dangerous class of future mothers hardly had fairer prospects than the Hoscroft boys, it is odd to find the Philanthropic gentlemen contending that 'the Female School is no longer wanted or appreciated by the friends of the Objects for whose benefit it is intended'. Indeed, some suspicions as to the veracity of their facts on the matter possibly led the Duke of Richmond to recommend that this branch the Institution:

> should be continued for a time in its present state to enable the concern and interest of the public in its maintenance be fully proved.

Astonishingly, expectations of a revival of interest were found to be 'without foundation'. Although the Female School had been built to accommodate at least 60 girls, only 18 remained by January 1845, several were ready to leave and only a few new applications had been received. Accordingly, as these were 'facts which shew strongly, how small a demand exists for the aid of the Society, on behalf of this class of Object', it was decided to disperse the girls. By June they had all gone.

As to the causes of this decline in demand? The Society now was prepared to be satisfied that:

> owing to various legislative and social changes, such as the extensive abolition of capital punishment, the adoption of reformatory instead of penal discipline in the treatment of offenders, and the alteration of the Poor Laws, the particular kinds of destitution and ignorance, which it was the special object of the Society to relieve

---

5. The conditions in which these boys were found closely reflect those which Philanthropic founders, like Robert Young and Dr. Lettsom, encountered in the 'Augean Stables' of London at the end of the 18th-century.

have diminished in amount, or from being otherwise provided for, now stand less in need of the charitable aid of such an Institution.⁶

Had there been a conspiracy afoot, however? There is no evidence to suggest that figures had been manipulated or that applications for admission were deflected. Nevertheless, as it seems curiously convenient for the society now to have spare capacity for 60 children—just right for the numbers Turner envisaged in an expanded Reform division—we need to consider other influences that had appeared over the horizon. These, importantly, were ripening the Philanthropic temper for engaging in a radical re-interpretation of its charter of incorporation. As Philanthropic members were reminded, the Act of 1806 allowed room for flexibility, as:

> the original intention of the founders was expressed to be the prevention of crime generally, without specifically defining the means to be adopted, or the class or age of the children to be benefited.

Government interest: Ups and Downs

To pick up these threads in the Philanthropic tapestry we must return to a meeting held in November 1844. On that occasion, committee member Mr. Gaussen surprised the society by announcing:

> [he] had received a communication from Mr. Forster, Treasurer for the Refuge for the Destitute, referring to a proposal for an Union of that Society with the Philanthropic and wishing for a conference on that subject.

This was not the first time an alliance of voluntary effort had been mooted. We may recall that, in 1793, 'old' Earl Grosvenor had suggested the Philanthropic and Robert Young's Society for the Reform of the Criminal Poor

---

6. Turner would retrospectively claim: 'That the changes in the laws relating to the relief of the poor, compelling the family of the transported or executed criminal to enter the Union House, instead of subsisting by aid of out-door relief, rendered the number of children of convicts (especially of the female sex) who applied for the Society's assistance very small' (*Report*, 1850).

'ought to cooperate and assist each other, as having the same object'. Yet, while that potential partnership had withered from view, this new proposal was spectacular in prospect. It was 'approved by Sir James Graham, the Secretary of State for the Home Department'.

Remarkably, although few details of the Plan of Union survive in the Philanthropic ledgers, documents uncovered in the National Archives reveal that the formation of a 'new Institution called the London Refuge for Destitute Youths' was in contemplation. This had the 'object' of affording:

> an Asylum, and the means of reformation, to young persons discharged from Prison, but who from destitution and loss of character, are unable to obtain employment.

This Plan of Union also adds to our understanding of the context of discussions surrounding the disappearance of the Philanthropic girls. To make the new arrangements 'effectual' it proposed that:

> the male Establishment of 'the Refuge for the Destitute' be abolished, and the Inmates therein transferred to the Premises of 'the Philanthropic Society', which shall become the Male Establishment of the New Institution and that the Female Branch of the 'Philanthropic Society' be in like manner abolished, and the Inmates transferred to the Premises now occupied by the Female Establishment of 'the Refuge for the Destitute'.

The plan was devised by William Crawford.[7] We last encountered that gentleman giving evidence to the 1817 Select Committee of enquiry into the State of Police in the Metropolis, along with Philanthropic Steward Russell and former Philanthropic committee member, Edward Forster, who was there to promote the Refuge's interests. Crawford was at that time secretary of the Society for Investigating the Alarming Increase of Juvenile Delinquency in the Metropolis and heavily involved in the associated SIPD. He had since acquired such an aura of expertise that, in 1833, he was asked by the government to undertake a study of the systems of reformatory discipline operating in American Penitentiaries and Refuges. The result of that par-

---

7. A copy of the plan was sent by Crawford to a later Home Secretary in 1847. The document is in a file relating to the Refuge of the Destitute held in the National Archives, HO 45/1000. This was discovered to contain some Philanthropic correspondence. .

ticular trans-Atlantic cross-fertilisation of ideas was a lengthy report which, in vigorously advocating the 'separate' (cellular) as opposed to 'silent' (associative) system of confinement, strongly influenced the climate of debate surrounding the Richmond Enquiry. The deliberations of that body shaped the rationalising provisions of the 1835 Gaols Act and, as we saw, had influence on the Parkhurst Prison Act of 1838. By the time this Plan of Union was broached, Crawford had not only been appointed one of Parkhurst's first visitors in the company of Dr. Kay-Shuttleworth, the Reverend Whitworth Russell and Lord Yarborough, but had become an Inspector of Prisons for the Home Division. In that capacity he had under his sights the new model Pentonville Prison. That State facility had been designed on the cellular system by fellow Parkhurst visitor, Joshua Jebb, and had opened in 1842.

1842 had not just cast gloom because of widespread want and unemployment. In that year (and with the help of his friend Bishop Blomfield of London) Edwin Chadwick published his *Report on the Sanitary Condition of the Labouring Population*. Confirming the extent of squalor existing in the richest country in the industrialising world, it also delivered a warning on the dire consequences flowing from ill-health. These had not evaded the notice of the Philanthropic founders who had embarked on their crime prevention quest amidst alarms about the health, welfare and security of the nation at the end of the 18th-century. Now, however, Chadwick's statistical evidence on the extent to which disease robbed many children of the moral guidance of responsible parents and left them to roam amongst Chartist mobs or take to crime, fed into fears about the 'Condition of England'. Indeed, to many anxious eyes, the spectre of the dangerous classes already seemed manifest by an explosion in the committal of juvenile offenders which peaked in 1842.[8] We cannot be sure whether Turner attempted to exploit such anxieties at the end of that year when he urged the Philanthropists to consider enlarging that 'most really interesting part of the Institution' — the Reform. He had, however, calculated that the number of criminal boys received during the last 20 years had 'been nearly double that of the sons of convicts'. This placed the society's trustees in 'obvious difficulty'. On one hand, they were trying to 'ensure and enlarge' its 'pecuniary support' by 'endeavouring to

---

8. Radzinowicz and Hood (1986:113) note that these were 50% higher than in 1836.

interest the Corporations, quarter sessions, individual noblemen and country magistrates in its maintenance'. At the same time, they were refusing 'eight or nine out of every ten applications made to them for the admission of juvenile offenders from such quarters'.

Although Steward Russell also had identified an excess demand for the admission of the 'criminal class' of boys when appearing before the Select Committee on the Police in 1817, the Philanthropic rejects of 1842 would have experienced difficulty in gaining entry to reformatory asylums privately established elsewhere.[9] An extension of such provision had been recommended in the Richmond Report of 1835 as a means of preventing minor offenders (like the Hoscroft brothers) from revolving in and out of local prisons on short sentences. It had failed to materialise. We may recall, besides, that even the Philanthropists had rebuffed Home Secretary Lord John Russell's tentative exploration of forming a State and voluntary agency reformatory partnership during 1838. In this context, it is particularly interesting to find that the proposed union was conceived in terms of an 'experiment' aimed at testing the viability of introducing a government Bill:

> [to] empower magistrates to defray from the County rates the expense of maintaining discharged juvenile prisoners in some reformatory Institution.

The union foundered. Although the Refuge managers quickly and 'unreservedly acquiesced' to the scheme, their Philanthropic counterparts were not so impetuous. A Special Meeting on the 11th of November 1844 did, indeed, support a new Philanthropic committee member in his motion to give approval 'on principle'. This came from Serjeant Adams who would later claim 'the honour of introducing into the Parkhurst [Prison] Act' the provision which 'gave the Queen power' to send convicted children to reformatory schools.[10] The meeting also acceded to a proposal from another new member and future Attorney General — Richard Baggallay junior — to obtain some

---

9. SC on the Police, PP (1817), Vol. VII., Minutes of Evidence, p.443.
10. SC on Criminal and Destitute Juveniles, PP (1852), Vol. VII., Minutes of Evidence, Q. 1854.

modification of the scheme.[11] By the end of the month, however, another Special Meeting was expressing concern that the plan:

> may possibly be unacceptable to the general body of subscribers (to whose revision and rejection all their proceedings are subject) on account of the absence in it of all details as to the power of general Courts, the age to which Objects are admitted & the persons from whom and the manner in which the first body of directors is to be elected.

To clarify what was encompassed in the plan, a Philanthropic deputation headed by the treasurer, Samuel Richard Bosanquet, was dispatched to the Home Department.[12] It was not altogether soothed by the Home Secretary. The society seldom admitted criminal boys over 12 years of age but Sir James was of the view that it was 'very important that persons of greater age than 14 or 15 should have the benefit of the Institution, and of the step which it would afford to them, as well as more Juvenile Offenders, from the Prison to society'. What was more, while he gratifyingly mentioned that the government's contribution 'would probably exceed in amount the £3,000 now granted to the Refuge for the Destitute', some strings were attached. These were linked to what seems an unusual government conception of State and voluntary agency partnership in this period. As Sir James explained:

> [the governing body] would be comprised of twenty four directors; eight to be nominated by the Treasurer of the Philanthropic Society; eight by the Secretary of State in consideration of the contribution from the public purse [and eight by the Refuge].[13]

An eruption of Philanthropic dissent put paid to the union. Such was the depth of indignation about the manner in which negotiations were being conducted that some members formally registered their objections:

---

11. Baggallay had been called to the Bar at Lincoln's Inn in 1843. Knighted in 1868 he also became a Lord Justice of Appeal.
12. Samuel Richard had led the investigation into the society's affairs and had been elected Philanthropic treasurer on the death of his father, Samuel junior, in 1843.
13. A variation on the ratio of representation is outlined by Crawford in a memorandum of November 1844, HO 45/1000.

being of opinion that the resolution on Friday the 17th Inst. [January 1845] relating to the Plan of uniting this Society with the Refuge for the Destitute and adopted by a very small majority should be submitted to the consideration of a General Court of the members, before the Secretary of State is led to take any further proceedings, in preparing a Bill for effecting such a Union of the two Societies.

Quite how the Home Secretary got wind of this state of affairs is unclear. We might, however, suspect that Mr. Gaussen played a part. He had expressed 'his own decided protest' against the idea of putting the matter before a General Court 'on the ground of it being in his opinion a breach of confidence with Sir James Graham'. Indeed, these two gentlemen held overlapping interests and moved in interlacing circles of acquaintance. Sir James had been a Philanthropic subscriber in 1814 and William Gaussen—who was related to the Bosanquet family—was a life-member of the society by that time. In 1843, Gaussen was elected to the Refuge Committee along with Crawford and Philanthropic John Henry Capper. The Refuge would then be favoured by having Sir James join former Home Secretary and now Prime Minister Peel as a vice-president, by 1846.

Unfortunately, when the Philanthropic gentlemen re-assembled on the 7th of February 1845, they found the following communication had been received from Sir James's Private Secretary in Whitehall:

> Sir James Graham having been informed that the Plan which he has submitted for the Union of the Philanthropic Society and the Refuge for the Destitute had not met with the general concurrence of the Committee of the former Institution I am directed by him to signify to you his desire to withdraw the proposition.

This withdrawal of a Home Department lifeline probably shocked the cash-strapped society. Just at that moment it had decided to dispose of the girls and discontinue its unprofitable bookbinding and printing trades. The communication did not, however, depress hopes of an accommodation being reached. The Philanthropists now offered to receive juvenile offenders on payment of £20 each per annum to cover board and lodging. They were, additionally, prepared to go further than mooted in the plan, by way of submitting the Philanthropic Institution to government inspection with the 'right' of nominating four new committee members vested in the Secretary of State. They also thanked Philanthropic vice-president Lord Radstock 'for his endeavours to bring the Society under the favourable notice of Sir James Graham'.[14]

The negotiations stalled. Even the efforts of vice-president Edward Harman were of little avail.[15] Having written a note to the Home Secretary clarifying what actually had been decided by the Philanthropic Society, he was tersely reminded that Sir James was:

> not at present prepared to recommend on the part of Government any interference with that Institution.

A worrying silence from the Home Department followed. As this was still sustained towards the end of the year, the Duke of Richmond was employed as the 'medium of communication' for a memorial of goodwill. This made no impact. Turner then made it his duty to draw the Home Secretary's attention to the subject of supporting the society's operations. Disappointingly, a letter of response was received from Under-Secretary, the Honourable Manners Sutton, which pointed out that:

> the Government already receives from the Refuge for the Destitute the accommodation it requires for juvenile convicts with a view to their being instructed in trades or manufactures by the exercise of which they may gain an honest livelihood and Sir James therefore must decline to hold out to the Philanthropic the prospect of a pecuniary grant being made on the part of the Government.

Fearing 'that the Proposition of the Philanthropic Society' contained in the memorial had been misunderstood, Turner swiftly composed a reply. This is worth reading at length for it confirms that the society was bidding for *per capita* payments rather than 'any fixed annual grant from Parliament such as the Refuge receives'. As well, in comparing the Philanthropic Institution's quality of provision with that offered by the rival Refuge, Turner firmly constructs the Philanthropic conception of a 'Juvenile Offender'. As he stressed, the 'Committee of the Philanthropic are fully aware that in consideration

---

14. Lord Radstock would also be elected a Refuge vice-president in 1845.
15. Edward Harman thus carried-on the Philanthropic vice-presidential tradition set by his father Jeremiah and grandfather John.

of a Grant of £3000 per ann.' the Refuge receives '40 or 50 Young persons whom the Government recommends to its protection':

> But in the first place These Objects are principally Females, & in the second place They are usually of a more advanced age than can properly be classed under the term Juvenile Offenders,–the Refuge receiving none under 12, & the average of its inmates being 15 or 16 years of age …
> The request of the Committee of the Philanthropic had reference, more especially, to the vast number of Boys under 14 years of age,- who are convicted annually in the Police Courts,–& at the Sessions, of the Metropolis & Large Towns.

Having boys 'who have been once or twice convicted of Crime' in focus and with 'the attention of the Public earnestly turned to the Duty & Necessity of Amending and Reclaiming as well as punishing this class of Criminals', the Philanthropic had, furthermore:

> such large means of Accommodation, Education and Employment, as are adequate to the Moral Discipline, and Industrial Instruction, of near 200 boys–with every requisite for their healthful physical development, & advantageous disposal in the World if only the expenses of the Boys' Clothing & Food could be provided for.

The Refuge, in contrast, had to struggle with so 'many drawbacks and impediments' in its 'confined situation and inconvenient accommodations' it seemed:

> impossible that that Establishment could, by any possibility, meet the increasing demand for some Public and systematic effort for the Prevention of Crime by the Reformation of the Young Offender.[16]

Indeed, the Philanthropic Society's offer to take boys on payment of expenses either defrayed by the magistracy from the local rates 'or any other public resources' should not be overlooked. There was, in Turner's view:

> little doubt that the measure would be one of economy–as well as Religious Benevolence–the Offender's Reformation being in every sense a far cheaper process than His repeated Detection, Trial and Punishment.[17]

---

16. The Male Refuge was located in an old sugar warehouse.
17. HO 45/1000 – letter dated 16/1/1846.

The Home Secretary did not budge. Perhaps we might surmise that Crawford's influence held sway on the matter. His views on the memorial's 'prayer' had been sought and were worded almost exactly as in Manners Sutton's communication.[18] If so, Crawford's stance is somewhat puzzling. This prison inspector was likely aware of the escalating rate of admissions to Parkhurst Prison which was jumping from 284 in 1844 to 540 in 1845 and on the way to 648 in 1846.[19] Not all, admittedly, were in the Philanthropic's target age-range and, after the closure of the *Euryalus* hulk in 1843, boys under 13 or 14 were accommodated in new junior wards built at Parkhurst. Nevertheless, a report on the transgressions of the youngest exiles, after leaving Parkhurst for the colonies, had borne such testimony to the failure of this prison's reformatory regime that, in early 1845, Crawford confided to Jebb it was a 'heart-breaking Document'. He continued:

> The disposal of the junior boys is a most anxious question, and we should meet immediately on your return to Town, to consider whether we should not recommend Sir James to stop at all events this part of the System. Magistrates sentence these children to imprism. under the impression that by being sent to Parkhurst they are providing for them.[20]

This sentencing preference—alongside the failure in forcing local benches of magistrates to set up their own reformatories—found Sir James attempting to stem the upward trend in admissions by insisting that Parkhurst be reserved for the more serious offenders of at least 14 years. Government sponsored boys, however, still did not come through the Philanthropic doors. Neither did boys supported out of county rates.

Importantly, a new troupe of Philanthropic recruits did appear. Associations of county magistrates now began raising money to maintain boys they referred from local prisons for Philanthropic reformation. This was a significant development.[21] With Staffordshire magistrates leading the way

---

18. HO 45/1649 – letter from Crawford dated 1/1/1846 to S. M. Phillips.
19. Taken from a Table derived from the Return of the Number of Convicts under Sentence of Transportation Confined on 1st January each year, cited in McConville (1981:198).
20. Cited in McConville (1981:209-10).
21. An exploration of the benefits of making a permanent partnership arrangement with the Sheriff's Fund was underway when the Philanthropic deputation had met Sir James. Aware

at the beginning of 1846—closely followed by the magistrates of West Sussex — it was a source of Philanthropic funding that would considerably increase. This new revenue stream would also be supplemented by way of implementing a scheme of payment by children's parents and friends. This further shift from the original practice of receiving all children gratuitously was first conceived in terms of a fixed charge of £20 per annum and then modified to allow payment of five shillings a week or a lesser amount considered 'proper'. Ironically, this policy did not always have crime preventing consequences. Having deferred the admission of John Flemming (twice imprisoned for stealing) until Mrs Flemming could 'endeavour to raise ... some pecuniary contribution towards the expenses of his board & clothing', the society found that:

> The mother of John Flemming (who applied in December last for the boy's admission but unsuccessfully as unable to pay towards his maintenance) appeared before the Committee, the boy having been again guilty of theft and imprisoned since the last application.

The Philanthropic gentlemen still insisted on charging one shilling per week.[22]

Whether this new means-tested strategy was also intended to overcome the long-standing problem of deflecting undeserving applications, raising even meagre sums through enforcing parental responsibility was important. Having decided it was now expedient to reduce the holdings of land at St. George's Fields and reorganise how the boys were trained on the premises, the society found that implementing the 'new arrangements' had involved unexpected costs. Plans for converting the Female School had also run into trouble when the surveyor discovered 'the drainage was so very deficient & the brick and timberwork in parts so decayed as almost to endanger the stability of the building'. The superintendent's 'habitation' was in equally bad repair. So too was the Philanthropic Chapel whose congregation had been further 'materially reduced' by the nearby 'conversion of several Dissenting chapels into Episcopal places of worship'.

---

of this – and dangling the enticing prospect of a government grant before them – the Home Secretary warned they should not be confident of getting better terms from that quarter.

22. Voluntary donations from parents or friends had been proffered – and accepted – from the earliest years.

The society was not altogether despondent. Its enterprise had attracted the interest of Viscount Ashley. Besides being deeply involved in the campaign to ameliorate hardships experienced by chimney-sweepers' boys and children working in mines and factories, Ashley was also interested in the crime preventive benefits of educating the children of the streets. Already president of the Ragged School Union, he agreed to be elected a Philanthropic vice-president in March 1846. With this impressive addition to the vice-presidential cast-list in place and £300 paid into a building account for the 'Chaplain's House and New Reform School', other improvements were put in hand. Indeed, having set out with the Reverend Dr. Rice to engage a 'suitable person to act as schoolmaster', Turner could report to a meeting on the 1st of July 1846 that:

> the Revd. T. Jackson, Principal of the Training College Battersea had informed him that the National Society would allow him to furnish a thoroughly efficient schoolmaster from that Institution on condition of the Philanthropic Society paying £25 to the fund for the Mining and Manufacturing School.

Extraordinarily, the road to Redhill suddenly hove into view. The Philanthropic enterprise had been embedded in St. George's Fields for nearly sixty years and looked set to continue there within the compass of its walls. Nonetheless, the catalyst of change was in the air and materialised when—at the very same meeting—the society resolved that:

> the Chaplain be requested to visit the Colonie Agricole at Mettray–to inspect the arrangements of the same, and report on them to the Committee.

An Experimental Opportunity

The visit allowed Turner and his Philanthropic companion—police magistrate, Mr. Paynter—to feast upon one of the grandest experiments of the time. They were not disappointed with the menu on offer. As their *Mettray Report* on the visit disclosed, that French enterprise was yet another fruit of an international cross-fertilisation of ideas. It had been founded through the 'benevolent exertions' of Monsieur Demetz who had 'visited and examined at various times, in previous years, the chief penitentiaries, and asylums of reform in America, England and Holland and Germany'. Interested in the moral and industrial education of juvenile offenders, Demetz had then formed a society for their 'protection' and on land provided by the Viscompt de Bretignères de Courteilles (a gentleman of 'considerable distinction and eminence') a Farm School had been established, near Tours, in 1839. By the time the Philanthropic gentlemen visited to make 'enquiries and observations', it was providing for between 400 and 500 children.

It was not these numbers, however, which gripped their imagination. Rather, these Philanthropic explorers were enraptured to find there the seeds of a novel opportunity to replant the Philanthropic enterprise in the countryside. As they enthused, not only was the French experiment conducted far from the temptations, contaminations and costs of town, but it had achieved the feat of retaining and reforming boys without resort to walls, sentries or harsh punishment. This success was due to what Turner delineated the 'five leading features' of its system that were 'entitled to the rank of fundamental laws':

1st The employment of improved and prepared teachers for the training and instructing of the boys;

2nd The dividing up of the inmates into families, into distinct classes of moderate extent, and separated not by mere difference of name or dress but by the substantial distinctions of separate dwellings, each forming a *home* for its inmates;

3rd The acting on the boys by persuasion, not by force;

4th The giving the boys such active and outdoor occupation, by means of gardening, agriculture, &c. as shall always thoroughly and healthfully employ them, and prevent that constant communication and intercourse which can scarcely be avoided when the boys are collected together in sedentary trades;

5th The combining together of the charity and interests of individuals with the support and sanction of the Government.

There were reservations, nonetheless. Although these 'laws of educational and moral agency' were the result of 'widespread and most intelligent enquiries', there could be no mere transplanting of the system into England. Whilst admirably adapted to suit the French nation's social and political circumstances, Mettray's regime was so coloured by a 'military disposition ... the spirit of their religious faith and the character of their religious habits' that, in consequence, Turner had to confess:

> the countenance and demeanour of the boys give me the impression, that they rather submitted to their instructor and employment, as part of a fixed scheme of discipline, from which there is no escape, than entered into as things of their own spontaneous pursuit, with which they felt their own interests identified ... The boys appear a little too much looked after on a system of police, and hardly thrown enough upon their own *responsibility*.[23]

This may have been satisfactory for boys who were afterwards dispersed, under Mettray's system of 'patronage', to French farms where a close 'domestic' surveillance on their welfare was maintained. It was not suitable, however, for Philanthropic boys whose 'best hopes and prospects of subsistence' would be by means of settlement in 'colonial dependencies'. As Turner explained:

> Voluntary, not forced, good conduct must be the object we aim at; for this alone will last. If we render the boy dependent on the superintendence and discipline which we subject him too, he will be but as a child in leading strings; and when the artificial support which he has been used to lean upon is necessarily withdrawn on his going forth into the world, he will be liable to fall at every step he takes in life.

Indeed, to 'prevent any misapprehension' on the matter, he desired:

> to state distinctly, that the Intention of the Report, is not to offer the Institution of Mettray as a PATTERN to be in all, or even in many, respects copied or closely imitated, but is rather to offer it as an EXAMPLE in which the true principles of the Religious and Industrial Agency that must be employed for the Reformation of young offenders, may be seen in action; and the study and analysis of which may enable those who are interested in rescuing our youthful poor from the grasp of

---

23. Foucault (1977:293-4) would choose Mettray to exemplify the carceral 'because it is disciplinary form at its most extreme, the model in which are concentrated all the coercive technologies of behaviour. In it were to be found 'cloister, prison, school, regiment ... [with its chiefs and their deputies] in a sense technicians of behaviour ... [whose] ... task was to produce bodies that were both docile and capable'.

crime and vice, to so design, and so carry on their operations, that their endeavours may be crowned with success.

If this language of scientific enquiry carries echoes from the past, Turner explicitly paid homage to the society's Enlightenment heritage when urging the establishment of an English Model Farm School. After all, the Philanthropic's original Institution, with its 'family division of the children; their distribution into distinct houses; the parental relation of their masters; the varied occupation, and agricultural character of the establishment', was 'in fact a Miniature Mettray'. Indeed, that mode of operation in Hackney, along with the idea of appointing 'guardians' in neighbourhoods where Philanthropic wards had been placed out:

> [showed] how singularly the views of the founders of Mettray were anticipated by the Enlightened Philanthropists who opened, sixty years ago, this Institution as an instrument for the diminution and prevention of crime.

Importantly, it could be further taken:

> as showing, too, that those, who of late have laboured to remodel and improve the system and the arrangement of the Philanthropic, have been labouring, not to *subvert* or to *destroy* its ancient constitution, but, in fact, to *renew* and *restore* it; to clear off the encumbrances and obstructions to its utility that time, and a forgetfulness of its founders original designs, have gathered around it.

Yet, although anxious to cast light on the way ahead, another worrying obstacle to success in English circumstances had been detected. This was the absence of legal control over the children. Lack of such power had long been a thorn in Philanthropic endeavours. The Mettray investigators had, however, discovered that under the French legal code, young offenders could be sentenced to 'long periods of detention in a house of correction' before being sent to Mettray. Even more intriguing was that the 'large number' of Philanthropic boys:

> who are received at once from the Police Courts without being committed to prison, and who are, therefore, innocent of serious and repeated guilt, although on the

threshold of it, correspond to that division of the boys at Mettray, who have been sentenced to detention, as being friendless, and vagrants.

Once there, moreover, the French law continued to exercise its own 'moral influence' by inculcating the 'fear of being sent back into custody without the chance of again returning to Mettray'. Convinced that this 'restraining power' — combined with the personal control which the Mettray directors had over the boys — was pivotal to dispensing with walls and guards, they 'earnestly' submitted to the committee:

> the propriety of bringing under the attention of Government, the importance of making such a change in the law regulating the treatment of Juvenile Offenders.[24]

Their revitalising recipes created a Philanthropic stir. This must have raised the hopes of William Gladstone who had been present at the committee meeting on the 1st of July during which the visit was proposed. A cousin of statesman William Ewart Gladstone, it was indeed he 'whose interest in Mettray, whose intimate acquaintance with its system, and whose desire to see something that may bear comparison with it established in this country' had sped Turner and Paynter on their journey.[25]

Excitement soon heightened. The door of the Home Department again opened. To the society's delight, Turner had been cultivating useful contacts. Not only could he relate that 'a friend' had offered to lay the *Mettray Report* before the new Home Secretary who had taken-up office in June, but that Sir George Grey had 'read it with much interest' and would be 'very happy' to receive some Philanthropic members if convenient for them to call. They

---

24. It is difficult to confirm whether they were correct in their grasp of how the English legal concept of *doli incapax* and the French concept of *sans discernment* were applied to the issue of juvenile responsibility in the two countries. As this point of jurisprudence continued to be the subject of circulating debate, it was felt necessary to attempt further clarification in the Philanthropic *Report* of 1854.
25. Turner and Paynter delivered their findings to the Philanthropic Committee in August 1846 and the *Mettray Report* was swiftly ordered to be printed for wider circulation. This account draws heavily on the revised second edition, of the same year, to which Turner added a Preface addressed to William Gladstone.

swiftly sallied forth and were accompanied by Turner's friend, the Honourable and Reverend R. Eden of Battersea.[26]

The Philanthropic party was initially disappointed. Upon Eden stating that 'one chief object of the deputation was to ask the Government to bring in an Act for the legal detention of young offenders, and for securing effectual control over them', Sir George replied that he would:

> be very glad to bring about some amendment in the present imperfect system, and that he thought such a power of detention by means of a conditional sentence could be given for such young offenders as had really incurred the penalties of the laws … [but] … he doubted the possibility of introducing a system so extensive as that of France or of sending any vagrant and delinquent boy to six or seven years detention: at least at present.

They were quite overwhelmed, however, to find an unexpected item on the Home Secretary's agenda:

> He then mentioned there were 70 or 80 boys in the Millbank Prison &c. sentenced to transportation but too young for Parkhurst by the new regulations there adopted and asked whether, if means could be found to send them to the Philanthropic, the Society could receive them

To which long-awaited invitation:

> The deputation answered, yes, at once.

This government bounty was not dispensed without the reappearance of a familiar figure. Sir George may well have told the Philanthropic gentlemen he was 'but too happy to put the boys he had spoken of in such good hands'. He also asked Crawford to account for any new circumstances — arising since 1845 — which might 'render it desirable that arrangements should be made with [the Philanthropic] for receiving a certain number of convict boys belonging to Government prisons'.

---

26. This is probably Robert John Eden (Baron Auckland), who was vicar of Battersea from 1837 to 1847, chaplain to William IV from 1831-37 and to Queen Victoria, 1837-47.

In response, Crawford would 'beg to state' that 'at that date' there had indeed existed 'great facilities in the disposal of criminal boys confined in the Millbank and Parkhurst Prisons, by sending them abroad'. Besides, the Refuge provision had been 'fully equal to the demands of the Home Office'. Now, however:

> since the suspension of Transportation further measures for providing for convict boys in this country have become necessary. I am therefore of opinion that it is desirable to accept the offer of the Committee of the Philanthropic Society to receive from the Government a certain number of criminal boys upon payment being made for their maintenance, and on the condition proposed by the Committee of subjecting their establishment to Government Inspection.–I consider that at the present time twenty five boys might be disposed of.

Whether this shift in stance was tinged by sensitivity to the whims of his new political master, Crawford retained a grip on the situation by suggesting:

> previously to any Number being sent to the Society, the Home Inspectors of Prisons should be directed to visit the establishment, and report … the description of boys whom it may be most desirable to select for admission.[27]

This, it transpired, was the class of boys who had been in prison 'for periods of two years and nine months and upwards, and have conducted themselves satisfactorily' but who were 'too young or too small, to be sent to the Colonies with a prospect of finding employment there on their arrival'. At least, that was what Crawford and that other influential Home Inspector of Prisons, Whitworth Russell, concluded after visiting St. George's Fields. Entertaining 'no doubt' that 'the religious and moral improvement of the boys there is well attended to', they found the 'general arrangements' were only suitable for the 'younger class of criminal boys who do not require to be subjected to a corrective discipline, in the means of enforcing which the Institution is essentially defective'. Indeed, while:

---

27. HO 45/1649 – letter to S. M. Phillips from Crawford, dated 16th November 1846, in reply to Sir George's enquiry of the 12th.

Agreeably to the Rules of the Institution, every Boy, on admission, is placed for a certain time in the 'Reform', or Probationary Ward, where he is associated with others.- As the Boys whom we now propose to remove to the Establishment are reported to be in a great measure reclaimed, we submit that the Committee would at once admit them into the General Establishment; by which means they will not be exposed to the contamination arising from association with other boys recently received from Prisons.[28]

Quite what Turner and treasurer William Gladstone thought of this criticism of Philanthropic arrangements is unknown.[29] Nonetheless, as the inspectors were assured of cooperation, the society soon was informed that:

Sir George Grey is prepared to sanction the proposed arrangement for the immediate reception of 25 boys from Parkhurst Prison at an annual rate of payment not exceeding twenty pounds each, which sum is to include the whole expense of their maintenance, superintendence and placing out on leaving the Establishment.-

Sir George Grey has requested that the Inspector of Prisons will select the boys for admission and communicate with the Secretary on the subject of their reception.-

Sir George Grey thinks it essential to this arrangement, that while any such boys are in the Establishment, it should as proposed by the Committee of the Society be open to the inspection of any gentlemen to be named by Her Majesty's Government for this purpose.-

At present it is intended that this duty should be performed by the Home Inspectors of Prisons.

It is also to be understood that the payment on account of such boys cannot in any case be prolonged beyond the expiration of the term of the original sentence of transportation or imprisonment.[30]

With terms agreed, the 'Queen's Boys' arrived on 26th December 1846.[31] They did not shy from engaging in a miscellany of misconduct and were soon at

---

28. HO 45/1649 – correspondence dated 30/11/1846.
29. Both met with the inspectors. Gladstone had been elected Philanthropic treasurer on 20th November in the place of S. R. Bosanquet who had resigned that 'office of so great honor and distinction'.
30. Letter from S. M. Phillips dated 10/12/1846.
31. Turner describes them thus.

the root of trouble encountered by the society's newly engaged drill sergeant. This may seem a surprising appointment considering the *Mettray Report* had condemned that French institution's military character — a reflection of which Turner had regretfully noted at Parkhurst when visiting there 'agreeably to the wishes of the Inspectors of Prisons'. But, drill *per se* had not been in contention. As we may recall, Turner had placed it on the Philanthropic curriculum in 1842. Hence, 'Corporal Hogg' took up position on the 3rd of February 1847. Within a few days he was outmanoeuvred by wily Queen's Boys who stole a key he had left in the washing room door 'by an oversight'. By August he was defeated. On this short 'experiment' Turner sadly reflected:

> In consequence of the state of feeling existing between the boys & the Sergeant Mr Hogg the latter has arranged to leave this day month. The Chaplain regrets to part with him but it appears to be impossible for him to make the drill for the boys what it was meant to be–a means of exercise and good order–he says he cannot deal with it in any but the strict military style–This is incompatible with the general system of the place–& produces so much dissatisfaction & resistance on the boys part–as to be very troublesome–there have been near 30 punishments during the last two months on acct. of complaints at Drill.

As for the grand Farm School experiment? Plans were still in a state of flux. Sir George had yet another surprising item on his agenda. Writing on the 16th November 1846 to confirm that the first Parkhurst cohort would be sent 'at once', he added:

> if the Philanthropic Society could agree to some plan of Union or combined operations with the Refuge for the Destitute, many obstacles to the Government[s] cooperation would be removed, and the adoption of larger and more effectual measures facilitated.

At this government steer, another Philanthropic deputation was dispatched to the Home Department. It was headed by Bishop Blomfield of London. Chadwick's friend and chairman of the Royal Commission that set out to reform the Poor Laws in 1832, Blomfield was an advocate of the poverty and crime preventive virtues of education for the children of destitute parents. He had been elected a Philanthropic vice-president in 1837 and was, conveniently, also a vice-president of the Refuge. The Philanthropists afterwards resolved:

> That in consideration of the wishes expressed by Sir George Grey and the strong recommendations on the subject by the Bishop of London, a special committee be appointed to consider a union of the two Societies.

This union courtship also failed. Not, this time, from any Philanthropic reticence. Rather, the Refuge managers were reluctant to be seduced. When they summoned their Philanthropic counterparts to a meeting on the 10th of December, the latter party were confounded to hear treasurer Forster say that his society's representatives would not 'in any wise, discuss or confer upon the subject of an Union' but could 'only receive' the Philanthropic proposition and relay it to the Refuge Committee.

This led treasurer Gladstone to confide in treasurer Forster that the 'disinclination which the Refuge managers had expressed' would not allow him 'to be very sanguine as to their cooperation'.[32] His foreboding came to pass. In March 1847, having assembled to discuss the scheme of union in more detail, the Philanthropists were interrupted by the arrival of a 'communication'. This informed them that the Refuge Committee could not justify 'abandoning the practical means they at present possess of reclaiming the Juvenile Offender for an experimental Institution which they consider inadequate'. Indeed, although willing to provide a London Depot for the transit of boys to an agricultural colony where 'vagrant, pauper and criminal youth are collected and employed upon the land', they nonetheless found themselves 'after mature consideration':

> of an opinion that whatever may be the result at Mettray, in regard to these various descriptions of youth, an Institution of this nature would not be adapted to the class of boys which it is the object of the Refuge for the Destitute to reclaim.
>
> The grounds for this opinion are: -
>
> 1st That in such a Colony, the personal detention of the boys could not be secured –
>
> 2^{ndly} That the Committee could not undertake the superintendence of an Institution not situated in the Metropolis–and

---

32. HO 45/1000 – letter dated 25/1/1847.

3rdly That such a Colony could not be founded or maintained without incurring a large expenditure–such indeed as would absorb the entire funded property of the Refuge for the Destitute.[33]

This sundering of the ways did not shake Philanthropic faith in the Farm School ideal. Nor was it dented by Crawford's attempt to cast blight by informing Sir George that he was:

> assured that unless due provision be made for the safe custody of the Boys when employed on the land (which will be scarcely practicable without the erection of walls) escapes will be frequent. The desire of personal liberty in these boys is irrepressible, and experience has shewn that moral restraints of any kind prove feeble whenever opportunities for escape are presented ... The success which has attended the exertions made at Parkhurst on the recapture of the boys who have endeavoured to escape, cannot be expected in ordinary localities.- These attempts have been defeated by the difficulty which the boys have found in leaving an Island–The shores of which are vigilantly watched, day and night, by a coast guard, to whom the notice of an escape is communicated immediately on its occurrence, and who have orders from the authorities under whom they act, to apprehend any boy who is suspected to have absconded from the prison.[34]

The similarity of reluctant sentiments expressed in these two documents reminds us that Crawford was a Refuge Committee member. But, despite the likely influence of his countervailing views on Home Department deliberations, favourable opinion could be detected elsewhere. The Philanthropic gentlemen may not yet have conceived this in terms of a reformatory movement on the upswing. We might imagine, nonetheless, they were aware that the *Mettray Report* had been endorsed recently by Matthew Davenport Hill when publishing his thoughts on the principles of punishment.[35] As well as having this adversary of a purely punitive approach to juvenile offenders onside, Turner could also relate that another reformatory advocate, Richard

---

33. Extract from the Refuge *Minutes* of 10/3/1847, copied into the Philanthropic *Minutes* of 13/3/47.
34. HO 45/1000–letter dated 31/3/1847 to Sir William Sommerville for Sir George's attention.
35. Hill had sent the Home Department a draft of his *Report* (1846) concerning the need for amending the criminal law so that 'reformation' was the 'object of secondary punishment' and would be best begun with juvenile offenders (HO 45/1471).

Monckton Milnes MP, had visited the Institution with 'Mrs Nightingale and friends'. On that occasion, Milnes informed him that:

> Sir George Grey had spoken of the Philanthropic to the deputation of the Refuge for Prisoners Society which had waited on him last week & had expressed himself as relying greatly upon its plans and efforts for enabling him to make some effectual provision for Juvenile Offenders.[36]

What was more, when Turner had called upon 'the Reverend Eden—and Mr Kay-Shuttleworth—to communicate the Refuge's resolution to the latter':

> Mr. K-S said that he felt confident Sir George Grey's interest in the subject was so great and personal that he wd. be anxious to sanction and assist the Philanthropic Society if they were able to offer a well-grounded and comprehensive scheme.

This opinion held an aura of authority. Kay-Shuttleworth had worked as an assistant Poor Law commissioner (beside Chadwick) before being appointed as one of the first visitors to Parkhurst (with Crawford) in 1838. That year, the commissioners' report on pauper education had condemned the neglected condition of children who were equipped only for a life of dependency by being taught in workhouse schools by other inmates. Believing, like Bishop Blomfield, that education of the rising generation was one of the most important ways to eradicate pauperism, Kay-Shuttleworth then championed the introduction of elementary district schools, staffed by properly trained teachers and subject to inspection. Appointed secretary to the Privy Council Committee on Education in 1839, he had a controlling interest in the School of Industry at Norwood which fed apprentice-teachers into the Normal College he helped found at Battersea in 1840.

Since it was to this training college that the Turner had turned in his quest for a 'thoroughly efficient schoolmaster' in 1846, it would seem that he had been moving in intellectual circles of awareness of Kay-Shuttleworth's endorsement of European innovations which made a point of educating the whole child (head, heart and hands) on the lines pioneered by Pestalozzi. Yet, although we can only speculate on the sources from which Turner distilled

---

36. Milnes courted Mrs. Nightingale's reforming daughter, Florence, until rejected.

his educationally improving ideas, we can be rather more certain that, soon after returning from Mettray, he had 'interviewed' with Mr Kay-Shuttleworth on the subject of the plans and operations of the society and found that gentleman 'sincerely interested and desirous of seeing' the Philanthropic proposals 'as soon as possible practically realised'. Kay-Shuttleworth may also have taken the opportunity to appraise Turner of the Privy Council Committee's plans for establishing a model training college, at Kneller Hall, in which masters of workhouse and penal schools could be made competent. Indeed, a mutually beneficial circularity of interests appears to have been in contemplation. On taking-up Kay-Shuttleworth's suggestion of sending Sir George a 'mature proposal' for an efficient reformatory establishment in the countryside, the society declared its intent was:

> to make the Institution publicly useful, not only in reclaiming the Boys received into it, but in the training of pupil teachers who may do good service to the country as Prison School Masters and Masters of schools in agricultural districts.

Another silence ensued. Even though the Home Secretary had been sent a detailed description of the Farm School's projected mode of operation (together with estimates of the government's anticipated contribution to its foundation and after-maintenance), nothing was heard until Philanthropic envoys obtained an interview in September 1847. They found Sir George had indeed 'proposed giving his answer previous to the dissolution, but that he had been prevented by the pressure of Public Business'.

Sir George's inattention to Philanthropic anxieties is understandable. The year 1847 had been a particularly busy one for the Home Secretary. Successfully introducing a Bill which took expression in the Poor Law Board Act, his hopes of reviving Sir James's plans for enabling counties to set-up reformatories out of local rates had been battered during stormy debate on a Juvenile Offenders Bill in the spring. Although an Act empowering magistrates to summarily sentence minor offenders in order to avoid 'the evils of their long imprisonment previous to trial' did pass in the summer,[37] Sir

---

37. An Act for the more Speedy Trial and Punishment of Juvenile Offenders.

George was also entangled in controversies surrounding the management of Millbank Prison and the hulks.[38]

With this portfolio simmering, Sir George most likely was also keeping a very close eye on the proceedings of the House of Lords enquiry on the Execution of the Criminal Law especially respecting juvenile offenders and transportation. This was instigated by Lord Brougham, whose masterly Parliamentary performance had impressed American visitor, John Griscom, in 1818. Involved with Matthew Davenport Hill (as well as Dr. Birkbeck) in forming the Society for the Diffusion of Useful Knowledge, Brougham's improving impulse had been behind the formation of the Poor Law Commission in 1832 and the provision of education grants to voluntary organizations in 1833. Brougham was now 'at the height of his influence'.[39]

If the Philanthropists were delighted to hear that the Home Secretary was now willing to send them boys from other prisons, they may not have been so happy to know that Crawford had cast further blight on their plans. Upon reading the Philanthropic's application for 'pecuniary aid' in setting up a Farm School, Crawford felt obliged to warn Sir George that acceding to the request would set a 'dangerous precedent' and might draw the Treasury into its 'continuance'. In his opinion, 'the friends of the Philanthropic Society' were 'not such as to justify the expectation that the Agricultural Institution could be carried on without material assistance'. Unsurprisingly, the Philanthropic *Minutes* of October then record that:

> [Sir George regretted] it would not be in his power to aid the Society with a grant of money towards the formation of a Country Establishment.
>
> That the measures he [still] proposed to bring forward would enable counties and boroughs to make provision for the reformatory Education and Discipline of the Juvenile Offenders of their locality, either by establishing Penal Schools themselves or by using such Reformatory Asylums as the Philanthropic elsewhere–the expense of the maintenance and education of the children being defrayed from the rates.

---

38. One result of the review on these matters was Capper's retirement as Hulk Superintendent. He had resigned from Philanthropic activity in 1845.
39. Radzinowicz and Hood (1986:173).

> That on this ground it would be impossible to give such a grant as the Society asked for as similar grants would be immediately applied for and expected in other localities ...

> That with reference to a loan–that lay with the Treasury Department, but the possibility of such assistance must depend on whether the Philanthropic could be considered one of those Public bodies to which loans from the Treasury were restricted.

This news failed to impede the Farm School's progress. The Philanthropic entrepreneurs now took the risk of venturing out on their own. Although the exact destination was unknown, in January 1848 a Special General Court 'unanimously' found it 'expedient' to plant roots in the countryside where:

> With a view to the thoroughly fitting the boys to maintain themselves in after life, they shall be taught to cultivate garden ground and fields–to look after cattle, to make and repair their clothes and shoes, to knit stockings, to plait straw hats and to be useful in ordinary housework, such boys as are peculiarly adapted for such employment being taught the business of carpenter, wheelwright, bricklayer and every boy being taught to read and cypher–and receiving as much other useful instruction as his employment allow of, and the religious instruction of the boys and the accustoming them to religious habits being a fundamental part of their training.

Upon this resolution, it was decided to open a public subscription with a view to founding the Farm School when £3,000 was raised. Philanthropic friends responded magnificently. By March 1848, £2,000 had been collected. Perhaps even more spectacularly, the Philanthropic Society was now able to send 'loyal and respectful thanks' to:

> Her Most Gracious Majesty and to His Royal Highness Prince Albert for their kind encouragement of the Society's efforts in condescending to become its Patrons and in so liberally contributing to its funds.

There were other pleasing portents. Sir George had personally contributed to the Farm School Fund and made a visit to the Philanthropic Institution in St. George's Fields. He then had 'given his personal testimony' on the society's 'efficiency and usefulness' before the House of Commons. What was more, the Right Honourable William Ewart Gladstone MP had become a vice-president and Monckton Milnes, MP had been elected to the committee.

The society could also summon a public meeting on the subject of the laws regarding juvenile offenders and see its guest-list headed by veteran legal reformer Lord Brougham. With campaigning Matthew Davenport Hill and a cluster of influential others also attending, a petition emerged which was presented to the House of Lords by Philanthropic president the Duke of Richmond and to the House of Commons by Monckton Milnes. And, if there was disappointment at finding this effort had been made 'too near the end of Sessions to allow for that general movement which would else have been made in favour of some alteration in the laws', Turner could report:

> that petitions agreeing in the prayer sent up from the Meeting ... had been obtained from the magistrates of Montgomeryshire, Norfolk and Sussex and also from Reading.

Meanwhile, the Farm School acquisition was underway. In searching for a suitable site, the Philanthropic gentlemen found nothing to suit in the vicinity of Epsom, Croydon or, indeed, Reigate. Two plots were then spotted near Uxbridge but the asking price was too high and so a farm near Farnborough was considered. Bereft of a house and with the land entirely bare of trees, this was thought unsuitable. As an 'advantageous site' was then 'lost from the managing committee not being in a position to at once make an offer for it' Turner, treasurer Gladstone and committee member Mr. Cattley were granted the necessary powers. The society also felt a need to escape the shades of nimbyism that had haunted Bentham's panopticon progress and agreed, in May, that:

> it being probable that objections may be raised by vendors to selling the land for such purposes as the Society have in view the Treasurer be requested to purchase the same and to convey it by resale to the Society if this course shall be found desirable.

By August the quest seemed at an end. The Duke of Richmond had been consulted on the subject and the sale of the London estate and chapel was cleared by an Act of Parliament.[40] The Society then sanctioned the purchase of a farm at Potters Bar. In this was in mind:

---

40. In September, committee member Richard Baggally junior was thanked for 'his kind and

That the proposed Farm School being intended especially as a Model Institution and being especially a school of spade husbandry and gardening for boys the three chief points to be looked into in deciding on a site should be–

It being very easily accessible and within view from some frequented line of Railway communication and of it being of a light soil such as young persons could be advantageously employed upon.

Although a design prize of £20 was afterwards won by Mr. Moffat who had 'most fully realised the domestic and rural character of the proposed Institution' and building tenders were received in October, the Philanthropic Farm School did not materialise in the 'English Country Farmhouse style' near the Great Northern Railway. On the 21st of December 1848, Treasurer Gladstone announced that:

he had received an offer of a Donation of £1,000 to the Farm School Fund on condition that the new Establishment shall not be fixed at Potter's Bar but be removed to some other locality where facilities for obtaining more land can be found and be placed at a distance of not less than 40 miles from St. Paul's upon the North side of London and not less than 12 miles on the south side–and that an estate near Redhill–on the Brighton Railway–which appeared, from the buildings on it, to be very eligible for the purposes of the Farm School–had been offered on a long lease, or to purchase.

This was not an offer to refuse and terms were quickly agreed. Indeed, the publicity value of this new investment was soon milked by inviting Prince Albert to lay the foundation stone of the first Farm School house. A public celebration of this event was also arranged to take place after Turner took-up residence in the existing buildings on the site. The ensuing festival was a roaring success. On Prince Albert's arrival:

the Royal Standard was immediately hoisted, and the band of the Royal Artillery struck up 'God Save the Queen', the immense assemblage, from the surrounding neighbourhood, as well as those from the Metropolis, drawn thither by the exceedingly

---

valuable services in gratuitously advising on and preparing the Act of Parliament ... the early and economical passing of which this Court feel strongly to be due to the clear and skilful manner in which the Bill was prepared'.

propitious weather, expressing their approbation by loud cheers and the waving of hats, &c. His Royal Highness was received by His Grace the Duke of Richmond, the President of the Institution, who formed into a procession, with the Committee, the boys now in the School, the clergy of this and adjoining districts, &c., by whom His Royal Highness was conducted to the stone, placed beneath a large pavilion, in which were about 600 ladies and gentlemen.

As they contemplated this happy scene, some Philanthropic trustees may have paused a moment to reflect on how their enterprise had come out of the shadows and into the light now shining on Red-stone Hill. It certainly had not decayed over the past decade. In many respects, this was a radically different Philanthropic Society to that which set out to nip crime in the bud at the end of the 18th-century. No longer including girls amongst its objects and intent on ending the admission of boys of criminal parentage, it was beginning to specialise in the reformation of male juvenile offenders. Having embarked on this English Reformatory Farm School experiment and with a closer relationship to the Home Department now forged, the Philanthropic gentlemen might have been delighted to know that their new venture was ripe for 'testing the mechanisms' of important legislative action. There was, nonetheless, still some stony ground to plough.

CHAPTER 7

THE LEGISLATIVE QUEST

A Fresh Start

Immense excitement pervaded the Farewell Anniversary Dinner when Philanthropic gentlemen speculated on the extent to which their very 'important experiment' would reveal:

> viz.- how far the free discipline and out-door occupations of a country school, conducted on the footing of an Agricultural Colony, can be successfully applied to the moral Reformation and Industrial Training of such youths as the Philanthropic seeks to rescue.

Relocating to the countryside also fulfilled the founders' ambitions. As Turner reminded the gathering, those eighteenth-century gentlemen had intended to employ 'agriculture' as a means of transforming outcast boys into hardy husbandmen, ready to cultivate 'waste lands'. What was more, their sentiments 'strikingly' coincided with those expressed by the 'Enlightened Mirabeau'. When writing to Romilly, in 1785, he had declared:

> All hospitals ... all Institutions for the reception of the Infirm, of Foundlings, Beggars, Lunatics, &c., are established near Towns. Why are they not removed from Towns which they infect, and which infect them, to the Country? ... let them be removed to the Country, where everything is cheaper ... Children bred there can only be brought up for Trade, and for Towns, while the sedentary employments of Trade kill the children, whose first want is to run and jump and play about ... These unhappy children, the produce for the most part of the vices of the Cities, will at least be brought up in the good and simple morals of the country.[1]

---

1. *Report* (1850). Curiously, the Philanthropic Farm School was located about ten miles north from where Robert Young planted the foundations of his British Settlement in Tilgate Forest, near Crawley, Sussex, in 1795.

Agricultural pursuits failed to philanthropically flourish after the transition from the asylum without walls at Hackney. The utility of cultivating the soil was, however, firmly embraced in other experiments improved at home and abroad. It had, for instance, been a fundamental feature of the cottage-based initiative for delinquent children established at the Rauhe Haus, near Hamburg, Germany by Emmanuel Wicherm in 1833. It also underpinned numerous Farm School schemes whose roots lay in the 18th-century Hanway Acts.[2] Besides encouraging parish schools to provide gardening plots, that body of legislation enabled parishes to board-out pauper children and apprentice them to masters in country trades in the hope that skills thus acquired would prevent them being a future drain on the poor rates. But, by the time the Poor Law Amendment Act was passed in 1834, a vast number of these schools had grown into large barrack-like Institutions to which Poor Law unions merely 'farmed' out their wards to contractors who were intent on making a profit. Neither agriculture nor horticulture featured prominently on the curriculum. Instead, the children were mostly occupied in sedentary trades, such as picking oakum or inserting bristles into brushes. One of the best of these establishments — Mr Aubin's School of Industry at Norwood — would be taken under the reforming wings of Kay-Shuttleworth and then developed to provide a model for pauper education in district workhouse schools.

While the views of Kay-Shuttleworth were consulted and the opinion of experts in agricultural management had been sought when the Farm School Plan began its progress, Turner had not been tempted to visit the countryside asylum without walls at Stretton-on-Dunsmore. His reluctance to inspect its arrangements seems reasonable. Although established, in 1818, on the initiative of Warwickshire magistrates who sent criminal boys there to be trained to earn an honest living through spade-husbandry, when its spokesperson appeared before the Richmond Committee, in 1835, he had to confess that this scheme had since lapsed as few farmers in the vicinity were willing to employ such lads.

---

2. Act for an Annual Register of all Parish Poor Infants (1762) and Act for the better Regulation of all Parish Poor Children (1767).

The thorny matter of after-disposal also beset Captain Brenton's Children's Friend Society. Commenced as a small agricultural establishment at West Ham — before removing to a larger site at Hackney Wick — this venture invoked the merits of *The Bible* and spade for the boys under its care. The Bible, broom and needle provided for the future of its girls who were settled into a Royal Asylum at Chiswick. Having discovered that many employers refused to take-on its children at home, the society's attention turned to sending both boys and girls to the colonies where a demand for labour had been detected. Successfully touting its wares and attracting a great number of subscribers, it also, we may recall, had even procured Philanthropic money by promising to give Thomas Brown a fresh start at the Cape of Good Hope in 1833.[3]

Yet, by the end of that decade, the Children's Friend Society was encountering the escalating ire of settlers at the Cape who suspected it was off-loading rather too many children with criminal backgrounds into the colony. It was also spinning into a crisis of public credibility at home surrounded by accusations of 'selling' children into conditions of exploitation and cruelty. This proved devastating. Not only was Brenton persecuted by the press but committee members had the frightening experience of being pelted with stones when going into a meeting. Indeed, as after Brenton's death, in 1839, his remains were 'insulted on their way to the grave by a mob who cried out that he had been a slave dealer under the pretext of charity',[4] we can appreciate why funds dried up and the society wound down.

Amazingly, this furore did not unnerve Turner from bringing the idea of emigration to the fore in 1843. Bending his mind to the 'most effectual method of lessening the cost of the establishment', he suggested that £900 a year could be saved if 'the great part' of the boys 'should be retained in it three years (or in some cases one year more) and then be placed out in the colonies'. This, admittedly, might appear a risky business after what had

---

3. This was not a new market in care and convenience. When the Virginia Company petitioned for a supply of London youth in 1618, the Lord Mayor had vindicated his readiness to send swarms of waifs, orphans and children with criminal tendencies across the Atlantic in terms of them being a 'nuisance' to authorities at home at a time when plantation owners were desperate for labour (Wagner, 1982).
4. Bradlow (1984).

befallen the Children's Friend Society. Nevertheless, he believed that no serious evil or difficulty would occur because:

1st The boys would be older averaging 14 years of age

2^d There would not be any money received for them

3^d Being criminals the protection and assistance of the government might be claimed and obtained for them, a point which all the information I can gain shews to be of primary importance.

Turner may well have mulled over the topic of emigration with committee member Mr. Capper. Still superintendent of the convict hulks at that time, Capper could have appraised him of his own — and even vice-president Holford's — belief in the benefits of 'exile'. In formulating the proposition, Turner possibly even paid reverence to the views expressed by Steward Russell when before the Richmond Committee. As we saw, Russell had supplemented his thoughts on the utility of sending juvenile offenders to reformatory asylums by suggesting it would be a 'wonderful benefit' to the boys — and to the public — if, after a few years within, they then were sent to the colonies.

The topic of emigration subsided from view. It did not rise again until fused into the *Mettray Report's* recommendations regarding the 'best prospects' for Philanthropic boys whose after-disposal tended to prove taxing. This certainly was in contrast to the French experience. As Turner and Paynter had discovered, the directors of the *Colonie Agricole* found no difficulty in providing for Mettray graduates 'there being more applications than can be satisfied' from farmers and tradesmen throughout that country. Hence, with emigration to British colonies conceived as a crucial component for implementing the Philanthropic Farm School Scheme, we can imagine why Turner would soon boast that he had communicated 'with the Under-Secretary of State for the Colonies, Lord Westminster' on the subject and had received an encouraging response.[5]

---

5. In a memorandum to Sir James Graham in November 1844, prison inspector Crawford mentioned that the Plan of Union had been drawn-up 'with the view of adapting the best parts of

That news might lead us to reflect on whether treasurer Gladstone had nurtured the contact with Whitehall. This could easily have been effected through the residual influence of his cousin, William Ewart Gladstone, who had just been replaced as Colonial Secretary in the summer of 1846. It is also feasible that the necessary introductions were made by the society's president. Besides taking an interest in prison reform and secondary punishments, in 1831 the Duke of Richmond had been one of the commissioners appointed to enquire into the subject of emigration to British colonies and possessions abroad. Still, as the Farm School Plan galvanised many erstwhile figureheads into action, we should not be too surprised to discover that the Philanthropic world already had embraced Lord Westminster as a vice-president. Having followed in the Grosvenor family's path of Philanthropic duty, his personal interest would extend to visiting St. George's Fields on quite a few occasions. Also giving Turner the pleasure of recording he had dined at Lord Westminster's in 1847, his lordship would be added to the Farm School Management Committee in 1848.

Although we cannot confirm which influential friend facilitated access to the Colonial Office, Turner also met with another Under-Secretary therein. This was Benjamin Hawes who informed him:

> That with reference to the emigration of boys from the Philanthropic School to the Colonies, every assistance would be readily given by the Colonial Office –
>
> That he thought there would be no difficulty in placing a very considerable number (100 or 200) annually in Port Phillip and South Australia and in securing them efficient protection for a year or two after their landing –
>
> But that boys would have little prospect of success if only trained to such sedentary trades and collective occupations as tailoring and shoemaking –
>
> That in fact to prepare them properly for such a destination they should be practised in trades and labours connected with agriculture and trained in a country establishment.[6]

---

the French system of Patronage' to provide juvenile offenders from the combined Institution with employment at home or in a British Colony. HO-45/1000.

6. Hawes had been a Surrey magistrate and was a commissioner of Pentonville Prison. He was also influential in establishing the Fine Arts Commission in 1841 and found time to patronise the development of the electric telegraph and Babbage's calculating machine.

The promised assistance proved elusive. We might, indeed, suspect Turner's tale was tinged by a desire to drive the Farm School project forward. The society would certainly pilot the scheme by sending a contingent of 19 boys to Swan River, Perth, 'under private arrangements' in August 1848. With their disposal successfully accomplished, Turner then was authorised to negotiate with the Colonial Office (now in the hands of Earl Grey) for help in sending a batch of 36 boys to Algoa Bay, at The Cape, in January 1849. Alas, he had to disappoint Philanthropic hopes of pecuniary reward by announcing that:

> [he] had communicated with the Emigration Officers agreeably to Earl Grey's suggestion ... [but] ... had reason to believe they would not be able to give the Society the aid applied for in the present instance, the arrangements for the boys' passage having been made independently of the Emigration Office.

This was as nothing to the shock of finding the second mass sortie of Philanthropic boys into the colonies had caused great 'outrage' amongst the settlers. Considering how fatal The Cape shore had been for the Children's Friend Society in recent memory, that destination had been rather audacious. The boys' landing, however, was a matter of particularly bad timing. As Philanthropic friends there made known, 'it was most unfortunate that the introduction of these boys in the Colony' had coincided with the arrival of news that:

> [the] dispositions of the Home Secretary just now is to make this a Convict Colony and at the moment the whole of the Colonists are extremely excited and using every constitutional means to resist the infliction they are threatened with. The excitement now is so great that we think was another lot of your boys to arrive just now they would not find masters.[7]

The awesome scale of resistance was confirmed by Her Majesty's Governor in Cape Town. He warned that:

> the feelings on the subject of convicts is so strong and so universal at present in this Colony that I feel it would be most inexpedient to send out any more boys, at least for some time to come–However moral might be their character, and perfect their

---

7. The Philanthropic friends at Port Elizabeth, Algoa Bay, had been asked to organize a committee for the reception of the boys and to 'protect and watch over them'.

reformation, they would most assuredly be regarded at this moment by the inhabitants with suspicion and the object of their emigration be at once defeated.

On hearing that alarming opposition had been mobilised by The Cape press, the society hastened to correct 'erroneous statements'. As the Philanthropic gentlemen retorted:

> This Committee desire and most distinctly and emphatically to state that they have no understanding or arrangement of any sort whatever whether public or private with the Colonial Office or Emigration Board as to the sending their boys out.-
> And that their connection with the Government is limited to the receiving into their Institution a few lads convicted at the Assizes or Quarter Sessions but pardoned and recommended to the Society's protection on account of the lightness of their offences and their favourable character. The only pecuniary contribution received in any way by the Society from the Government being the amount expended for such boys' maintenance, clothing and provision when apprenticed out; which is repaid by virtue of the arrangement agreed to by Secretary Sir George Grey three years ago … an arrangement made at least twelvemonths before the idea of the Society's pupils being sent out to the Colonies was in any way entertained.
> That in applying to the Emigration Board for aid towards the expenses of the passage of the thirty six boys sent out in February last the Committee acted under the impression that some part of the grant voted for sending out to Australia the boys selected from the Ragged Schools of London and its vicinity might be available for the lads of the Philanthropic, these being principally of the same class of destitute and neglected children as these schools contain.
> That in reference to the boys spoken of as recommended from County Associations and as paid from the funds subscribed by magistrates and others–this Committee desire it to be distinctly understood that these lads are not of such character as that the magistrates are willing to pay £17 a piece to get rid of them.[8]

Turner also took up arms. He was particularly stung by suspicions of the boys being used as a covert spearhead for government ambitions. Insisting that emigration was only offered to the most promising lads as the 'Prize of the Institution', he decried:

---

8. Vice-president Lord Ashley's successful bid for a government grant of £1,500 towards transplanting ragged school children appears to have hovered around Philanthropic calculations.

> The Colonial Press has attacked the Society as receiving JUVENILE CONVICTS from the Government, as being in league with the Colonial Office to introduce boys of this strictly criminal class into the Cape, under a charitable disguise. The Society's assailants overlook the essential difference between the boys received into the Philanthropic on Sir George Grey's recommendation, and those who are sent to Parkhurst; and they pass by altogether the important fact that the very reason why these boys are recommended for the Queen's pardon, and placed in the Philanthropic, is that, though nominally Convicts, they are not Criminals in the real sense of the word, and deserve and want the moral discipline and instruction of a School much more than the penal correction of a Prison.[9]

Whether this riposte punctured the 'assailants' outrage, at least some of the Philanthropic emigrants were repeat offenders. Amongst those who embarked for Port Elizabeth was:

> John Webb aged 13–admitted 10/2/1847 at £16 per annum paid by the Surrey Society–committed for misdemeanour–says he has been 19 times in prison–charged with vagrancy at Union Hall–5 weeks imprisonment in Brixton House of Correction with hard labour.

In March 1853, the society heard that John had been employed on a farm at The Cape and was 'doing well but addicted to drink'.

As 'convict' status was usually conferred on people who were sentenced to more than two years imprisonment or transportation, George Fossett undoubtedly fits into that category. He was received into the Philanthropic Institution, in 1847, after Home Secretary Grey agreed to extend the Parkhurst scheme by sending Queen's Boys from other prisons. George had been:

> convicted at Northerallerton Sessions on 20th June for stealing £21.10s.1d and a purse–sentenced to 7 years transportation–had been previously convicted of felony at the Sessions for York City in September 1844–recommended by Sir George Grey–reads and writes imperfectly–he was 3 months in York Castle before being removed to Millbank.

No details of what happened to George at The Cape are recorded. Neither do the Philanthropic ledgers show how the following boy progressed:

---

9. *Report* (1850).

> William Stanley – admitted 30/10/1848 – charged with stealing money (£3) from his employer–the Butty (or overseer) of the coal mine he worked in – sentenced at Staffordshire Sessions to 4 months imprisonment & hard labour in Staffordshire Castle–recommended by the Staffordshire Prisoners Reform Association–admitted at the rate of £16 per annum–this boy states he was persuaded to steal the money by a man who had been discharged from the Pit & who told him where to find it–a fine intelligent lad.

The ledgers do, however, reveal that this next boy did not stay overlong at The Cape:

> George James aged 15–admitted 29/1/1848–concerned with another boy in stealing–tried at Guildhall January 13th – complaint not pressed on condition of his being received into the Philanthropic on the Sheriffs' Fund–recommended by Alderman Sidney–£16 per annum on account of the Sheriffs' Fund, Ludgate Hill. This boy is very ignorant–& appears to have great difficulty in learning anything–but is very quick & very fond of talking–he is a native of St. Helena where he has an aunt 'Sally' alias Margaret James–in service with a person keeping a Public House.

The society later heard that George had been apprenticed at an hotel. He then 'got disgraced' and returned to St. Helena.

A fresh start for some other Philanthropic pupils still entailed being sent to sea. Finding suitable ships was an even more fraught task than it had been in the society's earliest years. To overcome this difficulty, treasurer William Gladstone offered to apprentice two boys and place them on one of his ships, *The Duke of Wellington*, trading to Calcutta. George Jackson was one of these lads. He had been tried at Leicester in 1843 and sentenced to seven years transportation. One of the first Queen's Boys sent from Parkhurst, George was found on arrival to be:

> Good. Quiet. Shy. Does well and is not anxious to have it recognised – diligent, attentive, obedient, respectful. A Christian Boy.

Unhappily, in 1849 the society was informed that George had 'accidentally drowned at sea'.

The outcome for the other boy, Dennis McCarthy, was better — but not glorious. Dennis was aged 15 when sentenced, in 1844, at the Central Criminal

Court (Old Bailey) to seven years transportation for stealing tobacco. He arrived from Parkhurst in July 1847 with 'good character' and 'good scholarship'. Yet, only too soon Dennis was:

> imprisoned for very gross misconduct & threatening to stab the Drill Serjt. Mr Hogg. The boy defied all other officers but submitted to the Chaplain.

In 1850, the society heard that the captain of the ship had expelled Dennis for 'his extreme violence of temper'.

As for John Hoscroft's outcome? We may recollect that this starving boy was received from the police pourt, in Worship Street, in 1844. John was not given a fresh start abroad. Nor did he cultivate waste lands at home. Deemed 'a dull boy — but improving' in 1845, he was trained in sedentary trades and placed with the tailor in the Manufactory Department for a while. In August 1846 he went on trial to Mr. J. Peters, Boot and Shoemaker, 20 Walmer Place. John was then apprenticed in September and the following month received a 'good character' from his master. In February next, the remainder of the apprenticeship premium was paid by the society and his master's residence was noted as No. 8 Exeter Street, Lisson Grove. In October, John's mother called at the Institution:

> to state that the boy had been for some months with her – having left his master who is said to have made away with his clothes & ill used him. The boy has been working for himself & earning 5/- & 6/- per week. But he is unsettled.

With favourable reports on boys sent abroad outweighing the many such disappointing outcomes achieved at home, emigration soon became a prominent feature of Philanthropic practice. Even so, in the aftermath of The Cape crisis trauma, the society revised its thoughts on seeking government aid in the sphere of colonial enterprise and decided the more 'privately' and 'unofficially' its emigration plans were worked out, the better it would be.[10]

---

10. Radzinowicz and Hood (1986:217) note that of the 3,809 boys discharged between 1849 and 1871, 1,032 emigrated from the Farm School.

Reformatory Returns

This retreat from partnership with the Colonial Office is of marked contrast to the Philanthropic gentlemen's tenacious cultivation of Home Department territory. By May 1850, their toil was reaping a fruitful financial harvest. Out of the 100 children then in the Reformatory Farm School, the society could record that:

> 29 were on Government account at the usual rate
>
> 10 were on Government account by special agreement from Westminster Bridewell
>
> 28 were on account from various associations
>
> 18 were on account of friends or subscribers
>
> 15 were on the Free List.

These 'accounts' reflect the society's ideas on the appropriate allocation of reformatory responsibilities. On that important matter, the authors of the *Mettray Report* had been convinced that:

> with regard to the formation and support of such Asylums of Reform, they should in all cases be, as much as possible, the result of *voluntary exertion* and *private benevolence*, and not simply *Government establishments*; but, as individual charity could not be reckoned on for supplying the funds required for their maintenance, either to a sufficient amount, or with sufficient certainty and regularity, that such a sum should be contributed either by the Government, or from the county or borough rates, on account of each boy received on the recommendation of the magistrates, or the Secretary of State.

Turner and Paynter had furthermore urged that in regard to Treasury funding:

> It would be advisable to have any such contribution *paid by head* ... and not in the form of an annual grant of a gross sum from the Government. The present experience of the Philanthropic, where boys are now received from country districts, in virtue of the subscriptions of the magistrates, shows that the plan of paying so much per head for the boy's expenses, does not interfere with private contributions; while

the experience of the 'Refuge' seems to show that an annual grant, and an apparent dependence on Government, discourages them.

The fate of the Refuge for the Destitute suggests the Philanthropic approach was not misplaced. We last encountered that long-standing voluntary enterprise resisting exhortations to agree to the proposed Plan of Union in 1847. Around that time, the Refuge was maintaining 106 boys in its Hoxton establishment and 102 girls at its Hackney Road branch. By 1850 it was reduced to catering for only 40 girls in the Manor House, Dalston.[11]

These figures make such a stark contrast to flourishing Philanthropic fortunes that it is tempting to believe the Refuge's reluctance to risk embarking on an experimental joint venture had led to this sorry pass. Merely to do so, however, would overlook some very significant contributory factors lurking in the background. Not least of these was a House of Commons Select Committee on Miscellaneous Estimates and Expenditure which had commenced its enquiries into government efficiency in 1847. Under particular scrutiny by 1848 was the Home Department, wherein resided a Home Secretary who was very much alert to the duty of getting good value for public money.

Since that important item of Executive interest appears to have had no small bearing on the Refuge's rapid decline, it seems fitting to bring treasurer Forster forward to ask—somewhat complacently—for the 'usual' government grant of £3,000 in January 1848. Unfortunately, in also directing Sir George Grey's attention to the 'state of the account, by which it appears that the expenditure during [the] last year exceeded the income by £1,578.1.11', Forster's application touched a sensitive Home Department nerve. He was swiftly requested to send a more detailed statement of the 'Objects' admitted into the Refuge under the Parliamentary grant in the previous year. As this revealed the shocking fact that only seven males and three females had been admitted under the Secretary of State's orders, Sir George sent his civil servants scurrying to provide him with a yearly breakdown of the grant

---

11. Having also catered for about 200 children, the Philanthropic had deliberately reduced its numbers preparatory to implementing the Farm School Plan.

received by the Refuge since 1814. They were also ordered to set the income thus derived against that accrued from annual subscriptions and donations.[12]

This Whitehall exercise did not prove a study in fiscal prudence. Research disclosed that charitable aid had dramatically contracted, with only £240 being received by the Refuge in 1847. Government contributions, on the other hand, had remained more or less steady and, in effect, were being used for general purposes.[13] The Treasury was hurriedly consulted and the outcome was a drastic reduction in the public money supply. As Forster was tersely informed:

> Sir George Grey is by no means disposed to underrate the usefulness of such an Institution ... [but he] ... is unable to satisfy himself that there are sufficient grounds to justify a continuance of the application to Parliament for an annual grant towards its maintenance, which as the [Select] Committee of the House of Commons observe is a subscription to its funds and which in fact entails the greater portion of its annual income. The effect of such grants appears to be to check the exercise of that private charity and benevolence from which the Institution derived its existence & on which it first depended for its support ... The payment from the Treasury should be limited to the amount requisite for defraying the expense of the maintenance of juvenile offenders sent to the Refuge by order of the Secretary of State, including some definite sum for the expense of their apprenticeship or outfit on leaving the Institution ... in the next estimates ... the sum proposed to be granted to the Refuge shall be reduced to £200.[14]

This news must have been something of a bombshell. To compound Refuge woes, cholera 'suddenly broke out' on the 14th February 1849 at its female establishment and 'raged for a fortnight with fatal malignity carrying off 13 of the inmates and two of the matrons'. Having dutifully attended the scene, Forster was inflicted and 'died on the 21st of the month after a short illness'.[15]

---

12. HO-45/1000–letters and internal memoranda dated January and February 1848.
13. The £1,500 Treasury grant, given to the Refuge on Home Secretary Sidmouth's recommendation in 1814, had been raised to £5,000 *per annum* in 1819. It stood there until reduced by Peel to £4,000 in 1827 and then £3,000 in 1828.
14. HO-45/1000–letter dated 12/10/1848 .
15. Refuge *Minutes*. The Refuge's decline in fortunes may also owe something to the loss of their champion in the Home Department. Prison inspector Crawford died when attending a Board meeting at Pentonville Prison in 1847. His colleague, Whitworth Russell, committed suicide in Millbank Prison that same year.

The Philanthropic enterprise was in a much healthier state. Some difficulty in obtaining competent masters who were intelligent, earnest and 'at the same time cheap men' had, admittedly, hindered efforts to put the family-based system fully into practice as intended. More happily, a doctor had not been required to attend any serious medical complaints and a 'kindly interest and goodwill' had replaced the 'hostile and distrustful feeling' expressed by some Redhill residents at the appearance of the Farm School on their doorsteps. What was more, the spectre of extinction that hovered over its diminishing subscriber base at the beginning of the 1840s had receded. Although funding worries would not entirely disappear, the society was now in a rather more favourable position to respond to risks arising from the sudden demise of any one of its partnership arrangements.

It also had a resident chaplain-superintendent-secretary who determinedly flourished his competence before Sir George Grey.[16] At least, that is, while treasurer Forster had been content to furnish the Home Secretary with a straightforward abstract of the Refuge's income and expenditure each year, Turner outshone by ensuring a detailed financial statement was submitted, together with a careful tally of the after-destinations and outcomes of the boys. This was capped by a cost-benefit analysis of Philanthropic reformation viewed from a variety of angles.[17] Turner's conscientious scrutiny of the extent to which the government had profited from its investment in the society's operations was, no doubt, appreciated. We might, indeed, consider Turner's Philanthropic apprenticeship duly rewarded. After the Reformatory Schools Act was passed in 1854, he was appointed as the first Inspector of Reformatory Schools. He took-up this position in 1857, the year that the Industrial Schools Act was entered on the statute books.

The Philanthropic Network for Reform: A Legislative Conundrum

The shaping of these entwined legislative landmarks in juvenile justice and welfare policy has been amply discussed elsewhere[18] and it is not the intention

---

16. Turner was given this expanded role, in 1847, to avoid an 'unfavourable appearance' being exposed when the existing secretary acted as the society's solicitor in pursuit of the revised Act of Incorporation.
17. HO-45/1649.
18. See, for instance, Owen (1964); Carlebach (1970); Pinchbeck and Hewitt (1973); Margery

here to retread this ground extensively. Nevertheless, as the Philanthropic Society's influence on the passage of the 1854 Act tends to be rather underplayed, it seems pertinent to bring this to prominence. For convenience, we will pick up the threads by returning to the year in which the *Mettray Report* provided an impetus for recasting the Philanthropic mould.

The legislative quest had gathered apace when a meeting of 'gentlemen and noblemen' convened in the Mansion House at the beginning of 1846. Had any Philanthropic trustees attended, they would, most likely, have been invigorated to hear Charles Pearson, solicitor to the City of London, expound on his solutions for checking the growth of juvenile crime and delinquency. Robustly advocating the establishment of a nationally organised system of asylums to which children under 'say 16 years, found violating the law, or in a state of destitution which will inevitably lead to crime' could be sent instead of being committed to prison, Pearson equally energetically endorsed the utility of 'market garden stuff and other productions of the soil' as a reformatory occupation.[19]

Around the same time, Captain Maconochie published a tract on the mark system of punishments and rewards he had devised for convicts in the penal colony at Norfolk Island, Australia. There, prisoners were encouraged into good conduct by having their sentences translated from the specified length of time to be served into an amount of labour to be worked. This publication, *Crime and Punishment: The Mark System*, was closely read by Turner who felt able to declare that Maconochie's methods provided 'admirable' incentives for the reformation of adult convicts. Even so, his experience of boys for whom 'the future is comparatively nothing, the present everything' led him to believe it was 'scarcely possible' to apply it to Philanthropic practice:

> because it is not possible to place before the boy ... an incentive sufficiently strong to arouse in him, and yet, sufficiently far distant to call out and exercise his fore-

---

(1978); May (1981); Radzinowicz and Hood (1986); Wiener (1990); Shore (1999); Duckworth (2002).

19. A copy of the paper Pearson presented was sent by the Lord Mayor to the Home Secretary for comment, preparatory to a general public meeting being held on the subject (HO-45/1471).

thought and continuous self-control; the *man* must live by *faith*, but the *boy*, I fear, must live by *sight*.²⁰

Convinced, instead, of the reforming effects that a more instantly gratifying portion of 'plumb pudding' had on Philanthropic boys, Turner had an opportunity to discuss and compare reformatory methods with Maconochie when that gentleman called at St. George's Fields in the summer of 1847. His visit took place just a few weeks before Sir John Pakington's Juvenile Offender's Bill was successfully steered through Parliament to allow persons, not exceeding 14 years, to be summarily convicted for acts of 'simple larceny'.²¹ That legislative concession to 'youth' was passed in the midst of Sir George Grey's very busy year and probably seemed like a beacon of encouragement to the gentlemen who composed the Philanthropic Petition in 1848. As we know, their plea for further legislative action was put in the bag at the House of Commons by Philanthropic committee member, Monckton Milnes and presented to the House of Lords by Philanthropic president, the Duke of Richmond. His Grace, however, failed to elicit a positive response from the Lords despite declaring it was 'not a party question' and that:

> When they saw what had been already done by the Philanthropic Society, there was a very cheering prospect that they might be able to extend their usefulness.²²

Philanthropic pressure was renewed the next summer. This came from Monckton Milnes who moved to bring in a Bill for amending the law relating to juvenile offenders. While we do not know quite how this poet, essayist and lion of literary salons came to be drawn to this particular subject, Milnes had voted for the abolition of capital punishment around the time he accompanied his friend William Makepeace Thackeray (an honorary member of the Philanthropic Society) to an execution at the beginning of the 1840s.²³ We might also imagine he had discussed the inter-linked topics of poverty, crime and delinquency with long-standing friends and

---

20. *Mettray Report* (1846) 2ⁿᵈ ed.
21. The age limit would be raised to 16 years in 1850.
22. *Hansard*/HoL-4/7/1848.
23. Milnes also amassed a vast collection of erotica.

Philanthropic vice-presidents William Ewart Gladstone and Viscount Ashley. Milnes, however, now took the opportunity of his slot in Parliamentary time to stress that:

> Amongst the various subjects which did and ought to occupy the time of the legislature of this country, there was no one of the social questions more interesting to the philanthropist than the discipline and reformation of juvenile offenders.[24]

Reminding members to 'particularly bear in mind, that in legislating on such a subject they were not dealing with any difficult question … the crime was petty larceny; the criminal, the children of the poor', he contended that confinement in contaminating local prisons was of 'utmost danger' to these offenders. As it did not prevent repeat offending it was also of 'great injury to society'. What was more, since all that was done at Parkhurst was 'chiefly to give the boy a strong impression of punishment, instead of awakening his conscience', Milnes wished to:

> press upon the Government the necessity of establishing some such asylum for the criminal youth of Great Britain as that of the Philanthropic Institution, which, under the able guidance of Mr Sydney Turner, had been made the equal of Mettray in France.

Remarkably, Home Secretary Sir George Grey was moved to say that he 'entirely concurred' in the 'eulogium' bestowed on the society and that 'Too much could not be said in praise of Mr. Turner, the excellent Secretary of that Institution'. His forbearance was not, however, bestowed upon Milnes's propositions. These were discarded with the scathing retort that:

> he should rather be disposed to accede at once to the Motion, if he believed that his hon. Friend had really a Bill in his possession. Everything in these matters depended, not on the expression of benevolent sentiments … but on the legal provisions which were necessary, and, at the same time, practicable, to give effect to these benevolent intentions.

---

24. *Hansard*/HoC-10/7/1849.

Sir George, indeed, felt obliged to protest against the assumption of the path of legislation being clear and easy. To his mind, it required a 'very nice hand' to balance the sentencing principles which ought to be kept in view; namely, 'the element which, by its deterring effect, repressed the commission of crime, and that which led to the reformation of those who were under punishment'. Nevertheless, as it was the duty of government to keep in view the reformation of juvenile offenders 'in a much greater degree than they were at liberty to do with criminals of a much more advanced age', he could assure Milnes that:

> he should be most willing to receive any suggestions on this subject; keeping in view the principle that crime required punishment, and that those who had been guilty of offences under the law ought not to be treated better than those who had not.

This legislative conundrum would not be satisfactorily resolved by Milnes. Admitting 'how difficult it was for individual members to grapple with a question of this kind', he had hoped his motion would prompt the Home Secretary to bring in a measure on the subject. With no movement evident from that quarter by the spring of 1850, Milnes attempted to bring forward an amended Bill.[25] This time, he confessed that:

> [his] connection with the Philanthropic Society had induced him to devote much attention to the dreadful state of the juvenile criminal population, the heavy cost and expense they entailed upon the country, while the means used for their reformation had proved inefficient.

He also invited members to see from the circumstances in which this 'class of boys' were placed that 'the wonder was, not that they were in prison, but that they were ever out of it'. Besides being a 'question of police', it was a 'Christian duty' to take care of the religious and moral education of those 'unfortunate children' by supporting his Bill. Indeed, its character could be described by reference to the inscription, placed by Pope Clement XI, over

---

25. *Hansard*/HoC-24/4/1850. Beforehand, Milnes had 'consulted' with police magistrates (including Philanthropic Mr. Paynter) and 'other persons of weight on the matter'.

the entrance to the industrial school for vagrant and delinquent juveniles attached to the Church of St. Michael in Rome:

> Perditis adolescentibus corrigendis
> Instituendisque,
> Ut qui inertes oberant
> Instructi Republicae Serviant[26]

His hopes were again shot through by the Home Secretary. Scattering withering criticism over Milnes's proposals, Sir George particularly doubted the expediency of establishing 'industrial schools' at public expense. Instead, he thought:

> such schools would be much more useful if supported by private charities, such as the Philanthropic Institution, which acted on this principle, but without ostentation. The Government sent juvenile offenders to it, on paying the expenses for which they would be chargeable if the prisoners had remained in gaol ... He had received only that morning a pamphlet from Mr W. Gladstone, the Treasurer of the Philanthropic Institution, containing a translation of a report presented to the National Assembly in France. Mr Gladstone differed to some extent from his views, but ... thought there should be two classes of these schools, one reformatory, and the other for the punishment of the wilfully criminal and vicious. The latter might be regarded as ordinary prisons, while the former, that gentleman thought they should be mainly founded by private benevolence.

Crushingly concluding that the 'machinery' of Milnes's proposed Bill was 'perfectly impracticable', Sir George added:

> it should not be forgotten that there was at this moment a Committee sitting upstairs on prison discipline, of which his hon. Friend was himself a member, and he thought it would be wise to wait for the report of that Committee before proceeding to legislate on the subject.

---

26. 'For the correction of young people who have lost their way/That whoever should experience it/Should, having been instructed/Be of service to the commonweal'. John Howard had been impressed by this industrial school/juvenile reformatory and, in his *State of the Prisons* (1777), had quoted another portion of inscription: *Parum est coerce improbus poena nisi probus efficas disciplina*—'It is doing little to restrain the bad by punishment unless you render them good by discipline'.

Notably, this Select Committee not only comprised Sir George and Monckton Milnes but Philanthropic committee member, Alderman Sidney. Also included were Sir John Pakington who had just presided at the Philanthropic Anniversary Dinner and city solicitor, Charles Pearson, who recently had descended on the Philanthropic Farm School with 'several other parties interested in the treatment of juvenile criminals and vagrants'.

By the end of the session, the Select Committee members were unable to offer any 'distinct recommendations' on the 'interesting question' of what system of prison discipline was best adapted to juvenile offenders. They were, however, 'of opinion' that a 'larger amount of industrial training and reformatory discipline might be advantageously adopted in their care than of ordinary criminals'.[27] In forming this view, they were to some extent guided by Captain Maconochie's evidence on how his mark system had been adapted for use in the then Borough Prison, Birmingham—from whence he sent boys to the Philanthropic on the 'Free List'.

The Select Committee had also listened to the Reverend Sydney Turner's views. This novice to Parliamentary proceedings was not given an altogether easy time. He was, unsurprisingly, able to provide a shining account of Philanthropic operations under questioning by Monckton Milnes and mentioned that the society now had only two children of convicts in residence. But, on parading the rigours of the Farm School's regime against the 'indulgences' enjoyed in prisons, Turner claimed that when the first Queen's Boys had come to the Philanthropic from Parkhurst:

> their complaints were endless; they had not the comforts they said, which they had before; they wanted more clothing; they wanted mittens, they wanted comforters around their necks. They wanted gruel at night and cocoa in the morning, and a variety of things of that sort.

At this, a keen nose for exaggeration—and an appetite for first-hand accounts—prompted the chairman to enquire whether he had 'actually ascertained' if the boys really had had those indulgences in Parkhurst. Turner then had to admit:

---

27. SC on Prison Discipline, PP (1850), Vol. XVII., Report.

I think they had not had the mittens or comforters; but they had been kept so much indoors that they did not feel the want of them; and at our place, where they had to go without caps, and to be in their common clothing in the open air for a great part of the day, they felt the influence of the weather.[28]

If this amendment skirted past the fact that the first Queen's Boys had been sent to toil within the Philanthropic Institution at St. George's Fields, other important visitors soon took time to actually ascertain how the Redhill Farm School experiment was being conducted. In September:

> Mr F. Hill Inspector of Prisons visited with Lord –Mr M. D. Hill Recorder of Birmingham, Mr Alcock, M.P. &c.–Mr Hill went very thoroughly into the details of the Boys discipline and employment and expressed himself much satisfied and interested.[29]

A similarly glowing accolade was received from 'Inspectors Mr Carleton Tuffnell and Mr Seymour Tremenheere' the next month. Both these gentlemen were inspectors of Poor Law schools. Edward Carleton Tuffnell (also Secretary of the London Statistical Society) had financially backed Kay-Shuttleworth's experiments in pauper education at Norwood and in the teacher-training establishment at Battersea. Hugh Seymour Tremenheere had been a revising barrister on the Western Circuit and was appointed one of the first inspectors of mines on the passing of Ashley's Mines Act of 1842. Like both Kay-Shuttleworth and Carleton Tuffnell, he had sympathy with educational ideas which advocated that habits of obedience should be fostered through affection rather than fear and had been consulted by Turner on these matters. He would also be thanked by the Philanthropic Committee gentlemen for recommending a schoolmaster from Cookham Union House for a situation at the Farm School.

Whilst the month of November saw Monsieur Ferras, Inspector General of Prisons in France, venture to Redhill, treasurer Gladstone took very great pleasure reporting, in June the next year, that:

---

28. SC on Prison Discipline, PP (1850), Vol. XVII., Minutes of Evidence, Q. 8290-1.
29. Frederic Hill was inspector of prisons for Scotland and the Northern District. He was brother to Matthew Davenport. Another brother, Rowland, found fame through Post Office reforms and innovations.

Mons. Demetz the celebrated founder of 'Mettray' had visited the Farm School and had expressed himself mighty interested and gratified with everything he had seen of its arrangement and management.[30]

Prince Albert then visited the Farm School in August. On that occasion, this royal Philanthropic patron:

> expressed himself highly pleased with the School and the state of the farm. He suggested that brickmaking, charcoal burning and grafting should be taught to the boys ... [and] ... has been pleased to signify his intention to bestow a Bounty of £10 per annum to be given in two sums of £5 each to the two lads who shall earn the best character in the School to be given to them at the end of twelve months service in North America and Australia respectively.

Soon afterwards, Turner was laid low by an 'infection of the chest followed by jaundice'. In September, he applied to the society for a few more weeks rest as his 'nervous system was so shaken'. He would later refer to this as a 'long illness'.[31] Hence, he may not have fully recovered by early December when a zealous band met at Birmingham, bent on swaying public opinion to the cause of reforming the laws relating to juvenile crime and delinquency. This national conference was convened on the initiative of Matthew Davenport Hill and Mary Carpenter. The latter personage had recently stimulated debate on the subject by publishing a book entitled, *Reformatory Schools for the Perishing and Dangerous Classes and for the Prevention of Juvenile Crime*. In this she called for the establishment of 'reformatory penal schools' under 'the guidance of enlightened Christian benevolence, sanctioned and mainly supported by government inspection and aid'.[32]

---

30. The visit provided an opportunity to cement links through an exchange of letters between the English and French boys. Perhaps Turner did not help over-much with the translation of the correspondence. Having again visited France in 1849, to 'renew and correct' his impressions of Mettray, he had thanked his travelling companion, treasurer Gladstone, for assisting 'most effectively with his knowledge of the language and his personal acquaintance with de Metz and de Courèilles'.
31. Turner's family had multiplied by this time. When the 1851 Census for Reigate was taken, in residence at the Farm School were: Sydney (36), Mary (40), Sharon (8), Gordon (6), Florence (5), Alfred (2) and George (3 months).
32. Carpenter (1851:349).

A Philanthropic perspective provides a fascinating insight on unfolding events. Indeed, as a further development in Farm School arrangements was entwined, we should note that on the 17th of December, treasurer Gladstone had waited upon Sir George Grey 'and had laid before him a proposition for the extension of the Society's operations in concert with the Government'. Turner then 'had gone up with the Deputation appointed by the Birmingham Conference — on Reformation Schools — to Sir George Grey', on the 27th of December, in the hope that the Home Secretary would bring in a Bill based on the conference resolutions. The deputation (which included treasurer Gladstone) met with a rather lukewarm response. Having assembled at the Ragged School Union Office and charging their spokesperson to confine his remarks to the conference resolutions, they headed-off to the Home Department. On returning, they agreed that Sir George had entertained discussion on the main points of the resolutions, but, had said:

> the Government would be ready to give its attention to any measure brought forward by gentlemen practically informed on the subject if the difficulty in the details could be overcome. He stated further that the Government had no general measure in contemplation and that if we thought it expedient he had no objection to a Parliamentary Committee of enquiry, but he considered that in many cases, such a course only tended to delay.

Sir George also intimated that he would be glad to hear details of the proposed Philanthropic scheme which, if 'practicable', he was disposed to help forward 'by all the means in his power'. As well, he was ready to see one or more of the society's members on the subject when the plan was 'more matured'.

Sir George seems not to have awaited a lengthy maturity. On the 24th of January 1852, he sped-off to visit the Farm School and conduct his own enquiries into the matter. An official letter from Whitehall shortly followed. As this clarifies otherwise cloudy details of the Philanthropic proposition and indicates how voluntary zeal could be reined in by government temperance, it is of interest to note that Under-Secretary Waddington relayed the following information:

> With reference to the proposal recently made by the Philanthropic Society to provide accommodation for 300 boys in the Society's Farm School at Redhill and also that the terms for the maintenance of such boys should be increased–I am directed by Secretary Sir George Grey to state that if the Committee of the Philanthropic Society can undertake to receive and provide for 100 boys to be recommended by the Secretary of State for the ensuing year, he will recommend to the Treasury that an estimate should be submitted to Parliament for the sum requisite to defray the expence of their maintenance for a year (irrespective of the term for which he may have been sentenced) at the rate of £18 a year together with the expence of the outfit or provision on leaving the School the amount however of such last named expence to be subject to the approval of the Inspector of Prisons for the District who will be instructed to inspect the School from time to time.
>
> I am to add that with respect to the proposal of the Committee to construct additional buildings, Sir George Grey cannot guarantee to the Committee the permanency of this arrangement, as it must be dependent on the sanction of Parliament.

Whether these provisos dampened the Philanthropic Society's ambition to be of extended 'public service', Philanthropic nerves were probably stretched on hearing that February had brought in a new administration. Upon this, Sir George was replaced by Spencer Walpole as Home Secretary. In March, however, prison inspector Captain Williams was able to assure Turner that 'the change in the Ministry will in no way disturb the arrangement'. A Special Committee of Philanthropic gentlemen also concluded that:

> With regard to these proposals we believe that they may be safely regarded as originating not solely from the heads of Departments liable to change, but in truth from the Executive Government which must be viewed as the Agent of the whole Community, the Public having been at length fully convinced that the time has arrived for active intervention and that no further delay should be allowed in adopting some practical and general measures for checking the growth and the spread of Juvenile Delinquency.

If we have wondered quite why the Home Department had been so supportive of the Philanthropic reformatory experiment and by now suspect it was being used to test the 'machinery' of legislative action, these gentlemen also took that matter into consideration. They continued:

> No doubt could ever have arisen that the most feasible and obvious measure would in the first instance be to offer aid to an Institution already well organised and in successful operation–

It would also seem probable that the course now decided upon has been determined not for the simple object of availing themselves of the assistance and Agency of the Philanthropic Society in the rescue of Juvenile Offenders upon the comparatively small scale on which it could be conducted by one Institution in one District, but mainly for the purpose of showing by the experience and proofs which will be afforded by the Redhill Schools what may be effected and at what cost in other parts of the Country by the exertions of Charitable Associations combined with the Government aid.[33]

This conception of the society's experimental piloting role is striking. Its echoes pervaded proceedings at the following Anniversary Dinner. That event reminds us, indeed, of how Philanthropic fortunes had blossomed since the gloomy 1820s when many such fund-raising occasions had been postponed for lack of support. On the 8th May 1852, however, the society could trumpet that a spectacular £1,400 had been pledged that evening in aid of an extension of the Farm School. It was also able to flaunt before the public gaze a very impressive guest-list of Philanthropic enthusiasts.[34] Despite many gentlemen being prevented from attending by the 'superior attractions' of the Mansion House (where the Lord Mayor was entertaining Prime Minister Earl Derby and Her Majesty's other Ministers), vice-president William Ewart Gladstone presided as chairman and was flanked by his brother-in-law, Lord Lyttleton, who represented the House of Lords on the night. Under-Secretary at the Home Department, Sir William Jolliffe, also took a prominent part in the proceedings as did prison inspectors Captain Williams and H. H. D. O'Brien along with Monckton Milnes and fellow MP, Mr. Charles Bowyer Adderley.

Just as strikingly, chairman Gladstone's speech encapsulated an increasingly influential currency of thought on the role of voluntary organizations in civil society. Flexing his powers of oratory to pay tribute to a Philanthropic undertaking that promised 'interesting results to the happiness and virtue of the country', he declaimed:

---

33. The Redhill Schools referred to were the houses in which different divisions of boys resided under the care of a master and a matron. Scattered around the grounds to mirror English rural style, their arrangement was of marked contrast to the Mettray Institution's rather formal setting and regimented design.
34. A newspaper report on the proceedings was ordered to be reprinted for wider circulation.

> It was a great characteristic of England, that in this land many problems were solved by private enterprise, by private benevolence, and by the spirit of the Christian religion. Difficult questions were first approached and were often finally solved by the efforts of individuals, with which the public law and the institutions of the country would never have ventured to grapple.

This, Gladstone added, 'had been the case with the question of the reform of juvenile offenders'. On that 'most difficult and, unquestionably the most interesting of all matters', the society had been 'ready to tread on unbroken ground' and had 'actually effected, had laid the foundation on which the officers of the Government might tread'. In doing so, it had not proceeded 'on any visionary theory, but on facts' such as those laid out in the latest Philanthropic Report. These showed that of the 114 boys now in the school:

> forty-five or less than the moiety, had both parents alive; 54 had lost either father or mother, and 15 were wholly orphans, and of those who had parents living some 30 of those parents were bad or indifferent characters.

Such 'figures', he continued, were 'a more conclusive demonstration than could be provided by any argument, however elaborate' that the 'principle of pity and commiseration were the sentiments appropriate to these children'. For them, the principle of punishment required 'modification', for:

> the strong hand of public justice was too rigid and severe ... it spared too little, and crushed too much ... when in the case of children you applied to them in its full breadth, the doctrine that man was responsible, and was to be made responsible ... Surely the common principle of responsibility must be modified as regards to them; whatever was said about the free agency of man, and however necessary it was to apply it to adults, yet in regard to these poor children, it was a mockery and cruelty to give it full course (loud applause). If that was so, then ... the promoters of the charity were not only giving free scope to a benevolent impulse, but were acting strictly on the logical deduction of the understanding, when they said 'Let us see if we cannot supply something which, whilst it will not induce and tempt to crime by laxity and indulgence, shall, on the other hand, mitigate the severity of public discipline by the elements of kindness and attachment–by something less stern than the countenance of a turnkey and the doors of a prison ...'

Did his audience appreciate how these reflections of the Philanthropic founders' sentiments were entwined with their Enlightenment ambition to solve social problems through the rational application of knowledge? While we cannot be sure they did so, we can be rather more certain that chairman Gladstone's evidence was gleaned on a recent visit to Redhill and a close perusal of the society's records. As his diary notes, he visited the Farm School on the 24th of April and made a short address to the boys. On that occasion, his Philanthropic treasurer cousin was in attendance along with Monckton Milnes. The entry for the 8th of May records: 'Read the Philanthropic Reports — & presided at their Dinner at the London Tavern, 5¾-11½. Lady Palmerston's afterwards'.[35]

Before departing, however, chairman Gladstone had extracted even more 'loud applause' from the Philanthropic diners when announcing that the House of Commons:

> [had] appointed a Committee to devote special attention to the question and, the first witnesses to be examined would be the enlightened and benevolent officers of this Society–to gather the fruits of their experience, and render them available in a wider circle.

The Philanthropic Network for Reform: Reasons to be Cheerful

And yes, the previous day a Select Committee on Criminal and Destitute Juveniles had met. Monckton Milnes, Mr. Adderley and Sir William Jolliffe were amongst the members who elected Mr. Baines of the Poor Law Board into the chair. They then briefly deliberated and, before adjourning, Adderley 'stated that Mr. Sydney Turner would be prepared to attend and give evidence'.[36]

There is no room here to note all the individuals who came forth to offer frequently contradictory opinion as to which children the principle of *parens patriae* should be extended; to what type of institution they should be sent; quite how the principle of *doli incapax* had been interpreted and whether the Napoleonic Code's concept of *sans discernment* had more merit.

---

35. As transcribed by Foot and Matthews (1974).
36. SC on Criminal and Destitute Juveniles. PP (1852), Vol. VII., *Proceedings*.

Although witnesses also tussled over the benefits a period of prior imprisonment might—or might not—bring to young offenders deemed deserving of reformatory treatment, Matthew Davenport Hill attended and disclosed he had:

> had occasion to pay a good deal of attention to the mode of treatment at Mettray and Redhill, which is the School of the Philanthropic Society, who have been so fortunate as to obtain the services of my excellent friend, Mr Sydney Turner.[37]

Hill would also mention the ominous lack of funds which threatened the survival of the Stretton-on-Dunsmore enterprise. So too did Serjeant Adams.[38] He also explained why he had left the Philanthropic fellowship. As this bluff character related:

> I withdrew my name from the Old Philanthropic Society for this reason; that they took the children of felons, and apprenticed them with premiums, sometimes amounting to 20*l*. to people at home. I said, 'You are in error from beginning to end; what right have you to be giving felons, and to the children of felons, 20*l*.; when you will not give 5*l*. to the children of honest hard-working people?'[39]

Serjeant Adams also claimed he had introduced into the Parkhurst Prison Act the provision which gave power to send convicted children to reformatory schools on conditional pardon. This, he confided, was taken from the system operating in the Children's Friend Society, but it:

> became a dead letter as the Prison Inspectors set themselves against it; they said that a child who had committed an offence was a child of the state, and not the subject of private benevolence. I remember saying to one of them, 'God bless me Sir! Is a child who had stolen a penny tart, to become a prisoner of the state.[40]

---

37. SC on Juveniles, PP (1852), Vol. VII., Q.415.
38. During the passage of the Reformatory Schools Act, Lord Brougham would regret to say that Stretton 'had, within the last six weeks, come to an end from the want of funds' (*Hansard*, HoL-11/5/1854).
39. SC on Juveniles, PP (1852), Vol. VII., Q.1873.
40. SC on Juveniles, PP (1852), Vol. VII., Q.1854-61.

That Clause XI had become a 'dead letter' seems a curious assertion. Particularly so if we have been correct in believing it was the legal foundation on which Home Secretary, Sir James Graham, sought to establish a union between the Philanthropic and the Refuge. It also had provided a statutory basis for Sir George Grey sending Queen's Boys to St. George's Fields. But, while Serjeant Adams may have been alluding to opposition initially expressed by prison inspectors Crawford and Whitworth Russell, it is reassuring to find Captain Williams now highlighting his role in 'extending' that 'very beneficial clause' in Philanthropic partnership. As outlined to the Select Committee, this prison inspector had applied it first of all to boys in Millbank 'who were really so diminutive, and also of an age which seemed to render them quite unfit for transportation at all or even being sent to Parkhurst'. On finding the majority turned out 'remarkably well' he had been 'induced' to pay more attention to the Philanthropic Society. He then:

> recommended to the Secretary of State that it should be extended to young offenders in the prisons of the metropolis and elsewhere. Sir George Grey was pleased to consent to this, and I have since that time been selecting a number of boys from the Westminster House of Correction principally, and also from other prisons, who have been sent to the Philanthropic Society at the charge of the Government, and the experiment is still working remarkably well; indeed, has far exceeded my utmost expectations.[41]

Equally remarkable, when asked about the 'principle' on which the boys were selected, Williams not only illustrated the referral process but revealed he had devised a special contract for them to sign. As he explained:

> When there are any boys required to fill up vacancies in the Philanthropic Society I go to the Westminster Bridewell or to the other prisons, and I confer with the Chaplain and the Governor upon the subject, and select a number of boys for examination. A boy is brought before me, in the presence of the Chaplain, and I ask him if he is willing or has any wish to leave the life he is leading. If he says that he has, I proceed to take his examination in writing, telling him that it is within my power to recommend him for a conditional pardon, on condition of going to this charitable institution, and going abroad afterwards, if he wishes it. I also tell him that he must enter into an agreement, I may say with myself, for it is a sort of agreement between

---

41. SC on Juveniles, PP (1852), Vol. VII., Q. 19-20.

him and myself, that he must tell me everything that he has done or committed during the whole course of his life, in order that I may know that he is prepared to lead a new life and speak the truth hereafter; that if I detect any falsehood the condition is broken between us, and I cannot recommend him. In some cases they consent to this; in many they do not. I then proceed with their examination.[42]

Then probed for an explanation of why some boys wouldn't consent, Williams cited an 'extraordinary case of refusal'. This, he knew, had been witnessed 'only that morning' by Adderley at Westminster Bridewell on the part of:

a little boy about ten or eleven years of age, who had been eleven times in that prison. He was not as high as this table. I had sent his brother previously to the Philanthropic Society, who is doing remarkably well; in fact, although completely a professional thief, he surprises me by the way he has already conformed to the rules. This little boy refuses to go. I have tried every inducement to get the boy to go, but he will not, nor will he give me any reason why not.[43]

That this resistance might have stemmed from the little boy's canny consideration of the indeterminate length of the Philanthropic Reformatory care package was not lost on committee members. They also heard Turner confirm that similar thoughts created a 'restlessness' which often caused boys to abscond. These defections continued to pose difficulties for the society. Although the 'prize' of going abroad provided an incentive to good behaviour, the Philanthropic still had no legal powers of control over boys who were not apprenticed. Nor did it have compulsory powers to detain boys sent on conditional pardon once their sentence term expired.[44] Nevertheless, the innovative contract was signed by many boys including S. Piggot, who

---

42. SC on Juveniles, PP (1852), Vol. VII., Q.22. The contract was as follows: ' I do hereby acknowledge that the clause in the above related Act has been read over and explained to me, and that of my own free will and accord do promise that I will conform to the rules of the Philanthropic Farm School. And will go abroad whenever I may be found sufficiently instructed for employment by the governors of that Institution, and that I receive my pardon upon such a condition' (at Q.61).
43. SC on Juveniles, PP (1852), Vol. VII., Q.43.
44. Clause XI had provided power to bring Queen's Boys who flouted the Institution's rules before a court and for them to be confined in a gaol or house of correction. For those who were not Queen's Boys, Williams mentioned the ruse of bringing re-captured absconders before magistrates and claiming that they had 'stolen the Chaplain's clothes'.

was aged 15 years when admitted in March 1852. Sentenced at the Central Criminal Court (Old Bailey) to 12 months in Wandsworth House of Correction for uttering false coins, he had been imprisoned before and was known as 'a regular smasher'. His mother and connections were 'all very bad'.[45]

James Splan, however, was delivered into the Farm School through an especially noteworthy route of private zeal. Even before delegates were summoned to the Birmingham Conference in 1851, he had travelled to Redhill on the recommendation of Miss Mary Carpenter of Great George Street, Bristol. James was ten years old when admitted on the 26th of September 1851 on terms of 1s/6d per week from his parents and £1.1s. annually by Miss Carpenter. As his Philanthropic record reveals, James had been:

> charged at Bristol–stealing–one months imprisonment Bristol Gaol–convicted twice before (both for stealing–twice with the same punishment)–schools attended: St James' Back Ragged School very irregularly.

This appears to be the 'Jemmy S.' referred to by Mary Carpenter before the Select Committee of 1852 as testimony to the need for reformatories conducted on the 'family' lines of the Philanthropic. It is thus of interest to find that the cords of love that she advocated, had not been altogether successfully applied to her protégé. Jemmy took an opportunity to abscond on the 3rd of November and, after being retrieved, was fined for swearing on the 21st of December. Again fined for swearing on the 12th of July 1852, he was then confined in the cells for robbing an orchard. As with boys who engaged in early Philanthropic escapades, this punishment did not deter him. On the 21st of August, he was whipped for getting through a window and again robbing an orchard. On the 30th of September, Jemmy was 'returned to Bristol (Miss Carpenter's School, Kingswood)'.

Much has been made of how Mary Carpenter's case against the coercive character of Parkhurst's regime was tarnished by the discovery that she had not visited this establishment and thus had not 'actually ascertained' it no longer used fetters of iron on its boys.[46] She could, however, speak with more

---

45. 'Smasher' was a cant term for the profession of people who passed false money.
46. Miss Carpenter's favoured philosophy would be re-articulated in her book *Juvenile*

authority on the Philanthropic experiment. The Farm School had not been omitted from her itinerary of personal investigation. Miss Carpenter had travelled to Redhill in July 1851 and, on leaving, she was accompanied to the railway station by James Shaughnessy. Aged 16 years when admitted, James was another former pupil of the St. James' Back Ragged School. Regrettably, this protégé returned from his chivalrous expedition 'totally intoxicated'.

Continuing bad behaviour—and the prospect of keeping him 'as a prisoner in the cell' if retained—led to 'the boy Shaughnessy' being discharged 'with as much shew of disgrace as possible for his great ingratitude to the society and Miss Carpenter'. James was then sent back to Bristol:

> in charge of an officer of the School by Government train to Hungerford leaving him to walk from thence to Bristol ... being about 17 years old & stout & manly–he will easily do this–the Chaplain gave him a route from Marlborough to Chippenham & gave him four shillings for his expenses on the road.

James successfully petitioned to return to Redhill the next June. He was supported in his request by Miss Carpenter who wrote to inform the society that James had 'behaved very well since his return to Bristol but from his having been before in prison [for felony] he has not been able to procure employment'. James was then helped emigrate to New York on the 12th of August.

Had James met Charles Dickens just before travelling over the seas? We might like to think so. A few days previously, that gentleman had talked to some of the boys as he toured around the Farm School 'with the intention of making it the subject of an article'. This was published in *Household Words* on the 11th of September 1852. It undoubtedly provided a vehicle for pricking consciences at the plight of the thousands of neglected children who languished in desolate urban courts and alleys and 'went to pieces for the want of mending'. It was also adeptly employed as a tool for lauding the Philanthropic enterprise in juxtaposition with castigating Parkhurst's 'blind reliance' on a rigid system of discipline. Indeed, Dickens was not only glad to find that at Redhill the 'rules were few, the punishments still fewer', but,

---

Delinquents (1853). It also had been embraced by John Brewster who, when advocating the utility of a penitentiary–rather than punitive–approach to offenders in 1792, had said: 'There are cords of love as well as fetters of iron' (cited in Ignatieff, 1978:74). This may be the Rev. John Brewster who recommended Jane Scorry/Scurrah to the Philanthropic Society in 1807.

in that Arcadia, the boys leaving-off work for dinner could 'gambol about, and roll over one another on the grass, with a confidence in meeting no check while they do no wrong'. And, if this inclined him 'then and there to strongly embrace the chaplain', he received it as another 'encouraging sign' that:

> the good chaplain does not deem it needful to put on his religion in the out-ward and visible form of a grievous waistcoat, or to make it known to all men by wearing a clear-starched dog-collar around his throat.

We do not know whether this intimate portrait of Turner made an equally favourable impression on all that journal's readers. Neither are we informed if the visit had been suggested by his friend and fellow advocate of social reform, Monckton Milnes. It might even have been sparked by Philanthropic vice-president Viscount Ashley, with whom Dickens had discussed a proposition for opening a ragged school. Nevertheless, another friend, the wealthy Miss Burdett Coutts, afterwards visited the Farm School 'two or three times' and donated £50.[47] In May 1853, the society had the further satisfaction of accepting treasurer Gladstone's offer to fund the erection of 'a Gas Works on the Farm, for the purpose of testing the manufacture of Gas from Vegetable Oil'.[48]

In June, Ashley (now Earl of Shaftesbury) offered the House of Lords yet another solution to the problem of juvenile crime and delinquency. It took the form of a Juvenile Mendicancy Bill. This sought to lay down the principle that children should be taken from parents who sent them into the streets to beg and then lived in 'idleness and profligacy' on the earnings. It also aimed to eradicate that 'evil' by holding those who acted that way 'responsible for the maintenance of their children in their persons and their purses'.[49] This, Shaftesbury claimed, was a remedy 'within compass'. The judicially experienced Mr. Serjeant Adams had assured him that 'the ability

---

47. Dickens and this heiress had been involved in setting-up the Urania Cottage for 'fallen women'.
48. This 'experiment' was conceived with the idea of adapting coal gas apparatus for the use of rape-seed oil–and hence lighting the Farm School premises as well as providing agricultural employment for the boys.
49. *Hansard*/HoL -28/6/1853.

of these parents to support their children was the rule, not the exception'. As well, the Bill had received 'the full approbation of that zealous and intelligent body—the police magistrates'.

Regrettably, even though Shaftesbury sought to 'strengthen his case' by a 'quotation' of these gentlemen's names, he did not carry the House.[50] The Bill was then put into the hands of the Poor Law Board for further consideration. Shaftesbury soon heard, however, that an 'insuperable difficulty' surrounded his suggestion of taking-up children found in a state of vagrancy and placing them in the workhouse. Fellow Philanthropic vice-president the Earl of Harrowby did, indeed, lend support by declaring the Bill's principle 'was to treat the children virtually as orphans, as having parents who were worse than dead'.[51] The Poor Law Commissioners, however, were 'of opinion' that:

> it would render these establishments distasteful to the poor if the feeling once got abroad that persons were placed there who were destitute and criminal.

The Lord Chancellor was inclined to agree. As well, he was disposed to rebut Shaftesbury's interjection of 'Not Criminal' with the comment that:

> The noble Lord has said these children were not criminal; but they are so nearly criminal, that it would be difficult to give any definition of criminality which did not include them.[52]

This blurring of distinctions was not new. It had resonated around the Philanthropic Society's early efforts to straddle the spheres of penal and pauper law and prevent children sliding from destitution or parental neglect into crime. It continued to cloud the matter of formulating legislation when Adderley introduced a Juvenile Offender's Bill in the House of Commons the next

---

50. The police magistrates again included the Philanthropic Mr. Paynter.
51. Before being elected vice-president in the place of his late father in 1847, Harrowby (then Viscount Sandon) had sent boys to the Philanthropic on payment by the association of Staffordshire Magistrates . He sat on the Farm School Management Committee with Lord Westminster and was chairman of the Society for the Promotion of Colonisation. He was also President of the Royal Statistical Society and a member of the Geographical Society.
52. *Hansard*/HoL–12/7/1853.

day. This, he argued, was a measure the country was 'ripe' to receive. It 'was but a corollary' to Pakington's Act of 1847. Its object was the establishment of reformatory schools to which 'young children detected in the commission of offences and vagrant children might be sent by magistrates'. Not only had magistrates and justices 'anticipated the legislation, and taken the law into their hands by adopting most of the provisions contained in the Bill', but:

> the House should remember that the theory of this Bill had already been adopted in this country. It was adopted by the Philanthropic Institution, which was first established in 1806, nearly half a century ago, by a private Act of Parliament.[53]

Viscount Palmerston did not swoop to rush the Bill through. This new Home Secretary did, nonetheless, bend far enough to 'trust' that a measure upon the subject would be passed the next session. He also proposed that:

> we might combine this with that measure—the Juvenile Mendicancy Bill—which came down from the House of Lords ... [and] ... the best thing which hon. Members can do in this matter is to read, during the recess, the evidence taken before the [Select] Committee ... If they do that, we shall be able, when Parliament meets again, to enter into a discussion of the question, with a view to some immediate and practical measure.[54]

With no draft legislation appearing by the opening of the session, the Philanthropic Network for Reform ensured that pressure did not wane by calling another Birmingham Conference. This was attended by the Reverend Sydney Turner who was charged with representing the society's views. On returning, he was happy to relate that:

> the proceedings as fully reported in the Daily Papers were of a most encouraging description, both as regards the general cause of Legislation for Juvenile Delinquency and as refers to the efforts of the Philanthropic Society and their appreciation by the Conference.

---

53. *Hansard*/HoC–13/7/1853.
54. *Hansard*/HoC–14/7/1853. The Administration had changed hands again in December 1852.

Meanwhile, the society had been exploring the advantages of forging links with the Privy Council Committee of Education. The overtures were led by Monckton Milnes and treasurer Gladstone and revolved around the belief that regular scrutiny by one of the inspectors of pauper and workhouse schools would 'stimulate the Teachers and Officers on one hand and give a satisfactory guarantee for the utility and efficiency of the system' at Redhill on the other. Hopes of capturing funds also entered their calculations.

In response, the Lord President of the Council found 'no difficulty' in directing Carleton Tuffnell to inspect and report on the Farm School. Disappointingly, as the society's operations were deemed not to fit into the scheme for pauper schools as set out in a Privy Council Minute of December 1846, Earl Granville was 'not prepared to advise appropriation of any part of the Parliamentary Grant for Education towards its maintenance'. But, as a new minute was in contemplation, he was willing to entertain the society's thoughts on combining with the Privy Council Committee:

> to promote the establishment of Practising Schools upon the Kneller Hall estate ... either by the promotion of a second school, or by the transfer of the Establishment from Redhill.

The potential of such a partnership had been recognised and pursued by the society at the beginning of 1847. Yet, upon the proposition now looming into view, the Philanthropic gentlemen decided:

> [it] would not only be to sacrifice a large portion of the outlay which the Society have incurred (£16,000) ... but would be to interrupt and suspend for a year or two the beneficial agency that they are carrying on–without so far as they can see, any equivalent advantages either as regards the Public, or as regards the Charitable trusts they are administering.

Attention again focused on the Home Department. Wishing to extend the Farm School's utility even further, the society sought to increase the number of boys received on the government account with the assistance of a 'moderate' building grant. By the turn of the year, a Philanthropic deputation could report that the Home Secretary was prepared to increase the number of government boys to 200 and had 'thought that there was every reason for the connection of the Government and the School being maintained and enlarged'. Home Secretary Palmerston also indicated he was willing to have the society's views on government help with building costs laid before him in writing.

This was duly done and the Lord Commissioners of the Treasury were soon occupied in considering 'the propriety of expending so large a sum of money upon the buildings of an Institution over which the Government possesses no direct control'. They were also anxious to know 'whether the Committee was willing to give any security that the accommodation created in the manner proposed shall always be held at the disposal of the Government'. As the Philanthropic was, indeed, willing to provide guarantees under its corporate seal, the Treasury conceded to an additional yearly payment 'in the way of rent of £2 per head … in consideration of the Society's gradually carrying out and enlarging the School from their own resources'. Whilst we are left to ponder upon the possibility of Philanthropic vice-president Gladstone — now Chancellor of the Exchequer — playing a part in these arrangements, the agreement was cemented in a letter received from Treasury Chambers on the 2nd of August.

On the 10th of August 1854, a Reformatory Schools Act finally arrived on the Statute Book. Defining the slippery concept of 'juvenile offender' as any person under the age of 16 years convicted of an offence punishable by law, either on indictment or on summary conviction, this Act for the Better Care and Reformation of Youthful Offenders in Great Britain, was hailed by Matthew Davenport Hill as the Magna Carta of the neglected child. Even so, pressure on Parliament did not abate. Having achieved this degree of success, the Philanthropic Network for Reform continued their quest for legislation that embraced other categories of children in the Philanthropic founders' sights at the end of the 18th-century. Based on a Bill laid down by Adderley, an Act to make better provision for the Care and Education of vagrant, destitute, and disorderly Children and for the Extension of Industrial Schools then passed through Parliament on the 17th of August 1857.

By then, Sir George Grey had been re-installed as Home Secretary. The Farm School extension was also underway with the help of a magnificent personal donation of £1,000 from treasurer William Gladstone. Even more dramatically, the year 1857 had dawned on the Philanthropic world with the 'zealous, clever, and active' Reverend Sydney Turner informing the society, that:

> Sir George Grey has been pleased to confer on me the Appointment of Inspector of Prisons with special reference to Reformatory Schools–and that after a careful consideration of the matter I have felt it to be my duty to accept the appointment.

CHAPTER 8

INTO THE FUTURE

The provisions of the Reformatory Schools Act of 1854 mirrored many of the 'mechanisms' which had been pragmatically tested by the Home Department in Philanthropic partnership. Recognising the merits of a union between voluntarism and government regulation and aid, reformatory schools were to be privately run institutions, the directors or managers of which had to apply to the Secretary of State for certification. Establishments whose 'Conditions and Regulations' proved satisfactory were, thereafter, to be subject to the surveillance of one of Her Majesty's Inspectors of Prisons 'from Time to Time'. Power was also given to the Treasury to defray, at a *per capita* rate, the whole cost of the care and maintenance of juvenile offenders or such portion of the cost that was not recovered from parents or step-parents. For those who had 'sufficient ability to bear the cost', the Act followed Philanthropic precedent by setting parental responsibility at a sum not exceeding five shillings a week. In addition, however, reformatory school trustees were provided with the long-elusive power of taking any absconding juvenile offender before a police magistrate or justice of the peace who could then commit the miscreant to any prison or house of correction for up to three months — with or without hard labour.

As an answer to the 'interesting question' of how to balance the deterrent and retributive principles of punishment with reformative and welfare-orientated sentiments, this legislation responded with an equally interesting compromise. On one hand, the Act empowered courts to send juvenile offenders to reformatory schools for a term of between two and five years and, on the other, declared that this could only take place once a mandatory sentence of fourteen days imprisonment had been served. This prior imprisonment proviso may not have pleased those amongst the campaigners who believed the coercive impact — if not the corrupting potential — of even such a short, sharp, shock of incarceration would undermine reformative outcomes. Even so, the Act did bow to the requirement of punishing wrongdoing with some certainty and also acknowledged that youthful offenders were in a state of dependency and not entirely responsible for their actions.

The Industrial Schools Act of 1857 again acknowledged the benefits of government and voluntary agency partnership. Certification and inspection was, however, placed under the aegis of the Privy Council Committee of Education and no provision was made for Treasury grants. Parents deemed able to do so were, nevertheless, expected to contribute the lesser sum of up to three shillings a week towards the maintenance, training and education of their children. In cases where a child previously had been 'taken into custody on a Charge of Vagrancy' but released on the parent's written assurance of being responsible for their good behaviour, when a further committal was attributed to parental neglect the courts could punish parents by the infliction of a fine.

Although these Acts laid down the tracks on which a system of state-aided but voluntary managed institutions would develop, a series of revisions swiftly followed.[1] Two further Acts of 1866 invoked particularly noteworthy amendments. In regard to the Act relating to Reformatory Schools, scope was provided for reducing the term of prior imprisonment to ten days. This legislation also revived the 'beneficial' Clause XI of the Parkhurst Prison Act by enabling the Home Secretary to send youthful offenders 'convicted of an offence punishable with penal servitude or imprisonment' to these institutions on conditional pardon. As for industrial schools: while Treasury funds had come their way in 1861, the consolidating Act of 1866 decreed that their regulation should shift to the purview of the Inspector of Reformatories. It also extended the 'classes' that could be detained under its provisions. Besides children beyond the control of their parents, those who were under 12 years of age and charged with offences other than felony were included. So too were children, maintained in workhouses or pauper schools, who were deemed 'refractory' or who had a parent 'convicted of a Crime or an Offence punishable with penal servitude or imprisonment'. The legislation also embraced children discovered begging on the street, of criminal parentage or who frequented 'the Company of reputed thieves'.

---

1. Children in Scotland and Ireland experienced the fruits of different legislative trajectories.

These categories of children had not been overlooked by the Philanthropic founders. Brought together by a common conviction that their crime prevention experiment would add to the sum of national happiness, these gentlemen of utilitarian bent would, nevertheless, have been astonished to see how specialised the Philanthropic remit had become. Although not averse to seeking a minimal level of government help in furthering the goals of their voluntary enterprise, they would have been just as amazed to discover how the society's funding arrangements now reflected a shift in conceptions about the appropriate roles of civil society and the State in solving social problems.

Caution, however, remained the watchword at the heart of State. Political will still fell short of taking the initiative in statutorily cementing partnership arrangements. Although the potential benefits had been recognised at the heart of the Home Department and an engagement of mutual interests took a leap forward under the auspices of Sir George Grey, the Colonial Office's reluctance to facilitate the emigration element of Philanthropic operations—as well as the Privy Council committee's hesitancy in providing an education grant—remind us that State intervention was undertaken mainly as a last resort.

With this political culture prevailing, it is conceivable that the Reformatory and Industrial Schools Acts would have been even more delayed had it not been for the Philanthropic Network's zeal in pressing the case for new laws before Parliament and the public. This constellation of Philanthropic friends and trustees—with interests in politics, the arts, penal and pauper law as well as health and education administration—embodied the Enlightenment modes of thought which had percolated through the interlacing circles of early Philanthropic acquaintance. Drawn together by a common concern for social improvement, many became leading lights in the National Association for the Promotion of Social Science (NAPSS). Established in 1857 with Lord Brougham at its head, the NAPSS was reminiscent of Philanthropic founder Robert Young's Social Union for the Improvement of Civil Society. Reflecting an English empirical tradition in social science that was 'eclectic in its choice of problems,'[2] its first 'departments' were devoted to gathering knowledge on jurisprudence and amendment of the law, education, punish-

---

2. Pinker (1971:65).

ment and reformation, public health and social economy. Its membership included Kay-Shuttleworth and Chadwick as well as Matthew Davenport Hill, Mary Carpenter, Sir John Pakington, Charles Adderley and Monckton Milnes. The Reverend Sydney Turner, who also was a member, delivered the inaugural sermon entitled *Responsibility in Aims and Means*. As Brougham explained in his opening *Address*, its labours could be regarded as 'ancillary to the action of the State' in aiming to aid legislation 'by preparing measures, by explaining them, by recommending them to the community, or, it may be, by stimulating the Legislature to adopt them'.[3]

That enlightened ambition was already supported in other practical ways. As Turner disclosed to the Philanthropic committee in 1855, he had joined a meeting of 'gentlemen interested in the Reformatory Movement', held at the residence of Barwick Baker at Hardwicke Court, Gloucestershire. In consequence:

> it had been resolved to form a Reformatory Association or Union of which the chief object would be to collect and disseminate information–to prompt & watch legislation, and to promote practical efforts–on the subject of the Reformation of Juvenile Offenders. To assist & watch over the young persons discharged from Reformatory Schools after they have left the Schools–and to secure the training & preparation of suitable Masters & Teachers.[4]

Turner also mentioned that he was instructed by that meeting 'to request the cooperation of the Philanthropic Society & that he had consented on the part of the Society to the use of their office up to Xmas for the purposes of the Union'. To this arrangement the committee readily agreed and, 'heartily' concurring with the proposed objects, recommended the Reformatory Union to the 'support of all the friends of the Society'.[5]

---

3. *Inaugural Address* (1858). Brougham had instigated the society's formation by calling a meeting at his house in July 1857, just before the Industrial Schools Act was passed.
4. The flush of reformatory schools established at this time included one founded by Adderly on his estate in Staffordshire and another which prison inspector O'Brien established in Newcastle-on-Tyne. Mary Carpenter also founded a reformatory school for girls at Red Lodge, Bristol.
5. The society had secured a London office in Crown Court, Threadneedle Street.

Surprisingly, the Philanthropic gentlemen had continued to manage the Farm School outwith the provisions of the Reformatory Schools Act. In view of their tenacious legislative quest we can scarcely resist noting that—shortly after the Act was passed—they had met to consider a communication from the Home Department. This informed them that:

> A case having recently occurred at the Quarter Sessions for the County of Worcester in which a boy named William Humphries has been sentenced to be imprisoned for one month–and at the expiration of that period to be sent to the Philanthropic's Farm School at Redhill for Five Years. I am directed by Viscount Palmerston to request to be informed whether the Society has any wish that the Institution should be certified under the provisions of the 17 & 18 Vict.–cap 86–Sec. 1.

They did not rush to be certified. Instead, Turner was instructed to reply that:

> The arrangements which Viscount Palmerston has lately sanctioned for the reception to the Farm School for a larger number of Juvenile Offenders on the recommendation of the Secretary of State–together with the Society's charitable operations in cases admitted gratuitously; or on the application of subscribers and others–will fully engage their means and resources of Reformatory action for some time to come.

The lack of certification did not hamper the dispatch of prison inspector Captain Williams to the Farm School next year. His visit was in response to an allegation (made by one of the masters) that Turner had flogged some boys until the floor was 'sprinkled with blood'. Refuting the accusation — declaring that it was 'all falsehood and gross exaggeration' and that 'no boy was ever punished by me more severely than he would be at any public school for any serious offence' — Turner was, no doubt, relieved to receive a reassuring letter from Under Secretary Waddington. This advised him that Home Secretary, Sir George Grey, had:

> received from Captain Williams a report of the result of his investigation into a statement made by Mr. Harries imputing to you cruelty in the punishment of whipping inflicted upon the inmates of the Philanthropic Society's Farm School. I am directed to state to you that the charge of undue severity seems from Captn. Williams's report to be quite unfounded.

Ironically, the impact of contemporary legislative reforms on sentencing practice appears to have given the Philanthropic gentlemen pause to reconsider their position. Also anxious that a shortfall between the government allowance and the actual maintenance expenses would leave an operating deficiency of nearly £2,000 each year, the Philanthropists soon were resigned to accept that:

> the practice of sentencing boys for short terms & dealing with them by Summary Conviction under the late Criminal Justice Act has so much increased, as to make it improbable that the Government would be able to increase the number of boys under Conditional Pardons, or even to maintain the present amount. The number now in the School on the Government account are 178 of whom many will leave in the next six months.[6]

They therefore concluded:

> That it would seem advisable under any circumstances to certify the Schools under the Act ... as this step would give the Committee power to have as many boys as they thought fit, at the rate of allowance which the Treasury might sanction. With any additional payment that they might be able to obtain from parties interested in the case; and at the same time would not oblige them to admit any others or any more than they deem desirable.

The Philanthropic Farm School was duly certified and, in November 1856, the society resolved that the 'Corporate Seal be affixed to the agreement with the Kent Reformatory Association for the reception of Juvenile Offenders into Society's School under the provisions of the Act'.

The society's financial arrangements at the beginning of the twentieth-century still broadly reflected those in place at the time the Reformatory Farm School was established. Its regime, however, had been gradually modified to incorporate new ideas on the treatment of troubled and troublesome youth that emanated from the developing disciplines of criminology, child-psychology,

---

6. Some forewarning was relayed by Jebb (now chairman of the Board of Directors of Convict Prisons) who intimated: 'The influence of the present measures with respect to juveniles is beginning to be felt in the diminished number of that class sentenced to Transportation and Servitude. I do not think therefore that I shall be enabled henceforth to recommend the removal of any but very exceptional cases to Redhill'.

psychiatry and the emerging social work and probation professions. When the Children and Young Persons Act of 1933 formally amalgamated Reformatory and Industrial Schools, the Philanthropic's Redhill Institution became an 'approved school' regulated by the Children's Department at the Home Office. In 1952, the society petitioned for and received the accolade of a 'Royal' title.

The Children and Young Persons Act of 1969 brought more significant change in its wake. The Royal Philanthropic School at Redhill was denominated a community home with education on the premises (CHE), regulation and inspection shifted to the Department of Health and Social Security and 'controlled' status was adopted. This meant that, while the society retained hold of its property and committee members comprised one-third of the management board, responsibility for finance and the day-to-day operation of the school effectively passed into the hands of a local authority, the London Borough of Wandsworth.

By the beginning of the 1980s, the Royal Philanthropic Society was engaging in another radical re-interpretation of its charter. Although the Children and Young Persons Act of 1969 anticipated a flourishing future for residential care and control, a rapid contraction of the sector had subsequently taken place as new ideas on the benefits of community care gained hold and cuts in government funding imposed restrictions on referrals. Once responsible for running one of the United Kingdom's largest campus establishments (where the needs of 300 young people 'in trouble' could be attended to in an assessment centre with remand facilities, an intensive care unit and the CHE) the trustees found their charitable resources were now tied-up in providing for only 30 boys. With a further decline in referrals looming and believing it was no longer adequately meeting the charitable objectives set out in the Act of Incorporation of 1806, the Society decided to sell its Redhill property and use the proceeds, in innovative ways, to help both boys and girls 'at risk'.

In 1987, the Royal Philanthropic Society re-launched into the community. Finding gaps in provision for vulnerable young people leaving local authority care, its first steps in developing supported housing schemes were taken in partnership with social services departments and housing associations in Surrey, Kent and Wandsworth. Together with juvenile justice agencies, it also initiated bail support schemes for young offenders who might otherwise have been remanded from court into custody. Forging relationships with professional forums active in these spheres, the society also revived its endeavours to influence government policy and provide expert guidance on good practice at home and abroad. Its links with Mettray were also renewed through involvement in Euromet: a network of European organizations working with young people.

In November 1997, a union of long-standing voluntary effort took place when the Royal Philanthropic Society incorporated the 19th-century probation pioneering Rainer Foundation. With that charity's extensive experience in preventing youth crime and re-offending, as well as its wide network of training, employment, accommodation and mentoring services, now combined with the Philanthropic's charitable funds, business acumen and growing expertise, this merger conducingly enabled more young people, in many more places, to be helped more effectively. With RPS/Rainer thus formed upon the union, the Philanthropic identity was completely masked, however, when the charity became known merely as Rainer, in 2003.

In 2008, Rainer merged with Crime Concern, a charity set-up on the initiative of Home Secretary Douglas Hurd in 1988. Primed with Home Office funding and aimed at extending the role of crime prevention in civil society beyond the remit of professional police, it had, since then, developed nationwide schemes for creating safer communities, in collaboration with policing and local authorities and in partnership with young people, their families and friends at a local level. Initially called Rainer Crime Concern, this newly-formed charity has been re-branded as Catch 22: Helping Young People Out and provides for around 40,000 young people living in difficult circumstances in 150 communities across the UK. It also forms part of a consortium which, in July 2010, signed the first prison building, regime design, management and resettlement service contract awarded by the Ministry of Justice to an alliance of the private and voluntary sectors. Thus responding in innovative ways to problems revolving around crime, antisocial behaviour, welfare dependency and social exclusion—and with the aim of creating 'safer, inclusive, crime-free communities for the benefit of the public'—Catch22's 21st-century concerns are, indeed, very similar to those of the Philanthropic founders who set out to nip crime in the bud at the end of the 18th-century.

BIBLIOGRAPHY

PRIMARY SOURCES

Philanthropic Society

Surrey History Centre and Heritage Archives, Woking

MANUSCRIPT SOURCES

Minutes of General Courts and Committees; 1793-1859
Abstract of Minutes; 1788-1840
Building Committee Minutes; 1792-5
Trade and Finance Committee Minutes; 1794-1848
Chapel Committee Minutes; 1803-1813
Registers of Admissions; 1788-1853
Description Books (boys); 1788-1849
Register (girls); 1789-1844
Girls' Conduct Register; 1812-1815
Visitors' Book; 1853-1942
Superintendents' Journals; 1793-1948
Matrons' Journals; 1812-1836
Leases and Plans of Property at St. George's Fields; 1793-1804

PRINTED SOURCES (in date order)

The First Report of the Philanthropic Society instituted in London for the Prevention of Crimes, September 1788, (1789)
The Second Report and Address of the Philanthropic Society ...containing remarks upon Education and some account of the methods adopted in the Reform for cultivating virtuous dispositions and habits in the wards of the Society (1789)

The Philanthropic Society instituted September 1788, for the Prevention of Crimes, and for a Reform among the Poor by seeking out, and, as Orphans, training up to Virtue and Usefulness in Life, the Children of vagrants and Criminals, and such who are in the Paths of Vice and Infamy: [Address] To the Public (1789)

Appeal and List of Subscribers and Benefactors to the Philanthropic Society, &c. (1790)

An Address to the Public from the Philanthropic Society instituted … for the Promotion of Industry, and the Reform of the Criminal Poor to which are annexed, the Laws and Regulations of the Society, &c. (1792)

An Appeal to the Public relative to certain Buildings proposed to be erected for the accommodation of the Children, &c. (1792)

An Account of the Nature and Views of the Philanthropic Society with Laws and Regulations, &c. (1797)

An Act for Establishing and well-governing the charitable Institution commonly called the Philanthropic Society … [22 July 1806]

An Act for enabling the President, Vice-Presidents, Treasurer, and Members of the Philanthropic Society to purchase from the Corporation and other persons entitled thereto the Lands and Hereditaments in the Parish of Saint George the Martyr, Southwark, in the County of Surrey … [17 June 1823]

Report of a Special Committee set up to consider the financial situation, &c. (1827)

An Account of the Nature and Present State of the Philanthropic Society (1829)

Report on the System and Arrangements of 'La Colonie Agricole,' at Mettray, presented to the Committee of the Philanthropic Society, St. George's Fields, 19th August 1846 (1846)

Report on the System and Arrangements of 'La Colonie Agricole,' at Mettray: Second Edition, Revised (1846)

An Account of the Nature and Present State of the Philanthropic Society (1846)

'Reformation of Juvenile Offenders': The Philanthropic Society Report &c. (1848)

An Act to enable the President, Vice-Presidents, Treasurer, and Members of the Philanthropic Society to sell and grant Leases of the Lands belonging to them, and to purchase other Lands; and for other Purposes relating to the said Society … [22 July 1848]

Report on the Occasion of the Farewell Anniversary Meeting in St. George's Fields (1849)

Philanthropic Farm School, Redhill, Surrey: an explanation of the aims and methods of the new Farm School, with list of subscribers (1849)
The Philanthropic Farm School, Redhill, Surrey: Report (1851)
The Philanthropic Farm School, Redhill, Surrey: Report (1853)
The Philanthropic Society Year Book :Report (1854)

OTHER PRINTED SOURCES

British Library
An Account of the Nature and Present State of the Philanthropic Society (1814)

Senate House Library, Goldsmiths Collection
The Philanthropic Farm School, Redhill, Surrey: Report (1850)
Anniversary of the Philanthropic Society for the Reformation of Juvenile Offenders, May 8, 1852 (1852)

Refuge for the Destitute

London Borough of Hackney Archives, Rose Lipman Library
Annual Reports
Minute Books
Short Accounts and Reports

National Archives

HO-45/1000: Refuge for the Destitute.
HO-45/1471: Asylum for Criminal Juveniles.
HO-45/1649: Discharge of Boys to Philanthropic Institutions.
HO-47/21: Judges' Reports

Parliamentary Papers

Reports of Select Committees, House of Commons and House of Lords, with minutes of evidence and appendices:
SC on the Laws relating to Penitentiary Houses, HoC, 1811, Vol. XX.
SC on the Police of the Metropolis, HoC, 1817, Vol. VII.
SC on the Police of the Metropolis, HoC, 1828, Vol. VI.
SC appointed to Inquire into the present state and management of Gaols and Houses of Correction in England and Wales, HoL, 1835, Vol. XII.
SC appointed to Inquire into the execution of the Criminal Laws, especially respecting Juvenile Offenders and Transportation, HoL, 1847, Vol. VII.
SC appointed to Inquire into the Rules and Discipline established with regard to the treatment of Prisoners in Gaols and Houses of Correction in England and Wales, and into any improvements which can be made therein, HoC, 1850, Vol. XVII.
SC on the treatment of Criminal and Destitute Juveniles, HoC, 1852, Vol. VII.

Newspapers and periodicals

Household Words: A Weekly Journal conducted by Charles Dickens
The Gentleman's Magazine
The Times
The Whitehall Evening Post

Contemporary books and pamphlets

Bentham, J. (1789) *Introduction to the Principles of Morals and Legislation*. London.
Bentham, J. (1790) *Outline of the plan of construction of a Panopticon Penitentiary House: as designed by Jeremy Bentham, of Lincoln's-Inn, Esq.* London.
Blackstone, W. (1769) *Commentaries on the Laws of England: Book the Fourth, Chapter the Second; of persons capable of committing crimes*. Accessed via. Avalon Project: Lillian Goldman Library, Yale Law School.
Brand, F. (1806) *A letter to the Right Reverend the Bishops of the United Church of England and Ireland, containing a counter-representation to the statements laid*

before their Lordships in a letter from the Committee of the Philanthropic Society, relative to their intended Chapel, etc. London

Brenton, E.P. (1837) *The Bible and Spade; or, Captain Brenton's Account of the rise and progress of the Children's Friend Society: shewing its tendency to prevent crime and poverty and eventually dispose with capital punishment.* London: J. Nisbet & Co.

Carpenter, M. (1851) *Reformatory Schools for the Perishing and Dangerous Classes and for the Prevention of Juvenile Delinquency.* Reprinted 1968: Woburn Press.

Carpenter, M. (1853) *Juvenile Delinquents: their condition and treatment.* Reprinted 1970: Patterson Smith Publishing Corporation.

Carrington, F.A. and Payne, J. (1833) *Reports of Cases argued and ruled at Nisi Prius, in the Courts of King's Bench, Common Pleas, and Exchequer, together with cases tried on the Circuits and at the Old Bailey; from the sittings after Trinity Term, 1831, to the sittings after Hilary Term, 1833.* London: S. Sweet.

Chadwick, E. (1842) *Report on the Sanitary Condition of the Labouring Population.* Reprinted 1965: Edinburgh University Press.

Colquhoun, P. (1796) *Treatise on the Police of the Metropolis explaining the various crimes and misdemeanours which at present are felt as a pressure upon the community; and suggesting remedies for their prevention.* London.

Colquhoun, P. (1806) *A New and Appropriate System of Education for the Labouring People, elucidated and explained, according to the plan which has been established for the religious and moral instruction of male and female children, admitted into the Free School, No. 19, Orchard Street, in the City of Westminster, &c.* London.

Dickens, C. (1837) *The Posthumous Papers of the Pickwick Club.* London: Chapman and Hall.

Eden, F.M. (1797) *The State of the Poor: or, an History of the Labouring Class of England ...* London.

Engels, F. (1892) *The Condition of the Working-Class in England in 1844: with preface written in 1892.* London: George Allen & Unwin Ltd.

Gilbert, T. (1781) *A Plan of Police: for the better relief and employment of the poor; for enforcing and amending the Laws respecting Houses of Correction and vagrants; and for improving the Police of this Country; together with Bills intended to be offered to Government for those purposes.* London.

Griscom, J. (1815) *Hints relative to the most eligible method of conducting Meteorological Observations.* New York.

Griscom, J. (1823) *A Year in Europe comprising a Journal of Observations in England, Scotland, Ireland, France, Switzerland, the North of Italy, and Holland, in 1818 and 1819: Volume 1.* New York: Collins and Co.

Griscom, J. (1825) *Monitorial Instruction: an Address, pronounced at the opening of the New-York High-School, with notes and illustrations.* New York.

Griscom, J. (1832) *School Discipline–an Essay.* New York: Collins and Hanway.

Hansard (1831-91) *Parliamentary Proceedings.* Third Series; Vols. 1-156. London.

Hanway, J. (1775) *The Defects of Police: The case of immorality and the continual robberies, particularly in and about the Metropolis: with various proposals for preventing hanging and transportation. Likewise for the establishment of general plans of Police on a permanent basis, with respect to common beggars; the regulation of paupers; the peaceful security of Subjects; and the moral and political conduct of the People; &c.* London.

Hart, N.C. (1832) *Documents relative to the House of Refuge, instituted by the Society for the Reformation of Juvenile Delinquents in the City of New York, in 1824.* New York.

Hill, M.D. (1846/1847) *Draft Report on the Principles of Punishment, presented to the Committee on Criminal Law, appointed by the Law Amendment Society, etc.* London: W. Clowes.

Holford, G. (1821) *Thoughts on the criminal prisons of this country occasioned by the Bill now in the House of Commons for consolidating and amending the laws relating to prisons; with some remarks, &c.* London.

Holford, G. (1826) *Statements and Observations Concerning the Hulks ... Part I. Containing reasons for inquiring into the State of the Hulks ... Part II ... A Review of the Acts of Parliament ... .* London.

Howard, J. (1777) *State of the Prisons in England and Wales; with preliminary observations ... .* Warrington.

Iatros (1818) *A Biographical sketch of the life and writings of Patrick Colquhoun Esq., LL.D.* London.

Jackson, R. (1828) *Considerations on the Increase of Crime in London, and the degree of its extent, &c.* London.

Lettsom, J.C. (n.d.) *Hints respecting the Effects of a Little Drop.* London.

Lettsom, J.C. (1780) *Hints respecting the Immediate Effects of Poverty.* London.

Lettsom, J.C. (1797) *Hints designed to promote Beneficence, Temperance and Medical Sciences* (vol.1). London.

Luson, H. (1786) *Inferior Politics: or, Considerations on the wretchedness and profligacy of the Poor: especially in London and its vicinity ... On the Defects in the present System of Parochial and Penal laws ...* London.

Maconochie, A. (1846) *Crime and Punishment: the Marks System, Framed to Mix Persuasion with Punishment, and Make their Effect Improving.* London.

Malthus, T.R. (1798) *An Essay on the Principles of Population or a view of its past and present effects on human happiness &c.* Reprinted 1888: Reeves and Turner.

Mayhew, H. and Binny, J. (1862) *The Criminal Prisons of London and Scenes of Prison Life.* London: Griffin, Bohn & Co.

National Association for the Promotion of Social Science (1858). *The Inaugural Addresses delivered by Lord Brougham, President; Lord John Russell, M.P.; Sir John Pakington, Bart., M.P.; Lord Stanley, M.P.; and Sir Benjamin C. Brodie, Bart., F.R.S.: together with The Sermon by the Reverend Sydney Turner.* London: John Parker & Son.

Paine, T. (1791/2) *Rights of Man.* Reprinted 1974: Citadel Press.

Pitt, W. (1797) *Bill for the Better Support and Maintenance of the Poor, proposed by William Pitt, Chancellor of the Exchequer. A Bill &c.* London.

Smith, A. (1776) *Wealth of Nations.* Reprinted 1980, Harmondsworth: Penguin.

Townsend, J. (1786) *A Dissertation on the Poor Laws: by a Well-Wisher to Mankind.* London.

Washington, G. (1779) *The Writings of George Washington from the original manuscript sources, 1732-1799.* Accessed via. Electronic Text Centre, University of Virginia Library.

Young, R. (1787) *An examination of the third and fourth definitions of the first book of Sir Isaac Newton's Principia and of the three Axioms or Laws of motion ...* London.

Young, R. (1788) *An Essay on the powers and mechanisms of Nature; intended by a deeper analysis of physical principles, to extend, improve, and more firmly establish, the grand superstructure of the Newtonian System ...* London.

Young, R. (1790a) *An Undertaking for the Employment, Regulation, and Reform of the Destitute and Criminal poor: intended to draw their support from their own labour alone and by this means relieve their sufferings, prevent crimes, and eventually remove the burthen of the poor's rates.* London

Young, R. (1790b) *British Settlement, for the Reformation of the Criminal Poor, Adults and Children* ... London.

Young, R. (1790c) *Transactions of the Social Union formed for the Improvement of Civil Society*. London.

Young, R. (1790d) *An Introduction to an Account of the foundation of the London Philanthropic Society and the Author's relations, thereto*. London.

Young, R. (1792) *Undertaking for the Reform of the Poor, of which a principal branch is the Asylum for Industry, consisting of eleven houses in East Street, Walworth, in the Parish of Newington Butts*. London.

Young, R. (1795a) *Mr. Young's Reports on the attempts made by the Usurpers of the Philanthropic Society, to Destroy the British Settlement, founded on Tilgate Forest, Sussex, for the self-support and reform of the destitute and criminal poor: being an extension of an original Design, by which several hundreds, criminal and destitute of all ages, have already been reclaimed and restored to usefulness*. London.

Young, R. (1795b) *First Report of the British Settlement ... and on the delinquency of the usurpers, and their utter subversion of that Society, as to its original purposes, and as to any real benefits to the community*. London.

Young, R. (1796) *Mr. Robert Young's Address to the General Body of Subscribers of the Philanthropic Society and to the Nation, on the unparalleled Abuses, and atrocious Delinquency of the Usurpers of the Philanthropic Reform* ... London.

Young, R. (1801) *Gnomia: or the Science of Society; in which Civil Society is considered in its actual state, and its capabilities of further improvement; ... being a new Science, embracing the whole Organisation of a Body Politic; a course of Instruction to form Youth, of higher Positions, for greater public usefulness; and, all, for fulfilling better the Duties of the Social State. Written in characteristic dialogue ... (Part 1)*. London: J. Long.

SECONDARY SOURCES

Acres, W.M. (1931) *The Bank of England from within, 1694-1900: Volume 2*. London: Oxford University Press.

Alabaster, A. (ed.) (n.d.) *A History of the Royal Philanthropic Society 1788-1988*. London: Straker & Sons, for the RPS.

Barnett, C. (1970) *Britain and Her Army, 1509-1970: a military, political and social survey*. Harmondsworth: Penguin.

Bayne-Powell, R. (1939) *The English child in the eighteenth century*. London: John Murray.

Bradlow, E. (1984) 'The Children's Friend Society at the Cape of Good Hope' in *Victorian Studies*, 27:155-77.

Briggs, A. (1959/1979) *The Age of Improvement 1783-1867*. London: Longman.

Brown, F.K. (1961) *Fathers of the Victorians: the age of Wilberforce*. Cambridge: Cambridge University Press.

Carlebach, J.I. (1970) *Caring for Children in Trouble*. London: Routledge & Kegan Paul.

Dictionary of National Biography; and as updated by the *Oxford Dictionary of National Biography*, 2004–2010. Oxford: Oxford University Press

Duckworth, J. (2002) *Fagin's Children: Criminal Children in Victorian England*. London: Hambledon and London

Foot, M.R.D. and Matthew, H.C.G. (eds.) (1974). *The Gladstone Diaries: Volume 4, 1848-1854*. Oxford: Clarendon Press.

Foucault, M. (1977) *Discipline and Punish: the Birth of the Prison*. Harmondsworth: Penguin.

Gatrell, V.A.C. (1994) *The Hanging Tree: Execution and the English People 1770-1868*. Oxford: Oxford University Press.

Gay, P. (1969) *The Enlightenment: an Interpretation: the Science of Freedom (Book 3) The Pursuit of Modernity*. New York: Norton & Co.

Hirst, J. (1995) 'The Australian Experience: the Convict Colony', in Morris, N. and Rothman, D.J. (eds.) *The Oxford History of the Prison*. Oxford: Oxford University Press.

Ignatieff, M. (1978) *A Just Measure of Pain: the Penitentiary in the Industrial Revolution, 1750-1850*. London: Macmillan.

Knell, B.E.F. (1965) 'Capital Punishment: its administration in relation to juvenile offenders in the nineteenth century and its possible administration in the eighteenth', in *British Journal of Criminology*, 5:198-207.

Margarey, S. (1978) 'The Invention of Juvenile Delinquency in Early Nineteenth-Century England' in *Labour History* [Canberra], 34:11-27.

May, M. (1981) 'A Child's Punishment for a Child's Crime': The Reformatory and Industrial School Movement in Britain c. 1780-1880. Unpublished Ph.D. thesis, University of London.

Milne, A.T. (ed.) (1981) *The Correspondence of Jeremy Bentham: Volume 5, January 1794 to December 1797*. University College: The Athlone Press.

McConville, S. (1981) *A history of English prison administration: Volume 1, 1750-1877*. London: Routledge & Kegan Paul.

McGowen, R. (1995) 'The Well-Ordered Prison: England, 1780-1865', in Morris, N. and Rothman, D.J. (eds.) *The Oxford History of the Prison: the practice of punishment in western society*. Oxford: Oxford University Press.

Owen, D. (1964) *English Philanthropy 1660-1960*. Cambridge, Massachusetts: Belknap Press.

Pinchbeck, I. and Hewitt, M. (1973) *Children in English Society: Volume 2, From the Eighteenth Century to the Children's Act 1948*. London: Routledge & Kegan Paul.

Pinker, R. (1971) *Social Theory and Social Policy*. London: Heinemann.

Radzinowicz, L. and Hood, R. (1986) *The History of English Criminal Law and its Administration from 1750: Volume 5, The Emergence of Penal Policy*. London: Stevens & Sons.

Roberts, D. (1969) *Victorian Origins of the British Welfare State*. Hamden, Conn.; Archon Books

Semple, J.E. (1993) *Bentham's Prison: a study of the Panopticon Penitentiary*. Oxford: Clarendon Press.

Shore, H. (1999) *Artful Dodgers: Youth and Crime in early 19th–century London*. London: Royal Historical Society

Wagner, G. (1982) *Children of the Empire*. London: Weidenfeld & Nicolson

Weinreb, B. and Hibbert, C. (eds.) (1983/1993) *The London Encyclopaedia*. London: Macmillan.

Wiener, M. J. (1990) *Reconstructing the Criminal: Culture, Law and Policy in England, 1830-1914*. Cambridge: Cambridge University Press.

ADDITIONAL READING

Andrew, D.T. (1989) *Philanthropy and Police: London Charity in the Eighteenth Century*. Princeton, New Jersey: Princeton University Press.

Beattie, J.M. (1986) *Crime and the Courts in England, 1660-1880*. Oxford: Clarendon Press.

Branch-Johnson, W. (1957) *The English Prison Hulks*. London: Christopher Johnson.

Chesney, K. (1970) *The Victorian Underworld*. London: Maurice Temple Smith.

Cunningham, H. (1991) *The Children of the Poor: Representations of Childhood since the Seventeenth Century*. Oxford: Basil Blackwell.

Emsley, C. (1987/1996) *Crime and Society in England 1750-1900*. London: Longman.

Evans, R. (1982) *The Fabrication of Virtue: English Prison Architecture, 1750-1840*. Cambridge: Cambridge University Press.

George, M.D. (1925) *London Life in the Eighteenth Century*. Harmondsworth: Penguin.

Grovier, K. (2008) *The Gaol: The Story of Newgate–London's Most Notorious Prison*. London: John Murray.

Highmore, A. (1810) *Pietas Londoniensis: the history, design and present state of the various public charities in or near London*. London.

Hughes, R., (1987) *The Fatal Shore: A History of the Transportation of Convicts to Australia, 1787-1868*. London: Harvill Press.

Innes, J. (1996) 'The "mixed economy of welfare" in early modern England: assessments of the options from Hale to Malthus (c. 1683-1803)', in Daunton, M. (ed.) *Charity, Self-interest and Welfare in the English Past*. London: University College London Press.

King, P. (2000) *Crime, Justice, and Discretion in England 1740-1820*. Oxford: Oxford University Press.

Linebaugh, P. (1991) *The London Hanged: Crime and Civil Society in the Eighteenth Century*. London: Allen Lane.

Low, S. (1850) *The Charities of London comprehending the benevolent, educational, and religious Institutions: their origin, design, progress and present position*. London.

May, M. (1973) 'Innocence and Experience: the evolution of the concept of Juvenile Delinquency in the mid-nineteenth century', in *Victorian Studies*, 17:7-29.

McGowen, R. (2007) 'Managing the Gallows: the Bank of England and the Death Penalty 1797-1821', in *Law and History Review*, Vol.25, No.2.

Palmer, S.H. (1988) *Police and Protest in England and Ireland, 1780-1850*. Cambridge: Cambridge University Press.

Pearson, G. (1983) *Hooligan: A History of Respectable Fears*. Basingstoke: Macmillan.

Picard, L. (2000) *Dr. Johnson's London: Life in London 1740-1770*. London: Phoenix Press.

Porter, R. (1990) *The Enlightenment*. Basingstoke: Macmillan.

Porter, R. (1994/2000) *London: A Social History*. London: Penguin.

Radzinowicz, L. (1956) *The History of the English Criminal Law and its Administration from 1750: Volume 3, Cross-currents in the Movement for the Reform of the Police*. London: Stevens & Sons.

Rawlings, P (1999) *Crime and Power: A History of Criminal Justice, 1688-1998*. Harlow: Addison Wesley Longman Ltd.

Shoemaker, R.B. (1991) *Prosecution and Punishment: Petty Crime and the Law in London and rural Middlesex, c.1660-1725*. Cambridge: Cambridge University Press.

Walvin, J. (1982) *A Child's World: A Social History of English Childhood, 1800-1914*. Harmondsworth: Penguin.

Webb, S. and Webb, B. (1922) *English Local Government: Volume 6, English Prisons Under Local Government*. Reprinted 1963, London: Frank Cass.

INDEX

A

Abbott, Rt. Hon. Charles 116
absconding x, 70, 78, 119, 130, 149, 150, 165, 166, 208, 246, 247, 255
abuse 17, 102, 146
accommodation 88, 90, 147, 172, 240, 253, 262
Act for Effecting Greater Uniformity in Practice, etc. (1835). 169
Act for the Better Care and Reformation of Youthful Offenders, etc. 253
Act for the Preservation of the Health and Morals of Apprentices 138
Act of Incorporation 113, 116, 118
　passed in 1806 125
Adams, Serjeant 191, 244, 249
Adderley, Charles 258
admission
　admission procedure 154
　Admission Registers 47, 148
affection rather than fear 237
after-care 92, 168
after-destinations and outcomes 230
after-disposal 220
agriculture x, 35, 46, 201, 218
　Agricultural Revolution 18
　Board of Agriculture 96
Albert, Prince 212, 214
　visit to Farm School 238
Aldersgate Church Wardens 121
Algoa Bay, The Cape 222
Allen, William 146, 147
alliance of private and voluntary sectors 262
alternatives to custody xiv
altruism 52
America 199
　American Penitentiaries and Refuges 189
　Anglo-American War 155
　United States of America xii
　War of Independence 18, 51
Amory, John 69
Angerstein, John Julius 39, 117
Anniversary Dinner 60, 83, 113, 159, 217, 236, 241
apprenticeship x, 64, 174, 225, 230, 246
　apprenticing-out 127
　refractory apprentices 67
approved school xi, 261
Arcadian idyll
　pursuit abandoned 46
Arden, Sir Richard Pepper 109
aristocracy 35
Arrogant, Daniel 55
Ashley, Viscount 198, 233, 249
assault 19, 29
assessment centre 261
Assizes 56, 223
　Oxford Assizes 135
　Reading Assizes 54

275

asylum 29, 31, 46, 77, 189, 198, 211, 227, 231
  Asylum for the Deaf and Dumb 147
  'asylum not a prison' 24
  Asylum of Industry 106, 114
  Royal Asylum, Chiswick 219
Attorney General 104, 108, 148
authority 18
Aylesford, Earl of 114

B

bad
  bad company 58
  bad members of the community 28
badge
  badge of disgrace 67
Baggallay, Richard (Junior) 191
bail support 261
Baker, Barwick 258
banishment 69
Bank of England 42, 60
Banner, Nathaniel 129
banyan days 83
Baron Eldon 124
Bates, William (beadle) 166
Battersea 209, 237
  Battersea Rise 115
  Battersea Training College 198
beadle 166
Beccaria, Cesare 31, 36

Beccarian exactness of punishment 75
Bedford, Duke of 97
Bedfordshire 40
begging 17, 19, 27, 30, 49, 69, 256
  'sturdy beggars' 29
Belgrave, Viscount 33, 115
Bell, Dr. (Dr. Bell's 'monitorial system') 137
Bellerophon 161
Bell, John Any Bird 53, 161
bells
  ringing of 148
'Beneficence, Temperance and Medical Science' (1797) 38
Benefit Sermons 120
benevolence xiii, 27, 97, 98, 150, 155, 195, 227, 233
  Christian benevolence 238
  private benevolence 242
Bentham, Jeremiah 35, 36, 39, 42
Bentham, Jeremy xiv, 34, 35, 42, 93, 114, 213
Bermondsey 47, 130, 132
Bernard, Thomas (Bishop of Durham) 38
best characteristics 28
Bible, The 123, 136, 146, 219
  Bible Society 115
Birkbeck, Dr. George 140, 180
Birmingham 236, 237, 238, 247, 251
Bishop of Winchester 122
black book xi, 62
Blackstone 17
blame 74

Blomfield, Bishop 190, 206, 209
Bloody Code 20
Boddington, Thomas 39, 42
bookbinding 193
borrowing 90
Bosanquet, Charles 114
Bosanquet, James 60, 173
Bosanquet, Samuel 60, 160, 173, 192
Botany Bay 21, 59, 73, 88, 167
Bow Street 99
   Bow Street Court 23, 50
Bradbury, William 92
Brady, James 58
Brand, The Reverend 124
breaking windows 73
Brenton, Captain 170, 219
bricklaying
   discontinued 63
bridewell 19, 49, 67, 99
   Bridewell Committee 162
   Clerkenwell Bridewell 50
   Emanuel Bridewell 41
   Westminster Bridewell 227, 245
Bridge House Estates Committee 159
Bristol 247, 248
British Settlement 101, 105, 106
   British Settlement for the Reformation of the Criminal Poor, etc. 33, 34
Brookham, George 135
Brougham, Lord 140, 146, 180, 211, 213, 257
Brown, Thomas 170, 219
Building Committee 90, 117, 128

building debt 122
burglary 143
Burn, Thomas 65

C

cane 75, 183
Cape of Good Hope 170, 219, 222
capital punishment 17, 143
   abolition 232
   extensive part abolition 161, 187
Capper, John Henry 161, 167, 193
carceral approach xii
care package 246
Carmarthen, Marquess of 24
Carpenter, Mary x, 238, 247, 258
carpentry 45
Carter, Christiana 58
case histories 47
Catch 22 viii, 262
catechism 138
cat-of-nine-tails 75
Cato Street Conspiracy 156
Causer, William 66
censorship 158
certainty 33, 256
certification 255, 256, 259
Chadwick, Edward 190
chapel 119, 176, 197
   Address from the Philanthropic Society to the Public on the Subject of Erecting a Chapel 122
   chapel collections 157, 164
   Chapel Fund 122

chapel keeper 125
floating chapels 128
pew rents 157
chaplain 131, 134, 249
   chaplain-superintendent 177, 179
   resident chaplain-superintendent-secretary 230
character 31, 47, 58, 65, 78
charity x, 22, 27, 117, 120, 153, 162, 227, 229, 235, 261, 262
   abuse of charities 146
   charitable 'bounty' 25
   charitable rivalry 121
   charity fatigue xiv, 121
   charity schools of industry 30
   charity sermons 96
   indiscriminate charity 31
   National Charity Company proposal 34
   pretext of charity 219
Chartist mobs 190
chevaux de frise x, 165
child
   child protection 151
   child-psychology 260
   child-saving 24
   Philanthropic children 47
   poor children 47
   rescue 25, 47
children 28
   Children and Young Persons Act 1933 261
   Children and Young Persons Act 1969 261
   children in need ix

Children's Friend Society 170, 219, 220, 222, 244
chimney sweepers 24, 38, 41, 198
   exploitation of 219
   mines and factories 198
   neglected children 31
   outcast children 30
   pauper children 31
   rescue of 28
   zero-sum children 28, 34
cholera 229
Church Building Society 128
Church of England 123, 130
citizen
   Citizen Service xiv
   duty of responsible citizens 23
City Corporation 94, 117, 118, 122, 147, 157
City of London 42, 46, 117, 231
civilising philosophy 181
class
   classes of labour, etc. 28
   of labouring poor 26
   superior class of mechanics and servants 28
   'the most degenerate class of poor' 29
classification 127, 184
Clause XI 171, 245, 246, 247, 256
Cold Bath Fields 55
collar 71
Collier, Superintendent 142, 163, 166, 169
Colonial Office 221, 222, 227, 257
Colonie Agricole 220

colonies 220
Colquhoun, Patrick 41, 137, 148
Commentaries on the Laws of England (1769) 17
commiseration 242
committee
    Building Committee 90, 117
    Chapel Committee 122
    Holford Committee 115
    Richmond Committee 170, 172, 190, 191, 218, 220
committee (and see Select Committee)
    Committee Minutes 47
    Committee of Enquiry 71
    Committee of Trades and Finance 126
    General Committee 89, 104, 116, 117, 126, 132, 141
    Special Committee 126, 130, 133, 142, 150, 157, 165, 173, 177, 240
common weal
    benefitting 23
communications
    evil communications x
    improper communication 120
community
    civil community 30
    community care 261
    community home with education 261
compassion 18, 43, 50, 77, 79, 81
complexity of imperatives 25
Condition of the Working-Class in England in 1844, The 186

confession 17
confidence 30, 169
confinement 67, 150, 155, 165, 166, 190, 233
    solitary confinement 167
Congreve, Sir William MP 145
consent 246
Considerations on the Increase in Crime and the Degree of its Extent 118
constable 42
    Constable or Peace Officer 125
contamination 129, 131, 147, 151, 233
contentment 62
contract management 115
contractors intent on profit 218
control 201
    no legal powers of control 246
    over-control 151
    self-control 232
Cooke, Frances 119
Cookham Union House 237
Cooper, James 55
corporal punishment 184
Corresponding Societies 81
corruption 31
    must inevitably be propogated 27
costs 234, 253
    cost-benefit analysis 230
cottage-based approach x
counterfeiting 66
Court of Chancery 103, 107, 108, 109, 146
Coutts Banking 103
Coutts, Burdette 249

Crauford (Crawford), William 155, 189
Crawley, Mary xiii
Crawley, Sussex 105, 217
credibility 29, 111
Cremorne, Viscount 114
crime 201, 232
   atrocious crimes 17
   Crime and Punishment: The Mark System 231
   Crime Concern 262
   crime-free communities 262
   crime prevention ix, 23, 30, 35, 43, 96, 137, 162, 188, 190, 197, 206, 257, 262
   perceptions of crime 19
   roots of crime 30
   trifling offences 20
criminal code
   severity of 155
criminality 42, 49
criminal law 26
criminal youth 207
criminology 260
cruelty 62, 219
Cupar's Bridge, Lambeth 114
curiosity 79
custody
   corrective custody 57
   Philanthropic custody 66

D

Dalziell, James 57

Dampier, Jane 148
dangerous classes 145, 187, 190
Davis, James 65
Davy, Sir Humphrey 146
death penalty 17, 19
   children 52
decay 28
deceit 154
decency 129
Defects of Police, The (1775) 23
deference 18, 144
degradation 130
delinquency x, 20, 113, 145, 155, 170, 231, 232, 235, 249
   grave delinquency 153
Demetz, Monsieur xii, 198, 238
Denbigh, Thomas 65
Dent, Jane 148
Department of Health and Social Security 261
dependency 26, 209, 256, 262
depravity 26, 147, 184
   early depravity 39
depredations 20
depression 158
   economic depression 186
Derbyshire 105
   'waste-lands of Derbyshire' 35
Description Books 47
desertion 66
desolation 26
despair 186
destitution 25, 187, 231, 250
deterrence 20, 234, 247, 255
Dickens, Charles 160, 248

diet xi, 83, 84, 86, 133
   bread and water diet 67
dignity 183
Dingle, James 173
disaffection 81
discharge 32
   Discharged Prisoners Act 1774 40
   prison from 21
discipline xi, 125, 164, 168, 182, 236
discontent 62, 137
discretion xiii, 20, 55
   erratic exercise of 153
discrimination 26
   selection processes 48
disease 40, 190
disgrace 248
dishonesty 17, 19, 62
disobedience 62
disorder 18, 43, 70
   disorderly and diseased 129
dispensaries 37
   General Dispensary, Aldersgate Street 40
   Surrey Dispensary 40
displacement
   populations of 18
Disraeli 187
dissent 40
   era of religious dissent 123
disturbances x, 166, 177, 184
diversion from the criminal justice system 55
Divine Service 122, 124, 143, 164
doli incapax 17, 202, 243
donations 156, 163

Dorchester Goal 148
Downes, Benjamin 135
Downing Street 32
drill 206
   drill exercise 183
   military drill xi
Durand, Superintendent 63, 68, 74, 142, 149

E

early life 31
East India Company 39, 115, 118
ecclesiastical discord 122
economy 46
   economic crisis 81
Eden, Reverend R 203
education xi, 39, 133, 135, 180, 206, 256, 258
   educating the whole child 209
   education grant 211, 257
   elementary district schools 209
   free education 40
   industrial education 199
   'menial servants' as 45
   moral education 136
   power of 61
   power to shape young minds 43
   rate-subsidised education 137
   want of education 155
'electing' children to institutions 158
Elizabethan times 29
elopement 78, 129
Emanuel Hospital

shoes for 96
emigration 219, 220, 221, 226, 248, 257
   Emigration Board 223
employment xi, 63, 168, 189, 262
   honest employment 28
   want of employment 155
energetic members 176
Enlightenment xi, 30, 35, 41, 61, 79, 96, 179, 217, 243, 257
   Enlightenment heritage 201
   Enlightenment Manifesto 34
environmentalist theory 30
envy 162
Essay on the Principles of Population (1798) 82
Euromet 262
Europe 35
Euryalus 161, 196
Evangelic brotherhood 41
evidence xi
   evidence-based ethos 133
   evidence-gathering tradition 173
evil 25, 26, 27, 249
   a solution for social evils 31
   evil communications 46
example 31
   example to others 28
excursions 70
execution xiii, 17, 19
exile 169, 220
experience 35, 46
experiment 181, 191, 198, 206, 207, 215, 217, 228, 240, 248, 257
   experimental enterprise 79

exploitation 17
ex-prisoners 33
expulsion 78

F

facts
   philanthropy based on 29
Faith and Duty, etc. 180
family
   changed family circumstances 59
   family-based approach x, 230
   family division of children 201
   'family' lines of the Philanthropic 247
   without family 48
farms
   agricultural colony 217
   Farm School 208, 210, 227, 236, 252, 259, 260
      Farm School experiment 206
      foundation stone of the first Farm School house 214
      Model Farm School 201
      public subscription 212
      tours of 199
Farnborough 213
fault 62
felony 17, 19, 20, 56, 153, 256
fetters 71, 76, 247
Fielding brothers 23
filth 30
fines 21
Fleet Prison 107

Flemming, John 197
flexibility 56
flogging xi, 67, 126, 139
food
    cheap food for the poor 42
foot patrol 23
Fordree, James 50
forgery 156
Forster, Edward 114, 155, 189
Forth, Reverend 142
Fossett, George 224
Fothergill, John 37
Foucault xii, 200
founders 45
Foundling Hospital 24, 41, 63, 95, 96, 117, 158
France xii, 18, 125, 155, 200, 233
    French Revolution 137
    war with 81
fraud 85, 153
free list 236
fresh start 217
friendlessness 48
frugality 83, 87, 111, 156, 162
Fry, Elizabeth 151
funding ix, xiii, 156, 163, 172, 244, 252, 256, 257, 261
    government funding xi
    Treasury funding 227

G

gallows 17, 39, 73, 77, 161
    alternatives to 53

gambling xi, 155
gaol
    Gaol Act 1823 161
    Gaol Acts 1774 108
    gaol fever 19, 40
    Gaols Act 1835 190
gardening 45, 199, 218
    cultivation of gardens 183
    'market garden stuff, etc.' 231
Garrow, William 152
Gaselee, Mr. Justice Stephen 160, 161
Gaussen, William 188, 193
'general preventive' 23
Germany 199, 218
Gilbert, Thomas 31
girls 78, 83, 85, 86, 87, 90, 186, 215
    cholera 229
    disorder 151
    Female Reform 91, 119
    Female Reform, Bermondsey 97
    Female School xiii, 113, 138, 141, 149, 181
        discontinuance 185
        Register of the Conduct and Improvement of the Girls 138
'giving ever has a return with interest' 27
Gladstone, William 202, 205, 221, 225, 253
Gladstone, William Ewart 202, 212, 221, 233, 241
Gnomian Review 110
Gnomia; or the Science of Society 110
going abroad

'prize of' 246
good 27
goodwill 230
Gordon Riots 18, 23
governance 125, 143, 164, 176, 178
   problems of 81
   shift to 'mild government' 183
government
   government efficiency 228
   government grant 92, 104, 161, 164, 172, 194, 226, 228, 256
   government temperance 239
Graham, Sir James 189, 193, 245
grammar 180
Granville, Earl 252
gratitude 62
Grey, Sir George 202, 205, 207, 209, 223, 230, 232, 233, 239, 245, 253, 257
Grindlay, Reverend John 114, 119
Griscom, John xii, 146, 211
Grosvenor, Earl 33, 101, 103, 114, 188
guardians 91, 92
guards 202
Guildford 162
Guildhall Sessions 41

H

habeas corpus
   suspension of 81
habit 31, 61
Hackney 201, 218
   Hackney Road 228

Hackney Wick 219
Hamilton, Reverend Dr. 120
hanging 20, 161
Hanway Acts 218
Hanway, Jonas 23, 34
happiness 23, 27, 33, 34, 36, 241, 257
Hardinge, George 39, 110
hard labour 224, 255
Hardwicke Court, Gloucestershire 258
Harman, Edward 194
Harman, Jeremiah 156, 157
Harnage, Colonel Henry 114
Harrison, Caroline 156
Harrowby, Earl of 250
Hatton Garden Police Office 55
Hawes, Benjamin 221
Hawkesbury, Lord 125
Hayman, Stephanie viii
head lice 139
health 40, 133, 138, 190, 199, 230, 258
   Health of Prisoners Acts 1774 40
Henry, Eleanor 148
Hicks, James 73
High Treason 156
Hill, Matthew Davenport 208, 211, 213, 238, 244, 253, 258
Hill, Reverend Rowland 96
Hoare, Henry 96
Hogg, Corporal 206
holford
   Holford Committee 148
Holford, George 115, 125, 145, 153, 162, 165, 184, 220
Holford, Henry 141

Holland 199
Home Department/Home Office 161, 167, 172, 189, 192, 194, 202, 204, 215, 227, 228, 239, 252, 255, 257, 259, 262
   Children's Department at the Home Office 261
homelessness 17
Home Secretary 161, 171, 192, 193, 196, 202, 210, 211, 222, 224, 228, 230, 233, 239, 251, 253, 256
home visits 150
honesty 62
   honest industry 26
horticulture 218
Hoscroft, John 186, 226
hospital 27
Household Words 248
House of Commons 212, 243
   petition to 213
house of correction 55, 132, 138, 169, 255
   Brixton House of Correction 224
   France 201
   Wandsworth House of Correction 247
   Westminster House of Correction 245
House of Discipline and School of Reform, etc. 151
House of Lords 249
   petition to 213
houses 45
   dwelling houses 47
housing associations 261

Howard, John 20, 37, 40
Hoxton 228
hulks 21, 22, 53, 73, 114, 128, 161, 167, 196, 211, 220
   t hulk 128
   Statements and Observations Concerning the Hulks 128
Humane Society 128
humanitarian concerns 43, 156
humanity 29
human nature 30
Humble, Henry 49, 73
Humean ideas 34
Humphries, William 259
Hurd, Douglas (Lord) 262

I

idleness 20, 24, 26, 39, 62, 82, 184, 249
   'the devil makes work for idle hands' 29
ignorance 187
impiety 62
impressment 68
imprisonment 256
   a lifetime of 17
   prior imprisonment proviso 53, 244, 255
impunity 17
incentives 231, 246
incorrigible 66
indenture 64, 127
indigence 42

indolence 26, 143
Industrial Revolution 18
industrial schools xiii, 235, 256
   Industrial Schools Act 1857 230, 256
industrial training 217
industry 39, 61, 62, 137
   Asylum of Industry 32
   Aubin's School of Industry, Norwood 218
   honest industry 30
   industrious habits 28
   School of Industry 58
   virtuous industry 27
infamy 27
infant offspring of convicts 152
Inferior Politics, etc. (1786) 31
influence 188, 221, 231, 241
ingratitude 62
iniquity 25
inspection xi, 193, 204, 205, 256
   inspectorate 164
   Inspector of Prisons 190, 204, 237, 254, 255
   Inspector of Reformatories 256
   Inspector of Reformatory Schools 230
insubordination 137, 177, 184
insurrection 145
Intensive Care Unit 261
intoxication x, 30, 165, 248
Introduction to an Account of the foundation of the London Philanthropic Society, etc. 99
investment
   return on 27
itch (the Itch) 139

J

Jackson, George 225
Jackson, Randle (barrister) 118
Jackson, Reverend T 198
Jackson, Richard 129
Jacobin plots 81
James, George 225
Jebb, Joshua 190
Jewell, Maria and Elhanan 137
Jolliffe, Sir William 241, 243
judge 90, 95, 172
jurisprudence 257
jury
   jury nullification 20
just deserts 167
'just pain' 182
juvenile ix, 169, 178
   juvenile crime 145, 249
      growth of 163
   juvenile justice 32, 161, 230
   juvenile justice agencies 261
   Juvenile Mendiancy Bill (1853) 249, 251
   juvenile offenders 199, 207, 211, 215, 220, 234, 255
      'slippery concept' 253
   Juvenile Offenders Bill (1847) 210, 232
   peak of juvenile offending 190

K

Kay-Shuttleworth, Mr. 209, 218, 258
Kent 261
    Kent Reformatory Association, etc. 260
kindly interest 230
kindness 62
King's Bench Prison 56
King's Navy 24
Kingswood, Bristol 247
Kneller Hall 210, 252
knitting 45
knowledge 28, 33, 35
    knowledge of God 30
    power of knowledge xi
Knox, William 93, 102, 120

L

labelling
    physical labelling 126
    use of badges 67
Lambeth
    Lambeth Asylum 60
    Lambeth Charity School 138
language
    decent language 62
    immoral language 62
last chance
    'one last chance' 57
law
    as a lottery xiii
    execution of the Criminal Law, etc. 211
    inefficacy of 20
    iron hand of 26
    law and order 145
Leeds, Duke of 74, 103, 105, 110, 113
Lee, Stephen 54
legacies 162, 163
legislation
    legislative conundrum 234
    legislative quest 231
Leicester 225
Lettsom, John Cloakley 37, 187
liberal 29
liberty 23
Library of Entertaining Knowledge 180
light 33
Lilley, William 52
Linnean Society 114
Lion, Edward 126
liquor 166
Lloyds 41
local authorities xiv, 262
Lockean convictions 30
lodging in barns 49
logging 76, 77
loitering abroad 49
London
    London Borough of Wandsworth 261
    London Depot re transit to agricultural colony 207
    London Dock Company 42

London Mechanics' Institution 140
London Medical Society 140
London Refuge for Destitute Youths (proposed) 189
Lord Chancellor 124, 146, 250
Lowe, William 65
loyalty 137
Luddite agitations 145
Ludgate Hill 225
Lunar Society of Birmingham 35
Luson, Hewling 31
lying 30
Lying-In Hospital 120
Lyttleton, Lord 241

M

Maconochie, Captain 231, 236
Magdalen Asylum 24, 41, 117, 128
magistrate 40, 55, 56, 64, 90, 95, 131, 152, 154, 172, 186, 191, 195, 196, 210, 213, 223, 227, 251
    magistrate's certificate 154
    police magistrate 250, 255
    Speenhamland magistrates 81
    Staffordshire magistrates 196
    Warwickshire magistrates 218
    West Sussex magistrates 197
Magna Carta of the neglected child 253
Maidstone 162
    Maidstone Assizes 161
maintaining order 23, 25

maintenance 256, 260
Mander, Mary 54
Mann, William 143
Manor House, Dalston 228
Mansion House 67, 231
Manufactory 113, 132, 138
    Manufactory Committee 138
Marine Society 24, 41, 60, 65, 78, 115, 128
mark system 236
masters 64
matron 229
McCarthy, Dennis 225
means-testing 197
medicine 139
Melbourne, Lord 98
memorial 97
Memorialists 94
mentoring xiv, 262
Merchant Marine 24
mercy 20, 171
merit 62
    merit and demerit 26
Mettray xii, 92, 198, 202, 207, 233, 238, 244, 262
    Mettray Report 198, 220, 227, 231
Michael, Archduke 145
Middlesex Bench 36
Middlesex Justices Act 1792 41
midnight incendiaries 29
Millbank Penitentiary xii, 115, 141, 145, 203, 211, 224, 245
Minimum Wages Bill (1795) 81
mining 225
    Inspector of Mines 237

Mines Actn 1842 237
Mining and Manufacturing School 198
Ministry of Justice 262
mischief 119
  mischievous behaviour x
mischievous discretion 17
misconduct 164, 184, 205
misery 26, 30, 41
  prevention of 24
mob
  spectre of 'the mob' 19
Monckton Milnes, Richard MP 208, 212, 232, 236, 243, 249, 252, 258
monitoring xi
monitors 137, 138, 166, 181
Montgomeryshire 213
Moon, Edmund 50
morality 34, 99, 129, 133, 136, 147, 149, 217
  immorality 23
  'Moral and Physical Thermometer' 73
  moral contamination 20
  moral discipline xiv
  moral education 28, 199
  moral improvement 62, 204
  moral influences 182
  moral responsibility 82
  morals and manners 36
  moral welfare 159
  'school of morals' 61
Morton Pitt, William 148
Moseley, Joyce viii
murder 17, 29

Murrell, Charlotte 149

N

Napoleonic Code 243
National Association for the Promotion of Social Science 257
National Charity Company 42
National Gallery 41
national prosperity 29
national security 23
necessity 31
neglect
  employers by 17
  parental neglect 17, 50
Neild, James 38
New and Appropriate System of Education, etc. 137
Newgate Prison 21, 40, 52, 66, 88, 143, 163
Newington Butts 32, 101
New South Wales 169
New World 35
New York 147, 248
  New York City House of Refuge 147
Nicholas of Russia, Grand Duke 145
Nightingale, Mrs. 209
night-watchmen 42
nimbyism 213
nipping crime in the bud 41
Nonconformists 37
Norfolk 213
Norfolk Island, Australia 231

Normal College 209
Norwood 209, 218, 237
Nottingham 53
nuisance 25
'Nunnery' 149

O

oakum-picking 131, 132, 218
obedience 62, 237
observation 35; 46
Observations Concerning the Hulks 168
Old Bailey 19, 54, 129, 247
    Old Bailey 'Intelligence' 20
Oldenburgh, Grand Duchess of 145
Old Sarum 39
Old World 146
orphans 250
outcasts 217
Outline (1790) 36

P

paedotrophium 34
Pakington, Sir John 232, 236, 258
Palmerston, Viscount 251, 253, 259
panopticon 34, 36, 93, 114, 213
pardon xiii, 22, 135, 168, 171, 223, 224
  conditional pardon 244, 246, 256, 260

parents ix, xi, 154, 155, 168, 242, 247, 249, 250, 255
  children beyond the control of 256
  criminal parentage 187, 215
  destitute parents 206
  dissolute parents 24
  execution of parents xiii
  fine on 256
  imprisonment of xiii
  parens patriae 243
  parental care and control 58
  parental guidance 147
  parental neglect 250, 256
  parental relation of masters 201
  parental responsibility 66
  payments by 197
  responsible parents 57
  transportation of xiii
  wily parents 153
parish
  indoor relief 49
  parish officers 39
  without parish support 48
Parkhurst experiment 171
Parkhurst Prison xii, 203, 205, 225, 233, 245
  junior wards 196
Parkhurst Prison Act 1838 145, 171, 190, 244, 256
Park, James Allen 127
parochial law 31
partnership 178, 189, 191, 192, 227, 230, 245, 255, 256, 261
passion 26

patronage 144
　Mettray system of 200
pauper 23, 207, 209
　boarding-out pauper children 218
　pauper education 218, 237
　pauper law 250
　pauper management 34
　pauper school 256
peace
　effect of 158
　peace, good order and personal security 27
Pearce, Thomas 68
Pearson, Charles 231, 236
Peelers 166
Peel, Sir Robert (junior) 161, 193
Peel, Sir Robert (the elder) 138, 145
penal
　penal law 20, 31, 250
　penal policy 169
　penal schools 210, 211
　penal servitude 256
Pendleton Mills 64
penitentiary 198
　Penitentiary Act 1779 37
　Penitentiary Act 1794 114
　Penitentiary Acts 93
　Penitentiary Committee 135
　penitentiary houses 42, 115
Pentonville Prison 190
perdition
　saving souls from 29
Perry, William James 49
personal connections ix
persuasion not force 199

Pestalozzi 209
Peterloo Massacre 156
petition 232
petty larceny 233
petty theft 133
pew rent 159
Philanthropic economy 84
Philanthropic Network for Reform 29, 251, 253, 257
Philanthropic Petition (1848) 232
Philanthropic Plan 24, 30, 34, 39, 137
Philanthropic Society 17, 24, 35
　Philanthropic Society Instituted for the Prevention of Crimes 25
　Royal Philanthropic Society (RPS) viii, 261
　Welsh Philanthropic Society 110
Philanthropic Society's Manufactory 130
Philanthropic system of discipline 81
philanthropy
　Temple to Philanthropy 27
picking pockets 133
Pickwick Papers 160
piety 62
Piggot, S 246
pilfering 50, 57, 148
Pinker, Robert viii
Pitt the Younger 23
pity 242
placement 64
Plan of Police (1781) 31
Plan of Union 189
'plumb pudding' 232

Plumb, Sarah 148
Plumer, Sir Thomas 148, 152
police 34
   defective state of 155
   Introduction to Police 113
   'most important object of police' 30
   Police and Convict Establishments (Select Committee, 1797) 42
   Police Bill (1785) 23
   Police Office 41
   police 'spies' 23
   policing 234, 262
   Policing Plan 29, 31, 43, 45
   preventive policing 39, 42, 99, 155
   resistance to professional policing 23
   social good 24
poor ix, 18, 24, 37, 81, 137
   Bill for the Better Support and Maintenance of the Poor (1797) 82
   poor-box 186
   poor children at loose on the streets 19
   poor house 37
   poor rate 27, 218
   State of the Poor (1797) 82
Poor Law 26, 34, 49, 63, 118, 145, 187, 206
   31
   escalating levels of expenditure 18
   'great defect' 26

Poor Law Amendment Act 1834 218
Poor Law Board 250
Poor Law Board Act 210
Poor Law Commission 211
Poor Law Commissioners 250
Poor Law Schools 237
   reform 40
Popham, Master 108
Port Elizabeth 224
porter 130, 134
Port Phillip, South Australia 221
Potters Bar 213
poverty 40, 42, 47, 49, 186, 206, 232
   practical responses 43
prevention
   'preventing future ills' 25
Prince Regent 116, 143
Principles of Morals and Legislation, Introduction to the (1789) 36
printing 63, 96, 193
prior imprisonment 256
prison 27, 37, 131, 138, 255
   prison conditions 161
   prison discipline 155, 161
   Prison Inspector 196, 245
   prison population 169
private sector xiv, 36, 255
   private enterprise 242
Privy Council 164, 252, 257
   Privy Council Committee on Education 209, 252, 256
prize money 69
probation 66, 184, 261
   probationary house 128

probationary jacket 130
Proclamation Society 36, 41
profanity 30
profligacy 25, 249
property 23, 36
'Proposals for Raising a Capital, etc.' 32
propriety 129
prostitution 30, 32
protection 17
psychiatry 261
punishment 62, 170, 182, 199, 248, 255, 258
   cruel 71
   evening school 71
   exemplary punishment 66
   need for 'modification' of 242
   punishment and reward 231
   scale of punishments and rewards 167
   secondary punishment 221
   sending boys to sea 65, 68, 78
Pusey, The Hon Philip 114

Q

Quaker xii, 37, 38, 140, 146, 155
quarrelling 30
Quarter Sessions 40, 56, 191, 223, 259
   Reigate Quarter Sessions 97
   Staffordshire Quarter Sessions 225
Queen's Boys 205, 224, 225, 236, 245

R

Radstock, Lord 193
ragged school 223, 249
   Ragged School Union 198, 239
   St James' Back Ragged School 247
Rainer
   Rainer Crime Concern 262
   Rainer Foundation 262
Rauhe Haus, Hamburg 218
reading 138
reason 30, 33
rebellion 176
recession 186
Redhill xi, 178, 179, 198, 214, 230, 240, 243, 244, 247, 248, 252, 259, 261
   Gas Works 249
   Redhill Farm School 237
   Red-stone Hill 215
referral order panels xiv
reform 28, 42, 180
   Age of Reform 144
   children of 25
   'common' but 'penitent' prostitutes 24
   criminal law, of 146
   ex-prisoners of 189
   female reform 64
   inmates of 120, 133, 134
   juvenile offenders of 215
   juvenile reformation (USA) 147
   juveniles of 172
   network for reform 243

new Philanthropic Reform 133
Parliamentary reform 164
prisoners of 23, 115
prison reform 221
Reform Act 1832 164, 173
reformation of offenders 258
reformatory asylum 211
Reformatory Farm School,
 Redhill 178, 179, 227
Reformatory Movement 208, 258
reformatory regime 130
reformatory schools xiii, 244, 251,
 254, 255
Reformatory Schools Act 1854 ix,
 230, 253, 255
Reformatory Schools Act 1866
 256
Reformatory Schools Acts 259
Reformatory Schools for the Perishing and Dangerous Classes,
 etc. 238
Reformatory Union 258
reform boys 130
Reform Department 176, 181, 184
Reform Department for boys 152
Reform School Movement ix
Reform, The 113, 132, 181
refuge
 House of Refuge 147
Refuge for the Destitute xiii, 114, 151,
 155, 161, 163, 174, 185, 188, 192, 206,
 207, 228
regimes ix, 133, 148, 196, 236, 247,
 260

Register of the Conduct and
 Improvement of the Girls 138
regulation 163, 165
relationships ix
release fees 40
religion 29, 130, 242, 249
 religious instruction 115
remand facilities, 261
repeat offending 57, 224
*Report on the Education, Discipline
 and Employment of the Children
 under the Society's Care* (1841) 179
*Report on the Sanitary Condition of
 the Labouring Population* 190
Representation of the People Act
 1832 164
reputation 56
 reputed thieves 256
residential care 261
residential institutions x
resources 152, 173, 185, 261
Responsibility in Aims and Means 258
restlessness 150, 151, 246
restorative justice xiv
Retford 63
retribution 255
revenue 156, 164, 197
revolution 187
Revolution Mill Company 63
reward 52, 62, 87, 150
 punishment and reward 231
 scale of punishments and rewards
 167
Rice, Reverend Dr. 176, 198

Richmond, Duke of 169, 177, 179, 187, 194, 213, 215, 221, 232
rights 17
   rights and liberties
      France 18
   Rights of Man 81
riot x, 156, 166, 167, 177
   riotous assembly 41, 70
robbery 20, 54, 247
   embryo robbers 25
Rochester Magistrate's Court 161
rod 75
Rome 235
Romilly, Sir Samuel 115, 146
Rookeries, London 59
rope-making 63, 138, 158
Ross, Francis 52
Rowley, Hannah 21
Royal Exchange Assurance Company 42
Royal Humane Society 40, 160
Royal pardon 20
royal patronage 261
Royal Philanthropic Society (RPS) viii, 261, 262
rule of law 21
rules x, 154, 165, 166, 205, 248
   Constitution of Regulations and Rules 32
   lack of 153
   'Rules for the Internal Management of the Reform' 131
Russell, Lord John 171, 191
Russell, Thomas 155, 220
Russell, Whitworth 204
Russia 36
Ryan, Patrick 52
Ryder, Richard 135, 143
Ryder, The Hon. Dudley 135

S

safer communities 262
sailors
   demobilised sailors 19
salving conscience 156
Sanderson, James 39, 40, 68
Sanders, William 50
sans discernment 243
school 39
   School for the Indigent Blind 147
   School of Industry 136, 209
science 35, 38
   scientific enquiry 30
Scotland Yard 56
scourging 129
scripture 138
sea x, 225
   seamen 32
   sending boys to sea 169
secure training centre xiv
security 23, 43, 190
sedition 18, 156
   seditious practices 136
Select Committee 145, 151, 155, 158, 163, 169, 236, 247
   House of Lords Select Committee on Gaols and Houses of Correction 154

Select Committee on Criminal and Destitute Juveniles 243
Select Committee on Miscellaneous Estimates and Expenditure 228
Select Committee on the Police 155, 162, 168, 189, 191
self-interest 29, 43
self-sufficiency 63
sentencing 22, 260
separate system 190
serious offences
  increasing number of committals for 169
serious offenders 196
servitude 78, 79
Sharpless, George Cornelius 53, 54, 139
Shaughnessy, James 248
Shepperd, Richard 49
sherrif 21, 40
  Sheriff's Fund 162, 163
shoemaking 45
shoplifting xiii, 54
Shoreditch 65
short, sharp, shock 255
Sidmouth, Lord 143, 161
silent system 190
simple larceny 232
Sims, Dr. 39, 68, 139
slavery x, 38, 146, 219
  Committee for the Abolition of the Slave Trade 38
sleeping in the streets 49
slop work 131

'small beer' 72
smallpox
  protrection from 139
Smith, Adam 31
Smith, Charles 57
Smith, William 166
social
  social character 61
  social economy 258
  social enterprise xiv
  social exclusion 262
  social science 33
  Social Union, etc. 33, 38
  Social Union for the Improvement of Civil Society 257
  social work 261
Society for Bettering the Condition and Increasing the Comforts of the Poor (SBCP) 38, 41
Society for Disseminating Useful Knowledge (SDUK) 140
Society for Improving the Condition of the Infant Chimney Sweepers 41
Society for Investigating the Alarming Increase of Juvenile Delinquency, etc. 189
Society for Promoting Christian Knowledge Among the Poor (SPCK) 43, 96
Society for the Diffusion of Useful Knowledge (SDUK) 211
Society for the Prevention of Pauperism (USA) 147

Society for the Reform of Juvenile Delinquents 147
Society for the Reform of the Criminal Poor 188
Society for the Supression of Juvenile Vagrancy 170
Society to Ascertain the Extent and Causes of Delinquency, etc. 155
soldiers 32
    demobilised soldiers 19
solitary confinement 50, 73, 77
Southgate, Reverend 60, 75
Southwark x, 63, 83, 97
spade-husbandry 218
Special Committee of Enquiry into Affairs of Trade and Finance 83
spelling 138
Spencer, Earl 114, 115, 125
spinning 45
Splan, James 247
squalor 190
Stafford Assizes 135
Staffordshire Castle 225
Staffordshire Prisoners Reform Association 225
Stanley, William 225
Starkey, Richard 76
state
    State despotism 23
State of Crimes and Punishments in London 21
State of the Prisons (1777) 20, 37
statistics
    statistical 'accounts' 22
stealing

and see theft 30
Stemp, Stephen 48
St George's Fields x, xi, 46, 59, 62, 72, 90, 117, 139, 143, 145, 148, 159, 184, 197, 204, 212, 221, 232, 237, 245
    chapel 113, 119
Still, James 66
St. Paul's Coffee-House 17
strategy 25
Stretton-on-Dunsmore 218, 244
'strong and restless impulses' 77
subordination 137
subscriptions 157, 163
Sunday school 39, 62, 96, 137
Superintendent's Journals 47
support
    supported housing 261
    thinning of 145
Surrey 261
    Surrey Quarter Sessions 118
surveillance 92, 130, 255
    domestic surveillance 200
    protective surveillance 149
Sussex 213
Sutton, Edward 59
Sutton, Manners 196
Swan River, Perth 222
swearing 247
sympathy 20

T

tailoring 45

Taylor, Robert (murder victim) 161
temper 226
　good temper 62
　ill temper 62
temperance 137
terminal crisis 145
terror 20, 31
　terrors of the laws 17
Teschmaker, Mr. 64
Thackeray, William Makepeace 232
Thames River Police Bill 42
theft 17, 57, 148, 184, 197, 225, 247
　beneath the gallows 26
　stealing a prayer-book 21
Thornton, Henry MP 38
Thoughts on the Criminal Prisons of this Country 153
threatening behaviour 73
ticket-of-leave 151
Tothill Fields 115, 132
Tottenham Court Road 51
Townsend, Reverend 31
trade 138, 157
　fostering trading profits 138
　'Holy War' of market forces 159
　sedentary trades 226
　slump in 158
　'sound principle' of 27
　trade accounts 174
　unprofitable trades 193
tradition
　empirical tradition 30
training 256, 262
transformation 135

transportation xiii, 21, 59, 88, 143, 156, 161, 169, 171, 203, 211, 224, 225
　children 53
　suspension of 204
Treason and Seditious Practices Act 81
Treasury 229, 253, 255, 256
　Lord Commissioners of the Treasury 253
Treatise on the Police of the Metropolis (1796) 42
treatment of offenders 187
Tremenheere, Hugh Seymour 237
trifling offences 169
Trimbath, Thomas 75, 86, 113
troubled and troublesome youth 260
truancy 149, 153
Tuffnell, Carleton 252
Turner, Reverend Sydney xi, xiv, 75, 178, 179, 217, 233, 236, 238, 244, 246, 251, 254, 258

U

uncertainty 21
Undertaking for the Reform of the Poor, etc. 32
undeserving applications 197
union 103, 191, 207, 245, 255, 258, 262
　Poor Law unions 218
University College 140
Urchin, Thomas 133

useful habits of work 131
usefulness 27
utilitarianism 34, 36
utility 34, 63, 82, 111, 115, 123, 181, 201, 218, 252, 257
Utopia 29
uttering false coins 247

V

vagrancy 25, 32, 48, 49, 135, 147, 149, 153, 202, 207, 235, 250, 251, 256
   children of vagrants 27
   vagrancy laws 49
value
   disvalue 27
   value for money 228
   values x
van Coulster, Michael 56
ventilation of prisons 40
vetting
   by the visitors 64
   of employers 64
vice 25, 26, 27, 36, 39, 42, 62, 151, 162, 201
   captive populations and 20
   perevention of 24
   vices of the cities 217
'vicious' propensities 58
vicious propensities 31
Victoria, Queen 212
vigilance 50
Village of Industry 81
violation of the Sabbath 155

violence 226
   use of as punishment 182
virtue 27, 33, 39, 61, 62, 241
   planting the seeds of virtue 26
vision 47
visitors 58, 59, 64, 97, 125, 129, 131, 153
   prison visitors 96
voluntary
   voluntary exertion 227
   voluntary organizations 241
   voluntary sector
      pitfalls for xii
vulnerable young people 261

W

Wagner, Dame Gillian viii
Walker, Matthew 133
walls x, 24, 46, 64, 69, 70, 176, 198, 199, 202, 218
Walpole, Spencer 240
wandering 49
Wandsworth 261
war
   waging war on, e.g. passions 26
wards 35, 46, 61, 158
washing of prisoners 40
waste of society 35
watchman 89, 166
wealth 29
   wealth of the nation 26
   Wealth of the Nations (1776) 31
Webb, John 224

welfare 26, 32, 43, 149, 159, 190, 200, 230, 255, 262
   public welfare 29
Wellington, Duke of (ship) 225
Wellington, Lady 148
Welsh Philanthropic Society 110
West Ham 219
West India merchants 42
Westminster, Lord 220
Westminster School 19
whipping 67, 247, 259
Whitbread, Samuel 39, 40
Whitbread, Samuel (junior) 40, 81
Whitehall Evening Post 21
White, Samuel 136
Wicherm, Emmanuel 218
wickedness 28, 31
Wilberforce, William 36, 38, 128, 146
Willett, Jeremiah 56
Williams, Captain 245, 259
Williams, Zylpha 149
wisdom
   wise and gentle policy 26
Withering, William 152
Woodman, Ann 157
   Woodman children 157
Woolwich 115
Worcester 259
work
   work incentives 87
workhouse 26, 49, 55, 131, 210, 250, 256
   workhouse schools 209, 218, 252
workshops 47, 138
Worlock, Mary Ann 140

Worship Street Police Court 226
wretchedness 59
wrongdoing 255

Y

York and Albany, Duke of 113
York Castle 224
Young, Arthur 96
young delinquents 20
Young Offenders Academy xiv
young people viii, 28
   young people in trouble ix
Young, Robert xiii, 24, 30, 38, 47, 58, 81, 188, 257
   disgrace and banishment from the society 32
   Mr. Robert Young's Address to the General Body of Subscribers, etc. 107
   naming and shaming 100
youth
   unguarded youth 39
   youthful iniquity 153
   youthful offenders 256

Z

zeal 247, 250, 257
   voluntary zeal 239
zero-sum children 28, 34

Putting justice into words...

Punishments of Former Days
by Ernest Pettifer

Thoroughly absorbing - This book transports the reader to a time when punishment was often brutal, unrestrained and unregulated by standards, fairness or consistency. It also looks at the sometimes strange logic that was applied by judges, justices of the peace and those charged with carrying out the task.

175 pages | 1992 | Paperback ISBN 9781872870052

Until They Are Seven
The Origins of Women's Legal Rights
by His Honour John Wroath

An absorbing account of the origins of women's rights to property and children. A true story which reads like a Victorian novel.

144 pages | 1998 | Paperback ISBN | Ebook ISBN 9781906534431

Browse our full list of history, biography, and crime and punishment titles at our website **WatersidePress.co.uk**

Putting justice into words...

Serial Killers
Hunting Britons and Their Victims 1960-2006
by David Wilson
Wilson writes that we are not all at-risk everyday from what he terms 'hunting Britons', rather it is people from a variety of vulnerable groups: the elderly, women involved in prostitution, gay men, runaways, 'throwaways' and children and kids moving from place to place.
Paperback ISBN 9781904380337 | Ebook ISBN 9781906534417
192 pages | 2007

Law, Justice and Mediation
The Legend of St Yves
by Bryan Gibson, Foreword by Marcel Berlin
The Legend of St Yves is not widely known in Britain, even though he is the patron saint of lawyers (among other things). In this informative account, Bryan Gibson places St Yves - born Erwan Helouri - on a par with Robin Hood, Jessie James and Ned Kelly in terms of their appeal to various national psyches - and up there alongside Joan of Arc and Bernadette of Lourdes as regards his native France.
Paperback ISBN 9781904380405 | Ebook ISBN 9781906534677
96 pages | 2008

Justice in Middlesex
A Brief History of the Uxbridge Magistrates' Court
by Eileen M Bowlt
This delightful book about the history of one of England's magistrates' courts also looks at the rich underlying backdrop of a part of the country that is central to the English legal system.
Paperback ISBN 9781904380399 | Ebook ISBN 9781906534448
96 pages | 2007

Putting justice into words...

Cesare Beccaria
The Genius of "On Crimes and Punishments"
by John Hostettler
A text on one of crime and punishments under-recorded and maybe unsung heroes. Will be of considerable interest to anyone wishing to trace the development of the rights of individuals charged with or convicted of crimes, and of the importance of fairness, proportionality, decency and similar matters which may be at-risk in the wrong hands.
Paperback ISBN 9781904380634 | Ebook ISBN 9781906534936
160 pages | 2011

Sir William Garrow
His Life, Times and Fight for Justice
by John Hostettler and Richard Braby
A comprehensive account of lawyer William Garrow's life, career, family and connections. The lost story of Sir William Garrow and its rediscovery will prove intriguing for professional and general readers alike and provides an invaluable 'missing-link' for legal and social historians.
Hardback ISBN 9781904380559 | Ebook ISBN 9781906534820
272 pages | 2010

Fifty Year Stretch
Prisons and Imprisonment 1980-2030
by Stephen Shaw
An absorbing and highly innovative work by one of the UK's leading experts on prisons and penal reform. This book charts developments across a fifty year time frame beginning in 1980 at the start of a growth in the prison population of England and Wales (and other parts of the world) and ends with a prospective view taking events up to 2030.
Hardback ISBN 9781904380573 | Ebook 9781906534844
134 pages | 2010

visit **WatersidePress.co.uk**